DEBATING SAME-SEX MARRIAGE

"The best part of this valuable point-counterpoint is John Corvino's patient, clear, and logical dismantling of every argument and insinuation made by the leading opponents of letting loving and committed gay couples and their families share in something we all agree is good. Corvino convincingly shows that the couples, children, kin, and communities deserve the simple Golden Rule of fairness and the civic respect that are part of America's promise of the pursuit of happiness, liberty, and justice for all, and that ending their exclusion from marriage would harm no one. No wonder a majority of Americans—including, notwithstanding Maggie Gallagher's arguments, 63% of American Catholics—have opened their hearts and changed their minds to support the freedom to marry."

—Evan Wolfson, President of Freedom to Marry
and author of *Why Marriage Matters*

"Maggie Gallagher has been one of the staunchest advocates for traditional marriage in our lifetime, and she has now added what may well be the most cogent defense of that venerable institution yet written. Combining her philosophical training with real world experience, Gallagher articulates quite powerfully the societal risk of transforming marriage from an institution rooted in the biological nature of men and women and designed to foster the procreation and rearing of children, to one that is simply about adult relationships. A must read for everyone grappling with the policy debate currently underway, but particularly for those judges who think the policy decision is theirs alone to make."

—Dr. John C. Eastman, Henry Salvatori Professor
of Law and Community Service and former Dean,
Chapman University School of Law

POINT/COUNTERPOINT

Series Editor
James P. Sterba, University of Notre Dame

Affirmative Action and Racial Reference
Carl Cohen and James P. Sterba

God? a Debate between a Christian and an Atheist
William Lane Craig and Walter Sinnott-Armstrong

Does Feminism Discriminate against Men?
Warren Farrell and James P. Sterba

Abortion: Three Perspectives
Michael Tooley, Celia Wolf-Devine, Philip E. Devine,
and Alison M. Jaggar

Debating Same-Sex Marriage

JOHN CORVINO
AND
MAGGIE GALLAGHER

OXFORD
UNIVERSITY PRESS

OXFORD
UNIVERSITY PRESS

Oxford University Press, Inc., publishes works that further
Oxford University's objective of excellence
in research, scholarship, and education.

Oxford New York
Auckland Cape Town Dar es Salaam Hong Kong Karachi
Kuala Lumpur Madrid Melbourne Mexico City Nairobi
New Delhi Shanghai Taipei Toronto

With offices in
Argentina Austria Brazil Chile Czech Republic France Greece
Guatemala Hungary Italy Japan Poland Portugal Singapore
South Korea Switzerland Thailand Turkey Ukraine Vietnam

Published by Oxford University Press, Inc.
198 Madison Avenue, New York, New York 10016
www.oup.com

Oxford is a registered trademark of Oxford University Press

Library of Congress Cataloging-in-Publication Data
Corvino, John, 1969-
Debating same-sex marriage / John Corvino and Maggie Gallagher.
p. cm.—(Point/counterpoint)
Includes bibliographical references (p.).
ISBN 978–0–19–975632–2 (alk. paper)—
ISBN 978–0–19–975631–5 (pbk. : alk. paper) 1. Same-sex marriage.
I. Gallagher, Maggie. II. Title.
HQ1033.C675 2012
306.84′8—dc23
2012000390

3 5 7 9 8 6 4 2
Printed in the United States of America
on acid-free paper

For Jennifer, Joe, and Tess
—John Corvino

For my grandchildren
—Maggie Gallagher

John Corvino, Ph.D., is Associate Professor and Chair of Philosophy at Wayne State University in Detroit, Michigan. As "The Gay Moralist," he was a regular columnist for the now-defunct 365gay.com, as well as a frequent contributor to pridesource.com, The Independent Gay Forum, and other online venues. He has contributed to dozens of books, and is currently completing a book entitled *What's Wrong with Homosexuality?* for Oxford University Press. An award-winning teacher, he has lectured at more than 200 campuses on issues of sexuality, ethics, and marriage. Some of his writing and video clips of his lectures are available at www.johncorvino.com.

Maggie Gallagher is a nationally syndicated columnist; the co-founder of the National Organization for Marriage, a leading voice in the movement to strengthen marriage as a social institution; and the author of three other books on marriage including (with University of Chicago Professor Linda J. Waite) *The Case for Marriage: Why Married People are Happier, Healthier and Better Off Financially*. *National Journal* named her to its list of the "most influential" people in the same-sex marriage debate. She writes a weekly newsletter on life, marriage, and religious liberty at www.culturewarvictoryfund.org.

CONTENTS

DEBATING SAME-SEX MARRIAGE

1

Introduction

IN MAY 2011, for the first time in Gallup's polling on the issue,
a slim majority of Americans favored legal recognition of same-
sex marriage:[1] 53 percent of those polled were in favor, with
45 percent opposed—almost an exact flip of the previous year's
results (44 percent in favor and 53 percent opposed). Compare
these numbers to those from 1996, when Gallup first tracked the
issue: 27 percent in favor of same-sex marriage and 68 percent
opposed. Clearly, attitudes have shifted—dramatically—in the
last fifteen years.

Nevertheless, at a time when Americans appear roughly
evenly split on the issue, only a handful of states allow same-sex
couples to marry, and none of these marriages are recognized by
the federal government.[2] Several other states permit same-sex civil
unions or domestic partnerships, with many of the legal rights and
duties of marriage. Two states—California and Maine—extended
legal marriage to same-sex couples but then reversed course
when citizens voted to amend their state constitutions to prohibit
such marriages. Over two dozen other states have passed similar
amendments, and in every state where the issue has been put to a
popular vote thus far, same-sex marriage has been rejected.[3]

There are also lively debates occurring in Australia, Great Britain, South America, and other parts of the world. The issue remains divisive, and by the time you read this, it is likely that the landscape will have changed further—sometimes in favor of same-sex marriage, and sometimes against it.

This book is a debate about marriage as a legal and social institution: should it include same-sex couples? It is not about whether there is a constitutional right to such marriage, or about whether particular religious denominations should bless same-sex unions, although some of its content will be relevant to those debates. The authors, John Corvino and Maggie Gallagher, come from different sides of the "culture wars." Corvino is a philosophy professor and a frequent speaker and writer on gay issues under the moniker "The Gay Moralist." Gallagher is a nationally syndicated columnist and the cofounder of the National Organization for Marriage, the preeminent national organization fighting to preserve marriage exclusively as the union of husband and wife. The two have debated each other—and various other opponents—in numerous public forums. In collaborating on this book, they aim not only to convince readers of their respective views, but also to promote dialogue in the face of a sometimes ugly division.

Gallagher and Corvino agree on several points, especially the importance of marriage. They disagree, often deeply, on many others. A good deal of their work herein is an effort to "achieve disagreement"—that is, to uncover exactly where they differ and why. This debate is challenging in part because of its implications for other large issues: the role of government, the significance of sexual difference, the needs of children, the function of social norms, the freedom of religion, and indeed, the nature of marriage itself. All of these are touched on here.

The format of the book is as follows: Each author puts forth his or her views in a main essay, and then each offers a direct response to the other. Corvino begins by arguing that allowing same-sex couples to marry would be good both for them and for society at large, since society has an interest in supporting committed, loving relationships for all its members; he also responds to many standard objections. Gallagher follows by making the case for how marriage, understood as the union between a husband and wife, is the fundamental cross-cultural institution for ensuring that children have mothers and fathers; she argues both that same-sex unions cannot be marriages and that treating them as such would gut marriage of this core purpose. In his reply, Corvino takes issue with what he calls Gallagher's "Definitional Objection" by arguing that marriage is an evolving and multifaceted institution; he then considers and rejects three reasons for thinking that same-sex marriage would undermine marriage's child-centered purposes. Gallagher concludes by detailing points of agreement and disagreement; she then clarifies and expands her argument for why treating same-sex couples as married requires a fundamental change in marriage's meaning, one that is detrimental to society's crucial task of linking mothers and fathers to children.

It has become almost cliché to say that this issue tends to generate more heat than light, but like most clichés, this one captures something true. The debate over same-sex marriage has been frequently vigorous, occasionally strident, and sometimes downright hostile. It touches upon deep human longings and convictions; it affects real individuals and families. The controversy is unlikely to subside anytime soon. Notwithstanding their many deep disagreements, the authors share the hope that this book will help promote a conversation that is spirited, rigorous, civil, and productive.

2

The Case for Same-Sex Marriage

JOHN CORVINO

■ □ ■

BOYD AND JOSH LOOK ANXIOUS. This is not surprising. Today is their wedding, and they are surrounded by 150 close and not-so-close family members, friends, and colleagues. Many are experiencing a "gay wedding" for the first time. But Boyd and Josh aren't having "gay wedding" jitters; they're having plain old wedding jitters. When the pair say "I do" in front of throngs of well-wishers, there will be stomach butterflies and teary eyes.

As Boyd and Josh walk down the aisle hand-in-hand, preceded by their parents, I notice that they're sweating. This is probably less from anxiety than from heat: it's June, and the old brick church where this is happening isn't air-conditioned. The couple are wearing smart black tuxedoes; their fathers are dressed in suits; their mothers in tasteful formal dresses. The sun is beating through the stained-glass windows, and many in the congregation are fanning themselves with their programs. Along the aisle there are simple floral arrangements tied to the pews with cream-colored ribbon. Everyone's smiling. Were it not for the absence of a bride, you'd have a hard time distinguishing the scene from any other wedding.

A wedding scene, gay or otherwise, is an unusual way for a philosophy professor to begin a book. I thought about opening by acknowledging the contentiousness of this issue, or waxing eloquent about the history and significance of marriage, or even spotlighting a rather different scene: a hospital emergency where a gay person is kept from a partner's bedside because their relationship lacks legal status. I'll get to these matters soon enough. But it seemed right that the starting point for the book be the starting point as typically experienced by same-sex couples: a happy occasion, when people in love commit to building a life together. The issue is personal, affecting real individuals and real families.

Let's acknowledge, however, that the issue affects not only gay couples and those who care about them, but everyone who has a stake in what family means—in other words, pretty much everyone. It does not affect everyone in the same way, or to the same degree—an important point to which I'll return later. But there's more to the story than how this impacts Boyd and Josh. There are decent people on different sides of the issue, including some guests at today's ceremony who quietly disapprove of what's going on but decided to attend anyway out of friendship. I don't doubt that they wish Boyd and Josh well. They wish them well, but...

But... lots of things. But, this all feels weird. The ceremony is taking place in a church, but there's no bride walking down the aisle. There might even be same-sex dancing at the reception! Marriage is a sacred institution, the cornerstone of society, and up until about five minutes ago (or so it seems) marriage meant male-female. We shouldn't mess with tradition. And what about children? If Boyd and Josh have them, there won't be a mother in the daily picture. There is indeed more to the story. Among other things, we need to distinguish between *why people get married* (often for love; sometimes for security, or money, or other reasons) and *why society recognizes marriage*.

We know why Boyd and Josh are getting married—or, if you prefer, "married." (Their ceremony is taking place in Michigan, which constitutionally bans same-sex marriage or "similar unions for any purpose.") They love each other and want to build a life together; they want to signal their commitment to their family and friends; they want others to acknowledge them as the family unit that they understand themselves to be. Most people understand such aspirations; they are a familiar feature of human life. But are they enough? Are they sufficient to justify expanding one of our most time-honored institutions?

This book is a debate about same-sex marriage, and my contribution will be to make the case for extending marriage to same-sex couples. I'm grateful for the opportunity to do that in conversation with Maggie Gallagher, one of the other side's sharpest advocates, and someone who continually pushes me to think harder about this issue. I hope that the book enables us not only to push each other, but also to move the ball down the field in the increasingly urgent national and international debate.

A word about terminology: Some of my fellow advocates avoid reference to "same-sex marriage" rather than to "marriage equality" or "marriage for gay men and lesbians" or just "marriage." The phrase "same-sex marriage" suggests the creation of a new institution rather than the expansion of an existing one, which (they argue, and I agree) is the better way to understand our goal: recognition, not redefinition. Gay men and lesbians don't want something new, a "special right": they want marriage. But "marriage for gay men and lesbians" is a clumsier phrase than "same-sex marriage," and sometimes I don't want to refer to "marriage equality," I want to refer to the same-sex half of the equation. So you will find me using different formulations depending on aims and context.

This book is about whether the law should recognize same-sex marriage and whether individuals ought to regard committed same-sex unions as marriages. Thus, it is about marriage as a both a legal and social institution. It is not about religious or sacramental marriage, a related but distinct issue. In the United States, people often have a hard time mentally separating religious marriage from civil marriage. We use the word "marriage" for both, and couples who want both usually do them simultaneously. Not all societies do it this way. My in-laws had two weddings in the Philippines: one in a courthouse, then one a month later in a Roman Catholic church. It is possible to have a legal marriage without having a religious ceremony, just as it is possible to have a religious ceremony (as Boyd and Josh are doing) without having a legal marriage. Gallagher and I will consider the implications of legal marriage equality for religious freedom, but we will not pursue a theological debate.

Nor will we pursue a debate about the morality of homosexuality, although that's something I've done at length elsewhere.[1] Gallagher does not rest her argument against same-sex marriage on the premise that homosexual conduct is immoral, and in that respect she is similar to the majority of prominent marriage-equality opponents. I'm not denying that they *believe* that homosexual conduct is immoral: in fact, most do. But typically, they do not use this belief as a premise in their public argument against marriage equality. Conversely, one can believe that homosexual conduct is immoral but also believe that the government should nevertheless extend marriage rights to same-sex couples, who ought to be allowed to make such decisions for themselves. (By analogy, one might believe that divorce is immoral, but still believe that a free society should permit it.)

However, although the debate over same-sex marriage is distinct from the debate over the morality of same-sex relationships, they are surely related at the practical level. If same-sex marriage becomes more widely recognized, same-sex relationships will likely become more widely morally accepted. That's one reason why advocates seek it and opponents fear it: the legalization of same-sex marriage will help to "normalize" homosexuality. And the causal arrow goes both ways: the push for legalizing same-sex marriage is happening now precisely because moral attitudes toward homosexuality are changing, as well as vice versa.

How the Law Matters

Legal marriage involves an elaborate package of rights and responsibilities that couples voluntarily undertake with each other, vis-à-vis the rest of society. Marriage is, of course, much more than the legal package. Glenn Stanton, a researcher at Focus on the Family whom I have debated many times, likes to point out that no one tells a bride and groom at their wedding, "Enjoy the legal rights and responsibilities, folks!" Of course they don't. That is not (typically) why people get married, and it's certainly not the focus of weddings. But it is an important part of how we as a society define the contours of marriage. To put it simply, legal marriage establishes a couple as family in the eyes of the law. Not "friends," not "roommates," but *family*.

Legally, marriage creates family in hundreds of ways large and small. The U.S. General Accounting Office has identified 1138 federal legal incidents of marriage.[2] Some of these involve rights, benefits, and privileges; others involve legal burdens and responsibilities. A small handful can be covered by the documents in the very expensive binder Boyd and Josh will soon receive from their lawyer, but many cannot. (A marriage license costs about $40; that binder—which details their legal relationship regarding healthcare decisions, inheritance, funeral decisions and the like—will probably cost them over $1000.) As I sit here at their wedding thinking of the things that separate this "marriage" from full-fledged legal marriage, I am struck by the differences.

For example, thanks to the binder, Boyd and Josh will be permitted to visit each other in the hospital and make decisions in the event of incapacitation. (In Michigan, that particular document is free.) They can do so, that is, if they happen to have their paperwork with them. But how many of us keep legal documents handy "just in case"? Typically, a wife can tell emergency-room doctors "He's my husband," and that's that. Not so for gay couples. And what if they're traveling in the middle of the night and the bank back home with the safe-deposit box containing the documents doesn't open until 9 a.m.? Tough luck.

Thanks to the expensive binder, when one of them dies, the other can make funeral decisions—though again, the survivor will be asked for paperwork, and families often contest such paperwork. And he'll inherit the other's estate, though unlike a legal spouse he'll pay a hefty tax on it. Even with the binder, neither can file a wrongful death suit regarding the other: after all, they're not legally married. Whether they get bereavement leave will depend on their employers.

It's unpleasant to be contemplating the disability or death of a groom at his own wedding. But although marriage is "for better or for worse," the law is often most needed during the "for worse." So while the minister drones on, let's consider some other possibilities for our real-life gay couple.

Boyd, who is 33, has just completed his neurosurgery residency and is about to embark on a challenging medical career. Josh, 29, will soon begin law school, having spent several years after college graduation teaching English in Japan. Suppose Josh forgoes law school in order to devote himself full time to being a homemaker. Suppose further that, years from now, Boyd predeceases him. In a legal marriage recognized by the federal government, the homemaker would receive the breadwinner's social-security benefits. In the actual situation, Josh would receive not a penny of those benefits. And no expensive document from the lawyer's office can fix that.

Boyd and Josh are both American citizens. But imagine that Josh had instead fallen in love with a foreigner while teaching overseas. If that foreigner were female, their marriage could help secure her U.S. residency; if male, nothing. This may not seem like a big deal, unless you happen to fall in love with a noncitizen—a situation challenging enough for straight couples but potentially devastating for gay couples. Again, no expensive document from the lawyer's office can fix that.

Since we're contemplating the "for worse," let's suppose one of them eventually gets into legal trouble. If married in the eyes of the federal government, they could not be forced to testify against each other—acknowledging a zone of privacy that often helps the "for better or for worse" stay better. In Boyd and Josh's actual case, such "spousal privilege" is not an option, regardless of their expensive legal documents.

How about financial trouble? So far I've been talking about the rights of marriage, but there are also responsibilities, including responsibility for each other's debt. Since couples often function as a financial unit, this is generally a good thing. Suppose Boyd spends lavishly, showering Josh with extravagant gifts and transferring most assets into his name. Then Boyd declares bankruptcy. If they were married, creditors could go after Josh's assets, which are part of the marital estate. In the current situation, not so. And Boyd, unlike his heterosexually married colleagues, is not required to disclose any significant stock holdings in pharmaceutical companies and medical suppliers as long as he keeps them in Josh's name. After all, Josh is not his legal spouse.

Since we've already brought up disability, death, criminal activity, and financial trouble, why not go all the way and contemplate their divorce? Nobody likes to mention such things—especially at weddings—but nearly half of all marriages end in divorce. Heterosexual couples have a complex legal system in place to help make divorce go smoothly. The system is far from perfect, but it's better than nothing. Gay couples have…nothing, except whatever they cobble together at the lawyer's office, and that's usually pretty limited.

So, for example, their house is in Boyd's name: he bought it before they started dating three years ago. Selling it is not viable given the recent real-estate crash, and getting Josh's name on the deed, if possible at all, would be expensive because of closing costs and tax issues. Nevertheless, Josh contributes his fair share to the mortgage and household expenses. Suppose they eventually split up, and Boyd kicks Josh out. As things now stand, Josh would have no legal recourse. The two are not family in the eyes of the law.

I raise all these unpleasant possibilities with the full hope that Boyd and Josh will flourish together "until death do us part." They're a great couple, truly meant for each other. If anyone has what it takes, these guys do. We contemplate the "for worse" because it's possible, not because it's expected or likely. But contemplate it we must. Part of what legal marriage does is to provide security during the inevitable rough spots, and part of why gay men and lesbians experience its denial so painfully is that the law mostly abandons them in those rough spots. The expensive binder is no substitute.

***

I am jarred from my daydreaming when I hear the minister say "Repeat after me…" and I realize we've reached the important part. All eyes are on the couple.

"I, Boyd, take you, Josh, to be my husband, to have and to hold from this day forward, for better or for worse, for richer, for poorer, in sickness and in health, to love and to cherish; until death do us part."

(I'm pleased that they've decided to use the traditional vows. I'm old-fashioned that way.)

"I, Josh, take you, Boyd, to be my husband, to have and to hold from this day forward, for better or for worse, for richer, for poorer, in sickness and in health, to love and to cherish; until death do us part."

Just as I predicted: scarcely a dry eye in the place.

***

The essay that follows is divided into five parts. In Part 1, I make a preliminary case in favor of marriage for same-sex couples. In Part 2, I consider several versions of the "Definitional Argument" against same-sex marriage: the idea that, whatever we call these unions, they simply cannot be marriages. I also briefly review the diverse history of marriage. In Part 3, I consider the argument that extending marriage to same-sex couples would be bad for children. In Part 4, I explore what is sometimes referred to as the "slippery-slope" argument against same-sex marriage: that allowing such marriages would leave us no principled reason for prohibiting polygamy, incestuous marriage, and so on. Here I also respond to those who argue that the institution is itself irredeemably problematic and that we should instead look "beyond marriage" to alternative family forms. In Part 5, I consider how letting gays marry affects religious freedom and other cherished values.

1. WHAT MARRIAGE IS FOR

As noted above, Boyd and Josh love each other and want to build a life together; they want to signal their commitment to their family and friends; they want others to acknowledge them as the family unit that they understand themselves to be. That's why they're having a wedding, or, as some refer to it, a commitment ceremony. (I'll use "wedding" because that's what we, their friends, have mostly been calling it.)

Indeed, Boyd and Josh are not just having a wedding, they're having a big wedding, complete with rehearsal dinner, church ceremony, and reception for 150 guests. They've registered at Williams-Sonoma, Crate & Barrel, and Macy's; they've sent out fancy multipart invitations with useless sheets of tissue paper inside. "Why do you want such a huge production?" I asked Boyd one day. A few reasons, he told me. Partly it was because his siblings also had large weddings, and both he and Josh love big parties. But mainly it was a way for them to signal to family and friends, "This is real. We mean it. Take it seriously."

Before we turn to the issue of "Why marriage?" it might be worthwhile to ask "Why weddings?" Weddings are, at one level, absurd affairs: the gaudy pageantry, the forced intimacy with distant relatives and acquaintances, the cheesy running commentary from the DJ. They're expensive, sometimes outrageously so. One designer friend of mine has done a wedding with a $38,000 budget—*for the flowers alone.* We dress in clothes that we never wear otherwise; we rent limousines and big reception halls; we send out invitations requesting the "honour" of people's presence and the "favour" of their reply, as if we've all suddenly become members of the British aristocracy. Why do we make such a fuss?

We do it because, like Boyd and Josh, we want to say "This is real. We mean it. Take it seriously." Yes, we can (and often should) do that with simple affairs, and we can certainly do it with American spelling. But fanfare has its uses. If your friends and relatives are going to fly from all around the country and buy you expensive presents and sit through a long service that's all about you, you'd better be pretty damn sure about what you're doing.

But what *are* you doing? Weddings help to transform partners into spouses, a relationship into a marriage, legal strangers into legal family. But why should we seek such transformation? What is marriage for, anyway? Gallagher often claims that we cannot address the same-sex marriage issue without considering the question of marriage's purpose(s). On this, she and I agree.

We will not settle this question by a simple glance at history. Marriage has evolved over centuries, rather than being enacted all at once to solve some discrete crisis. The reasons for its evolution are messy, sometimes contradictory, and often inarticulate. In other words, the answer to the question "What is marriage for?" will not look like the answer to the question "What is that orange cone in the road for?" There was no historic "Relationship Council" that pondered the challenges in human relationships and concluded, "This shacking-up thing isn't working very well. Here's an idea! Let's invent marriage!"

Marriage-equality opponents often speak as if the opposite were true, as if something in the anthropological record settles once and for all what marriage is for, and that it isn't for same-sex couples. In the next section I'll consider the history of marriage and discuss its relevance to our present concern. For now I want to approach the question in a different way. I want to ask what good(s) might be achieved by extending marriage to same-sex couples—for them, for their families, and for society at large. Let's imagine that we were starting from scratch: that *we* are the historic "Relationship Council." Would there be good reasons to invent marriage and to include same-sex couples in its purview?

I argue that there are. My argument will be a preliminary, or prima facie, case, meaning that it's subject to revision as we consider further evidence. Sometimes we find good reasons for doing something only later to find even better reasons for not doing it, and we will consider the arguments against same-sex marriage soon enough. But first I want to flesh out the case in its favor.

Let me begin by stating what the case is not: it is not merely that same-sex partners fall in love. As Jonathan Rauch explains in his book *Gay Marriage: Why It Is Good for Gays, Good for*

Straights, and Good for America, you may or may not love your spouse, but "the two of you are just as married either way. You may love your mistress, but that certainly does not make her your wife."[3] Though love may make a family, as the pithy slogan goes, it doesn't make for good marriage policy, and it never has. One does not need the cooperation of the state merely to celebrate love.

But perhaps this dismissal is too brisk. Perhaps the point of marriage is not to *celebrate* love, but to help sustain a certain form of it. After all, true love is challenging. It is not a mere feeling, but an ongoing activity. I'm referring here not to the love that gives you stomach butterflies when your beloved shows up (or leaves you waiting) at a candlelit restaurant early in the relationship, but to the love that keeps you up all night tending to him when he's so sick that he can't keep dinner down. Surely a key part of the rationale for marriage is to support that kind of steady, enduring love even as romantic bliss waxes and wanes. Such love is good for people, and society has an interest in promoting, honoring, and reinforcing it. Marriage fortifies such love. It does so legally, by giving people tools for caregiving (spousal privilege, hospital visitation, bereavement leave, and so on). And it does so socially, by creating a web of expectation, encouragement, and support.

One might try to sum up this rationale for marriage by saying that "Marriage helps to provide reliable caregivers." The danger in that (entirely true and important) statement is that it oversimplifies, as pithy descriptions often do. Yes, marriage provides reliable caregivers. My HMO also provides reliable caregivers. Marriage is more: It involves the couple's commitment to each other and to society that they are each other's main line of defense in the world, for life. It is an exclusive commitment, not in the sense a spouse doesn't care for other people (children, friends, parents), but in the sense that only one person can be your Number One Person. Here is the "special someone" that you will have and hold, for better or for worse, for richer or for poorer, in sickness and in health, until death do you part. Here is the one that you will come home to at night, wake up with in the morning, and share life's joys, sorrows, and challenges with. Here is the one that you will be most intimate with physically, emotionally, socially, sexually—elements that are difficult to tease apart in practice, because they are mutually reinforcing. Nothing creates, signals, and sustains this kind of relationship the way marriage does. If we were starting from scratch, this would be a strong rationale for inventing marriage. For convenience, I'll refer to it as the "mutual lifelong caregiving" rationale, with the important caveat about oversimplification. Maybe calling it the "family-building" rationale would be even better. When Boyd's mother remarked at the rehearsal dinner, "I was worried about Boyd: he works so hard and lives so far from us, and I'm so relieved that he has a special someone," everyone knew exactly what she meant.

As one recent book on marriage put it, discussing the "myth" that "marriage is mostly about children," there is substantial data "documenting the powerful effect getting married and staying married has on the well-being of adults.... [F]or some people, marriage can literally make the difference between life or death."[4] That book, incidentally, is *The Case for Marriage: Why Married People are Happier, Healthier, and Better Off Financially*, by Linda J. Waite and Maggie Gallagher. Yes, *that* Maggie Gallagher.

Marriage-equality advocates are sometimes challenged for an explanation why letting gay people marry would benefit society at large. Here it is. When there's someone whose job it is to take care of someone else, that's good for the two of them, obviously. But it's also good for their neighbors. Married people are, on average, less likely to burden the public purse.[5] The things that make them healthier and happier at home also make them more productive members of society. It's a win-win: good for the married couple and good for those around them. From a social-policy point of view, we should aim to promote this sort of thing for as many members of society as possible, straight and gay alike.

It is worth noting that even if extending marriage to gay people did nothing for straight people in particular, it would still benefit society in general. Gay people are part of society, and any policy that helps them without hurting anyone else involves a net gain to society. Too often, marriage-equality opponents understand "society" narrowly to mean "straight people" and leave gays out of their accounting entirely. I remember once being challenged at one of my debates by an audience member, a proud Christian conservative: "What good is this for people like me!?" I was tempted to respond, "Um, it's not all about you." Gay citizens are citizens, too.

Some marriage-equality opponents ask why "mutual life-long caregiving" needs to be tied to romantic or sexual relationships.[6] In general, it doesn't. But human beings (straight or gay) have a tendency to pair off romantically, melding their lives and their property, and good social policy needs to take account of that fact. Sexual intimacy is an important part of such pairings, not just because (in the heterosexual case) it might extend the family by producing children, but also because (in all cases) it can be a way of expressing, replenishing, and furthering intimacy at other levels. While the connection between sex and other kinds of intimacy is complex and often obscure, it is folly to ignore that connection when thinking about the caregiving function of marriage.

But what about the other functions? One that I haven't mentioned yet is that which Gallagher and other traditionalists see as primary: protecting children. Others include settling the young (particularly males) and providing a safe harbor for sexual intimacy.[7] All of these are important, and I'll devote the entirety of Part 3 to the issue of children.

For now it's worth noting that marriage succeeds in its other functions largely, if not entirely, because of its mutual-lifelong-caregiving function. Marriage provides a good environment for children—why? Because it binds the parents together permanently in stable mutual support. Marriage settles young people, especially males—why? Because it gives them primary responsibility for another person, and vice versa. (As Rauch writes, "'It's one a.m. Do you know where your spouse is?' Chances are that you do.")[8] The myriad benefits of marriage accrue largely because it is an exclusive, presumptively lifelong, mutually supporting partnership.

I am not denying that some of these other benefits may have additional explanations. For example, some have argued that marriage settles males not because of the domesticating influence of marriage, but because of the domesticating influence of *women*. There may be something to this. But it remains clear that the way to settle gay men like Boyd and Josh is not to marry them off to women. On the contrary, that would likely be unsettling for everyone involved, the women especially. How many closeted gay politicians must have awkward "coming-out" press conferences with their wives in the background before we learn this? The best way to achieve marriage's "settling" function is not to promote heterosexual marriage for everybody, but to promote heterosexual marriage for heterosexuals and gay marriage for gays—that is, to promote marriage equality.

The issue of children is more complex, and I'll discuss it in more detail later. Here, I want to acknowledge unequivocally that the welfare of children is a supremely important rationale for marriage. There is no serious debate about this. The only question is whether it is the *sole* important rationale for marriage, one that renders all others irrelevant, as Gallagher sometimes seems to think. (Only sometimes: other times, as in her book with Waite, she recognizes this to be a myth.)

Walter is a neighbor of mine, a widower in his 70s. Recently, he announced that he was getting married, to a woman similar in age. What did we all say to Walter? We said "Congratulations," of course. Were we just being polite, secretly thinking "Why bother"? At their age, Walter and his new wife won't be having children. And yet his marriage makes sense—indeed, it seems like a very positive thing. Why?

Elsewhere Gallagher writes,

> It is also true, as gay-marriage advocates note, that we impose no fertility tests for marriage: Infertile and older couples marry, and not every fertile couple chooses procreation. But every marriage between a man and a woman is capable of giving any child they create or adopt a mother and a father. Every marriage between a man and a woman discourages either from creating fatherless children outside the marriage vow. In this sense, neither older married couples nor childless husbands and wives publicly challenge or dilute the core meaning of marriage. Even when a man marries an older woman and they do not adopt, his marriage helps protect children. How? His marriage means, if he keeps his vows, that he will not produce out-of-wedlock children.[9]

Congratulations, Walter. If you keep your vows, you won't produce any out-of-wedlock children. That's awesome. Let's have a toast!

Obviously, that is *not* what we meant when we congratulated Walter. We congratulated him—and regard his marriage as a good thing—because Walter now (again) has someone special to take care of him and vice versa. Mutual lifelong caregiving is a good reason for promoting marriage whether or not children are on the horizon.

Having acknowledged that children's welfare is an important rationale for marriage, I want to take the argument a step further. Children's welfare is an important rationale, not just for straight marriage, but also for gay marriage. I'm not just talking about gay kids, who ought to be able to aspire to "happily ever after" in marriage someday—although their welfare is quite relevant, and too often overlooked in this debate. I'm talking about the several hundred thousand mostly heterosexual children being raised in the United States by gay (single and partnered) parents.[10] Some of these parents have their children from prior heterosexual relationships, others have them by adoption, still others by insemination. Like Gallagher, you might think that in an ideal world such situations wouldn't exist. But in the real world, these kids do exist and their welfare matters.

Letting same-sex couples marry would help these children for all of the reasons already mentioned, and then some.[11] It would promote a more stable, happy, healthy family life. It would increase their material well-being, because of the financial security that accrues to married couples. It would also signal that their family deserves equal treatment in the eyes of the law. Not even Gallagher thinks that we ought to take these children away from their gay parents. And all else being equal, it would surely be better for them if their parents—the people who are actually raising them—had the prospect of marriage.

Of course, Gallagher denies that all else is equal, and we now turn to arguments for this claim. We do so, however, armed with a strong preliminary social-policy case for marriage equality: *Marriage promotes mutual lifelong caregiving in a way that no other institution does, a task that is important for gay and straight citizens alike. Put simply, it builds family.* In achieving this aim, marriage also accomplishes various related aims: it settles the young, assisting their transition into adulthood; it provides a safe harbor for sexual intimacy; and it creates a stable environment for any children who might arrive or already be present. If we were starting from scratch, this case would be good reason for us to invent marriage. As things stand, it *is* reason for us to sustain marriage, and specifically to endorse the sort of marriage appropriate to each person: heterosexual marriage for straight people, same-sex marriage for gay people. It is reason to provide various social and legal supports for marriage. And it is reason to say "Congratulations," not just to Walter and his bride, but also to Boyd and Josh.

2. THE DEFINITION OF MARRIAGE

There are doubtless some readers who will think that the entire discussion thus far has been confused. I have been arguing for extending marriage to same-sex couples, people like Boyd and Josh. But many readers will think that this is impossible. Sure, Boyd or Josh could get married. But in order to do so, they would need to find *women*, because marriage by definition is the union of a man and a woman. Call this the *Definitional Objection* to same-sex marriage. In this section I will clarify and respond to the Definitional Objection. But first, I want to spend a little time discussing marriage's diverse forms throughout history.

The History of Marriage and the Argument from Tradition

Many people oppose same-sex marriage on the grounds that marriage has "always and everywhere" been between a man and a woman. Call this the *Argument from Tradition*: marriage has always been a certain way; therefore it should remain so. In this bare-bones form, the Argument from Tradition is not very compelling—after all, traditions can and sometimes should change.

Claims about how marriage has always been are generally rather selective, and often simply false.[12] For instance, the majority of cultures in recorded history have preferred polygamy (and specifically, polygyny) to monogamy.[13] It's not "one man/one woman": it's one man, several women, and perhaps some concubines for good measure.

In many cultures, marriage has been arranged by parents, frequently without their children's input or consent. It has more often been understood as an economic alliance between families, specifying rules for inheritance and division of labor, than as a romantic commitment between spouses: indeed, the romantic view of marriage is a relatively recent invention. It virtually always imposes sexual norms, though these vary from culture to culture. At times it has been deeply oppressive to women, treating them as the property of their fathers and husbands. For example, ancient Assyrian law declared that "a man may flog his wife, pluck her hair, strike her and mutilate her ears. There is no guilt."[14]

Marital living-arrangements vary considerably, as do parenting responsibilities. In some cultures, husbands and wives reside in separate homes, with their children raised by one spouse's family. In others, children are cared for collectively by the tribe. As historian Stephanie Coontz reports, "When Jesuit missionaries from France first encountered the North American Montagnais-Naskapi Indians in the early seventeenth century, they were shocked by the native women's sexual freedom. One missionary warned a Naskapi man that if he did not impose tighter controls on his wife, he would never know for sure which of the children she bore belonged to him. The Indian was equally shocked that this mattered to Europeans. 'You French people,' he replied, 'love only your own children; but we love all the children of our tribe.'"[15]

Sometimes marriage is ceremonially formalized; other times it is not. It is usually presumptively lifelong, with varying degrees of tolerance for divorce. Yet some Arabic cultures have permitted *mut'a*, or temporary marriages, where traveling men could acquire a "wife for a day" in order to have a sexual partner without incurring penalties for nonmarital sex. Any children born of these marriages are considered legitimate.[16]

Only one recorded culture, the Na people of the Yunnan Province of southwestern China, appears not to practice marriage in any form.[17] Instead, brothers and sisters live together, jointly raising the children born from casual sexual encounters with outsiders. (Incest is strictly forbidden.) While the Na have rules and customs related to sex, child-rearing, inheritance, household division of labor, and so on, they lack one key feature seen in every marriage culture: *in-laws*. (Some readers are no doubt thinking, "Sexual freedom and no in-laws? Sign me up!")

Same-sex marriages have been documented in a handful of cultures, notably in African and Native American cultures.[18] Significantly, these groups grant such marriages the same legitimacy as heterosexual marriages, and they use the same terminology for both.[19] Consider the following account from the anthropologist Edward Evans-Pritchard, published in 1951, regarding the Nuer people of East Africa:

> What seems to us, but not at all to Nuer, a somewhat strange union is that in which a woman marries another woman and counts as the pater [father] of the children born of the wife. Such marriages are by no means uncommon in Nuerland, and they must be regarded as a form of simple legal marriage, for the woman-husband marries her wife in exactly the same way as a man marries a woman. When the marriage rites have been completed the [woman-]husband gets a male kinsman or friend or neighbor, sometimes a poor Dinka, to beget children by her wife and to assist, regularly or when assistance is particularly required, in those tasks of the home for the carrying out of which a man is necessary. When the daughters of the marriage are married he will receive for each a "cow of the begetting" and more beasts if he has played any considerable part in the maintenance of the home.[20]

Opponents sometimes respond that other cultures' same-sex marriages are different from "gay marriage," in part because they regularly involve a kind of gender transformation of one partner: a man "plays the wife" or a woman "plays the husband."

But this response is a red herring. Sure, same-sex marriages in these cultures look different from ours in various respects—but so do their heterosexual marriages. In particular, their marriages (both heterosexual and homosexual) tend to exhibit strict gender roles in a manner that is increasingly uncommon in the West. In any case, it is doubtful that opponents would abandon their objection to contemporary same-sex marriages as long as partners agreed to adopt complementary gender roles.

Note, too, the circularity in the opponents' approach: they base the question of whether same-sex marriage is legitimate on the issue of whether it occurs throughout history, and then they refuse to recognize any same-sex unions in history as legitimate same-sex marriages, simply because they do not conform to contemporary patterns of marriage. They also ignore the problem of historical censorship. The fact that gay and lesbian lives tend to be erased from recorded history complicates claims about the way marriage has been "always and everywhere."

So the history of marriage shows that no argument for marriage's future can be limited to looking at its past. Marriage's history is various and complex, and it often diverges from the egalitarian, monogamous male-female union that we tend to think of as "traditional." Moreover, there's a difference between *how marriage has been* and *how it should be now*. Even if same-sex marriage were an entirely new idea—which it is not—that fact by itself wouldn't make it better or worse than old ideas: like any proposal, it needs to be evaluated on its merits.

But can we really evaluate marriage on its merits? There is another, more sophisticated way to understand the Argument from Tradition, and it challenges the presumption that we can step back and scrutinize marriage's logic in the requisite way. The argument has been expressed most clearly by marriage-equality advocate Jonathan Rauch, who calls it a Hayekian argument, after the award-winning economist Friedrich August von Hayek.[21] The idea is that our customs and traditions have a kind of internal practical logic to them, encoding far more information than any individual mind can process. This logic may not always be transparent. But the tradition evolved the way it did for a reason, and we tamper with it at our peril.

It is worth noting that, from the fact that something evolved as it did for a reason, it does not follow that it evolved as it did for a *good* reason. I am reminded here of the old Craig Claiborne story about the woman who received a ham and was disappointed that she didn't own a saw.[22] Although she had never cooked a whole ham, she knew that her mother always prepared hams for cooking by sawing off the end, and she assumed it had to be done this way. So she called her mother, who explained that she learned to cook from her mother, who always did it that way—she had no idea why. Perplexed, the pair then called the grandmother and asked, "Why did you always saw the ends off of hams before roasting them?"

Surprised, the grandmother replied, "Because I never had a roasting pan large enough to hold a whole ham."

My point is that the Hayekian argument against same-sex marriage requires several leaps of faith. It assumes not only that there is a good underlying rationale for our exclusively heterosexual notion of marriage, but also that the rationale still applies—not just for maintaining heterosexual marriage but also for prohibiting same-sex marriage. After all, no one is arguing that same-sex marriage become *mandatory*. Whatever reasons there are for marriage's evolution might continue to operate—indeed, might even be better served—by maintaining marriage for straight couples while simultaneously extending it to gay and lesbian couples.

Rauch goes on to explain that the Hayekian argument can be understood in two ways. In its strong form, it states that we should never tamper with tradition—but that form, clearly, is untenable. Many obviously flawed institutions, and some outright evil ones (such as slavery), are part of our tradition. In its moderate form the argument states that, when modifying long-standing tradition, we should proceed with caution. I agree, as does Rauch. But we should not confuse a reasonable caution with obstinacy or complacency. Marriage has changed in many ways over the centuries—often for the better—and the history of debates over those changes is filled with Chicken-Little-type warnings. E. J. Graff captures the panic nicely, quoting from jurists, church leaders, and others in those prior debates:

> Naturally, conservatives are dragging out the rhetoric that has been hurled against every marriage change...Allowing same-sex marriage would be like allowing married women to own property, "virtually destroying the moral and social efficacy of the marriage institution." Or it would be like legalizing contraception, which "is not what the God of nature and grace, in His Divine wisdom, ordained marriage to be; but the lustful indulgence of man and woman.... Religion shudders at the wild orgy of atheism and immorality the situation forebodes." Or it would be like recognizing marriage between the races, a concept so "revolting, disgraceful, and almost bestial" that it would lead directly to "the father living with his daughter, the son with the mother, the brother with his sister, in lawful wedlock"—and bring forth children who would be "sickly, effeminate, and...inferior." Or it would be like making wives the legal equals of their husbands, a proposal that "criticizes the Bible...degrading the holy bonds of matrimony into a mere civil contract...striking at the root of those divinely ordained principles upon which is built the superstructure of society." Or it would be like allowing divorce, "tantamount to polygamy," thereby throwing "the whole community...into a general prostitution," making us all "loathsome, abandoned wretches, and the offspring of Sodom and Gomorrah."[23]

When Gallagher writes that allowing same-sex marriage means "losing American civilization," it is hard not to suspect similar fearmongering.[24] As Graff's quotations make clear, previous generations saw many changes as disastrous to the meaning and future of marriage. And yet, not only does marriage endure, it is arguably better for these changes.

Meanwhile, not allowing same-sex couples to marry has consequences as well, consequences that can at times be devastating. Exclusion from marriage is no small deprivation.

The Definitional Objection

Which brings us to the Definitional Objection. According to this objection, what we are denying to gays is not *marriage*, since marriage is by definition the union of a man and a woman. Sure, we could call Boyd and Josh's union a "marriage," but we ought to use scare quotes when doing so, since a same-sex union can in fact no more qualify as marriage than a union between a man and a bicycle—that's just not what marriage *is*. Like Abraham Lincoln, who reportedly asked "How many legs would a dog have if we called its tail a leg?" and then insisted (correctly) that the answer is four, proponents of the Definitional Objection claim that calling same-sex unions "marriages" involves a conceptual error.[25] As Gallagher puts it, "Politicians can pass a bill saying a chicken is a duck and that doesn't make it true. Truth matters."[26]

The Definitional Objection is one of those areas where each side tends to see its position as not merely correct, but *obvious*. Marriage-equality opponents say that marriage has been male-female pretty much forever, and you can't just change the meaning of words at will. Marriage-equality advocates say that marriage is an evolving legal and social institution, and if the law and society recognize same-sex couples as married, then they are in fact married. The Definitional Objection is also challenging because it's immune from empirical testing: it is not about the *consequences* of changing marriage, but about the meaning of the word itself.

In its barest form, the Definitional Objection contends that same-sex marriage is simply impossible. As Alliance Defense Fund attorney Jeffery Ventrella puts it, "[T]o advocate same-sex 'marriage' is logically equivalent to seeking to draw a 'square circle': One may passionately and sincerely persist in pining about square circles, but the fact of the matter is, one will never be able to actually draw one."[27] And again, "The public square has no room for square circles, because like the Tooth Fairy, they do not really exist."[28]

It is tempting to respond that we don't normally pass legislation or constitutional amendments banning impossible entities: why worry about something that not only doesn't exist, but can't possibly exist? Committed same-sex relationships certainly exist, and some jurisdictions grant them legal recognition under the name "marriage." So the debate seems to be less about whether something exists than about what to call these existing things.

By analogy, consider a modified version of Ventrella's "square circles" example. Surely there is no such thing as a square ball (or cubical ball, to use a more precise but clumsier term). Yet some tennis coaches have their players practice with irregularly shaped rubber "balls," whose bouncing behavior is erratic, in order to improve their reflexes. Suppose that some of these "balls" are cubical, and that coaches and players refer to them as "square balls." Now it might be an interesting academic question whether these or any objects could possibly be square balls. But that question has little relevance to whether people should continue to call them "square balls," and it certainly has no relevance to whether players should continue to practice with them. These objects exist (we are supposing), and "square balls" is a handy term for them. In a similar way, committed same-sex unions exist, and "marriage" is a handy term for them. What's the problem?

Conservative writer Robert H. Knight has tried to explain the problem with an analogy: "When the meaning of a word

THE CASE FOR SAME-SEX MARRIAGE | 29

defined is lost. For instance, if the state of Hawaii decided to
extend the famous—and exclusive—'Maui onion' appellation
to all onions grown in Hawaii, the term 'Maui onion' would
lose its original meaning as a specific thing. Consumers would
lack confidence in buying a bag of 'Maui onions' if all onions
could be labeled as such."[29] In his public debates, Institute for
American Values president David Blankenhorn makes a similar
point using a different example, asking audiences to imagine
what would happen if the word "ballet" were used to refer to all
forms of dance.

Knight's and Blankenhorn's examples are revealing. Yes, it
would be bad to use the term "Maui onion" for all onions or the
term "ballet" for all forms of dance, but that's because doing so
would frustrate reasonable human aims. If you go to the the-
ater expecting ballet but end up getting Riverdance, you may
be disappointed. The same is true if you go to the grocer asking
for Maui onions but getting plain white ones, or asking for a
chicken but getting a duck. Indeed, Knight makes the frustra-
tion problem explicit: "Consumers would lack confidence in
buying a bag of 'Maui onions' if all onions could be labeled as
such."

Would extending marriage to gays and lesbians frustrate
human aims in a similar way? Not directly. No one worries that,
if society extends marriage to same-sex couples, then grooms
will meet brides at the altar, lift their veils, and exclaim in shock,
"Damn, you're a dude!"

But perhaps the similarity is indirect. Same-sex-marriage
opponents often contend that stretching "marriage" to include
same-sex couples would have bad consequences, such as severing the institution from its child-centered functions. Notice,
however, that this contention represents a rather different sort
of argument: a consequentialist argument based on same-sex
marriage's alleged harms. (We will cover such arguments in

subsequent sections.) Recall that the point of the Definitional Objection is not that treating same-sex unions as marriages would lead to bad consequences, but that doing so is *wrong in itself*, amounting to a kind of lie or confusion. It says that such marriages are not possible, which is different from saying that they're not desirable.[30]

Knight's "Maui onions" example is misleading precisely because it obscures this distinction. "Maui onion" is a label that vendors attach to a distinctive variety of onion grown on the island of Maui. Suppose that a genetically identical variety could be grown on the island of Kauai, and that the resulting onion was indistinguishable in taste, texture, shelf life, and so on. In that case, it would be not only possible, but perhaps even sensible, for vendors to apply the "Maui onion" label to the genetically identical onion. Or consider how Americans often use the term "classical music" broadly to refer to all traditional Western instrumental music, not just music created during the Classical Period (as distinct from the Baroque and Romantic periods). Words are symbols, and speakers may use them in whatever ways serve their communicative aims.

Knight would doubtless respond that the cases are disanalogous: whereas traditional Maui onions and the hypothetical Kauai-grown "Maui onions" are genetically identical, traditional (heterosexual) relationships and same-sex relationships lack an underlying structural similarity. Perhaps so. But it doesn't follow that same-sex relationships are *so* different that they are ineligible for marriage. The problem with the Definitional Objection is that, instead of arguing for this conclusion, it simply asserts it. Eligibility for marriage is precisely what's at issue here. Yet the Definitional Objection says that same-sex couples cannot marry because same-sex marriage is impossible. That's a circular argument if anything is.

Another problem with the Definitional Objection is that it confuses a conceptual issue with a moral one. To see why, consider what I call the Marriage/Schmarriage Maneuver. Imagine a marriage-equality advocate who, after hearing the Definitional Objection, responds:

> You know what? You're right! This thing we're advocating isn't marriage at all. It's something else—let's call it schmarriage. But schmarriage is better than marriage: it's more inclusive, it helps gay people without harming straight people, etcetera. We'd all be better off if we replaced marriage with schmarriage. Now, it's unlikely that the word "schmarriage" will catch on—and besides, it's harder to say than "marriage." So from now on, let's have schmarriage—which includes both heterosexual and homosexual unions—but let's just call it by the homonym "marriage," as people currently do in Massachusetts, Canada, South Africa, and elsewhere. Okay?

Marriage traditionalists will surely respond "Not okay"—but why? The answer is that they reject the idea that the more inclusive institution—schmarriage—is better than marriage. Without some further argument for why it's morally important to maintain an exclusively heterosexual notion of marriage, the Definitional Objection looks like a mere academic quibble, akin to the "square balls" issue discussed earlier.

The Marriage/Schmarriage Maneuver is not entirely hypothetical. Many marriage-equality opponents are willing to grant gays (some or all of) the legal rights and responsibilities of marriage under a different name, such as "civil unions" or "domestic partnerships." In effect, they are willing to grant "schmarriage"—or a pared-down version thereof—for same-sex couples as long as they can keep "marriage" for opposite-sex couples. The semantic distinction matters to them because the underlying "real" distinction matters to them as well. In mirror image, marriage-equality advocates argue that calling same-sex unions by a different name suggests a difference that isn't present, and in turn creates a legal hierarchy: "separate-but-equal" never ends up being equal. Both sides agree that the word "marriage" matters morally because the reality that it signifies matters morally.

What about Civil Unions?

I should digress for a moment to say a bit more about "civil unions" and other attempts to provide same-sex couples a legal status similar but not identical to marriage. "Civil union" was a term invented by the state of Vermont in 2000 in order to give same-sex couples the statewide legal incidents of marriage without using the word "marriage"; since then, a handful of other states have followed suit. Civil unions do not include the (very important) federal legal incidents of marriage—such as social-security and tax benefits, spousal privilege, immigration rights, and so on—they are not portable across state lines (except to jurisdictions that explicitly recognize them), and they do not include the less tangible but crucially important nonlegal incidents of marriage—the history, significance, and social currency of the institution. They're a compromise, and like other historical attempts at providing "separate-but-equal" status, they fall far short of equal.

Suppose, however, that there were a federally recognized, portable civil-union status that genuinely granted *all* of the legal rights and responsibilities of marriage—a "robust" civil-union status. I'm not sure that this is practically achievable in the United States (though the United Kingdom and other European nations seem to have tried it under various names), but if it were achievable, what would I say to that?

I'd say that it would be far better than what we have now. I'm an incrementalist and a pragmatist: I'm willing to take half a loaf now while continuing to work to get the full loaf later—although perhaps a better analogy for "robust" civil unions would be taking virtually the full loaf now and not calling it bread.[31]

But the "virtually" is key. Marriage is much more than a legal status, and its legal meaning affects its social meaning. Insofar as civil unions, domestic partnerships, and other legal arrangements lack the same social significance as marriage, they involve unequal treatment under the law. Even if the legal incidents were identical, their effects would not be. We have seen this problem in a number of real-life cases, where hospital administrators, funeral directors, and other providers have discriminated against civil-union couples despite their alleged legal parity.[32] (Note that this objection would not apply if the state were to get out of the "marriage" business altogether and simply offer civil unions to everyone.[33])

I also think that such a "robust" civil-union compromise would only work to the extent that people didn't think too hard about it. For if it makes sense to grant same-sex couples truly *all* of the legal rights and responsibilities of marriage under a different name, wouldn't it make as much (or more) sense to grant them legal marriage, period? That is what has since happened in Vermont and Connecticut, which within a decade realized that a "separate-but-equal" system was untenable—legally, morally, and practically—and came around to granting marriage to same-sex couples.

The New-Natural-Law Objection

So proponents of the Definitional Objection believe that there's a reality—marriage—that is necessarily heterosexual. They believe that calling other things by the same name would obscure that reality, with the result that people would become less able to recognize and appreciate it. We still need answers to the following questions: What is this distinctive reality called marriage? Why must it be exclusively heterosexual? And why would it be wrong—not just conceptually, but ultimately morally—to replace it with a more inclusive alternative, whatever we might call it?

One way of answering these questions is to appeal to divine intentions: God sets the boundaries of marriage. But since this book is about civil marriage equality in a non-theocratic society, we will steer clear of theological debates. Another is to argue that the moral boundaries somehow exist in nature. The best attempt at this approach comes from a group of theorists known as the *new-natural-law theorists*, to whom we now turn.[34] They provide the most developed available argument for the idea that marriage *by definition* requires the sexual complementarity of one male and one female.

Although the new-natural-law theorists have intellectual roots in the "old" natural-law theory of St. Thomas Aquinas, their argument is rather different. Aquinas opposed homosexual conduct on the grounds that it violates the sexual organs' "natural purpose" of procreation. By contrast, the new-natural-law theorists rightly acknowledge that even though sexual organs are *for* procreation in some sense, it doesn't follow that it's wrong to use them for other reasons.[35] To say otherwise would have absurd implications—for example, that it's wrong to walk on one's hands, as acrobats sometimes do.[36]

Instead, the new-natural-law theorists appeal to the notion of "basic goods." Among these is marriage, understood in a special, prepolitical sense: a comprehensive two-in-one-flesh union of the reproductive kind. While marriage may result in happiness, emotional and physical health, and so on, its function is not reducible to any of these. Nor is it reducible to procreation. According to the new-natural-law view, sex and marriage are not properly chosen merely as a means to some other thing, including children. They are to be chosen for the sake of the comprehensive union—marriage—itself.

As a comprehensive union, marriage unites the partners along multiple levels, which reinforce each other. On the mental/volitional level, it requires a loving, permanent, exclusive commitment between the spouses. On the physical level, it requires that the spouses unite biologically in reproductive-type acts. In such acts, the male and the female become "literally, not metaphorically, one organism."[37] The new-natural-law theorists refer to the resulting view of marriage as the *conjugal view*:

> Marriage is the union of a man and a woman who make a permanent and exclusive commitment to each other of the type that is naturally (inherently) fulfilled by bearing and rearing children together. The spouses seal (consummate) and renew their union by conjugal acts—acts that constitute the behavioral part of the process of reproduction, thus uniting them as a reproductive unit.[38]

So their basic argument against same-sex marriage looks like this: Marriage is, by definition, a comprehensive union. A comprehensive union requires uniting on all levels, including the biological level. The only way in which human beings can truly unite biologically is in conjugal acts (i.e., coitus). Because same-sex partners cannot engage in coitus, they cannot achieve the comprehensive union that is marriage. And it would be wrong for the state and society to treat their unions as marriage, since the state is responsible for the well-being of its citizens.[39] Notice how the new-natural-law theorists integrate the conceptual issue with the moral issue: because marriage is a fundamental good, it is morally important not to obscure or distort it.

For many people, there's something intuitively attractive about the idea that sexual acts make spouses "literally" one organism. (Others find the single-organism idea controversial, if not incoherent.[40]) The idea fits nicely with familiar wedding rhetoric about how "the two become one," for instance.

There's also something attractive about the new natural law's emphasis on our bodily origins. While the importance of biology can be overplayed, and while other kinds of familial connections matter at least as much, if not more,[41] the fact that each of us is a bodily person who exists because of the bodily (sexual) actions of other persons—connected to our parents and grand-parents and so on in an unbroken biological chain—is admit-tedly awe-inspiring. This widely shared attitude explains why most people would be curious to meet a previously unknown biological brother or sister in a way that they would not be curi-ous about, say, a childhood neighbor with whom they had never crossed paths.[42] It also explains why people who have the most wonderful adoptive parents often nevertheless seek to know their biological parents. It's not that their adoptive families aren't "real" or good: it's that, in addition to those families, they want to know the persons from whom they bodily emerged. (Borrowing from the feminist philosopher Sylviane Agacinski, David Blankenhorn frequently refers to this parental connec-tion as the "double origin" of the child.[43]) Biological connections tend to matter to people, and the new-natural-law view places moral weight on the sexual acts behind these connections.

The standard objection to the new-natural-law view con-cerns heterosexual partners known to be sterile. Consider a woman whose cancerous uterus has been removed. Her sex with her future husband cannot result in procreation, and they both know it. How, then, can they engage in reproductive-type acts? Consistency seems to require either that they cannot marry or that the same-sex couple can.

The new-natural-law theorists respond that although the sterile heterosexual couple cannot reproduce, their sexual acts—unlike the same-sex couple's—can still be "of the reproductive type." Because their coitus is still coordinated toward the com-mon good of reproduction, it can still unite them in marriage. In a much-cited recent article entitled "What is Marriage?" Sherif Girgis, Robert George, and Ryan Anderson attempt to explain with an analogy:

> When Einstein and Bohr discussed a physics problem, they coordinated intellectually for an intellectual good, truth. And

the intellectual union they enjoyed was real, whether or not its ultimate target (in this case, a theoretical solution) was reached— assuming, as we safely can, that both Einstein and Bohr were honestly seeking truth and not merely pretending while engaging in deception or other acts which would make their apparent intellectual union only an illusion.

By extension, bodily union involves mutual coordination toward a bodily good—which is realized only through coitus. And this union occurs even when conception, the bodily good toward which sexual intercourse as a biological function is oriented, does not occur.[44]

The problem with this explanation is that there's a big difference between a goal that "does not occur" even though people are "honestly seeking" it, and a goal that *cannot* occur, and which thus cannot be honestly sought by anyone aware of its impossibility. Unlike Einstein and Bohr, who are genuinely intending a solution, the heterosexual couple who know they are sterile cannot intend reproduction—and in that sense, they seem to be in the same boat as the same-sex couple.

Much ink has been spilled on the sterile-couples objection, and I don't want to spend excessive time on it here.[45] What is clear is that when the new-natural-law theorists say *reproductive-type*, they don't mean that reproduction must be intended, and they don't mean that it must be possible. What on earth, then, do they mean?

As far as I can tell, what they really mean is *coital*—in other words, penis-in-vagina. (Or possibly, "*uncontracepted* coital": the new-natural-law theorists appear to differ on whether contraception undermines the reproductive character of otherwise conjugal acts.[46]) Unlike, say, amoeba reproduction, human sexual reproduction requires complementary male-female pairing in coitus. It requires a number of other biological factors as well—such as a functioning uterus—but those are irrelevant to whether sex is of the "reproductive type": the salient factor here is coitus. Only in coitus do the spouses' "bodies become, in a strong sense, one," which is what the comprehensive marital union requires.[47]

If marriage requires procreative-type acts, and "procreative-type" means "coital," then it indeed follows that sterile heterosexual couples can engage in procreative-type acts whereas same-sex couples cannot. But other unpalatable conclusions also follow.

Consider the following case. While engaged to marry Jill, Jack has a horseback-riding accident that paralyzes him from the waist down, rendering him unable ever to perform coitus. Nevertheless, the two legally marry and spend the next several decades raising children that they adopt. Although coitus is impossible, they engage in other acts of sexual affection. Are Jack and Jill married? It seems obvious that they are. But according to the new-natural-law conjugal view, they are not. Jack's inability to form a "bodily union" rendered him ineligible for "real marriage," as the new-natural-law theorists understand it. And since "the state is justified in recognizing only real marriages as marriages,"[48] its recognition of their "marriage" is unjustified.

(Incidentally, while I think that the new-natural-law theorists have no choice but to admit that paraplegics cannot marry in principle, I suspect they'll offer some pragmatic argument having to do with privacy invasions to avoid the unpalatable conclusion that the state should exclude paraplegics from legal marriage. But the initial bullet-biting would be a breathtaking concession.)

There are other counterexamples to the new-natural-law view. For example, its gloss on comprehensive unions implies that those who divorce and remarry are not really married to their second spouses (as long as the first ones are living) and that the state should not recognize them as such; the view is thus untenable for anyone who accepts divorce and remarriage.

In some versions, including those of Robert George and John Finnis, it also implies that spouses who permanently contracept—say, if the male has a vasectomy before the wedding—are not really married.[49] But the paraplegic case is sufficient to establish the conclusion that relationships can merit the label "marriage" even if they do not include—indeed, cannot include—coitus.

Once we acknowledge that conclusion, however, we abandon the new-natural-law theorists' main argument for insisting that same-sex unions cannot be marriages—namely, that marriage requires "bodily union... which is realized only through coitus."[50] The very same factors that lead us to recognize Jack and Jill as truly married—their love, sacrifice, commitment, romantic companionship, and so on—allow us to recognize Boyd and Josh and other same-sex couples as truly married.

What Marriage Is

Early in our collaboration Maggie Gallagher e-mailed me with the following challenge, "What's *your* definition of marriage? If you're going to use a word, you need a definition of the word."

I doubt that.

After all, most English speakers can competently use the word "yellow," but ask the average person to define the term (without merely pointing to examples) and watch him stammer. Then try words like "law," "opinion," "religion," and "game" just for fun. It's quite common to have functional knowledge of how to use a term without being able to articulate its definition.

Okay, you say, but as someone deeply involved in the marriage debate, surely I have some definition to offer? Yes and no. I have *definitions* to offer, not a single definition.

As already noted, marriage is multifaceted. It can be variously understood as a social institution, a personal commitment, a religious sacrament, and a legal status. It looks different from the spouses' perspective than it does from the outside; it looks different respectively to anthropologists, philosophers, theologians, lawyers, and so on. Each of these perspectives can tell us something about what marriage is; none of them is complete or final. So my rejection of a single, final definition stems not from the fact that I don't know what marriage is, as critics will doubtless allege, but from the fact that I do.[51] As one writer helpfully puts it: "There is no single, universally accepted *definition* of marriage—partly because the institution is constantly evolving, and partly because many of its features vary across groups and cultures."[52]

That writer is David Blankenhorn, in his book *The Future of Marriage*. It's a surprising concession, since Blankenhorn—a marriage-equality opponent—spends most of the rest of the chapter railing against marriage-equality advocates for offering definitions that he calls "insubstantial" and "fluttery." Blankenhorn's main complaint is that these definitions are too focused on love and personal commitment. By contrast, he wants to define marriage by its social function, particularly its role in providing for children. He offers the following:

> In all or nearly all human societies, marriage is socially approved sexual intercourse between a woman and a man, conceived as both a personal relationship and an institution, primarily such that any children resulting from the union are—and are understood by the society to be—emotionally, morally, practically, and legally affiliated with both of the parents.[53]

Blankenhorn's definition starts off a bit oddly: "marriage is...sexual intercourse." It seems more natural to say that marriage is the relationship that provides the context for such intercourse. (Perhaps Blankenhorn had the new-natural-law conjugal understanding of marriage in mind.) "Socially approved sexual intercourse" is certainly one angle from which to understand marriage, and not an illegitimate one (pardon the pun). But it's scarcely the sole one, as even Blankenhorn seems to recognize. On the very next page, he acknowledges a counterexample—raised by Christian theologians, no less: Marriage can't be *necessarily* (that is, always) sexual, since if it were, the Virgin Mary's "marriage" to Joseph would not be a marriage. And one could point to plenty of contemporary sexless marriages that are nevertheless marriages. Moreover, Blankenhorn's own definition includes the hedge-words "nearly all" and "primarily," acknowledging that marriage has multiple goals, including goals beyond connecting parents with their biological offspring.

Are there strictly necessary conditions for a union's being a marriage? Yes. For instance, there must be at least two persons. (I say "at least" because polygamous marriages are still marriages, whatever other objections we might have to them.) The partners must at some time understand themselves to be married. Sexual relations between them are prima facie permissible, though not, despite the contrary claims of Blankenhorn and the new-natural-law theorists, required. Beyond those requirements, and maybe a few others, we find a host of typical features: romantic and sexual involvement, a shared domicile, mutual care and concern, the begetting and rearing of children, the intention to make the commitment lifelong and exclusive. But "typical" does not mean "strictly necessary," and for any one of these features, it takes little imagination to conceive of a genuine marriage that lacks it. A "marriage of convenience" is still a marriage, legally speaking. A childless marriage is still a marriage. A marriage on the brink of divorce is still, for the time being, a marriage. What marriage-equality opponents deride as "insubstantial" definitions are actually scholars' attempts to provide analyses broad enough to capture all of the different things that we identify as marriages: loving and loveless, parenting and childless, monogamous and polygamous, domestic and long-distance, same-sex and other-sex. Such definitions may appear to lack specificity. But the alternative is either to pack the definition full of hedge-words ("nearly," "typically," "primarily," "often") or else to leave it vulnerable to counterexamples. Blankenhorn's definition actually exhibits both "flaws," although I'm not sure it's right to call them flaws. The looseness is a feature, not a bug.

In the context of this debate, those who challenge others for definitions (or cite definitions of their own) typically do so with the ulterior motive of proving that same-sex unions either can or cannot count as marriages—which means that their definitions often beg the question against the other side. I'd rather not take the bait. Instead, when people ask me for a definition of marriage, I usually begin by pointing to the standard vow. Marriage is the institution in which people live out the commitment...

*to have and to hold; from this day forward; for better or
for worse; for richer, for poorer; in sickness and in health;
to love and to cherish; until death do us part.*

These are the words my parents used; indeed, that many Americans use. They are the words that Boyd and Josh used. Obviously, they do not provide any kind of complete or perfect definition. We would need to flesh out what it means "to have and to hold," for instance, explaining why that phrase captures a relationship with a spouse but not with, say, a sister. But the vow tells us something important about what people are committing to when they commit to marry.

I shared some of these thoughts in my weekly column once, which prompted an animated e-mail from Blankenhorn. He wrote,

> I invite you to look back at the entire world history of anthropological thought on the topic of what is marriage, and point out to me even ONE example of ONE scholar who has, based on ethnographic data, said, actually or in effect, since recorded history

began, that marriage in human groups is properly defined as the promise of abiding love. If you can identify even one reputable scholar in the history of the world who has made such a statement or implied such a thing, I will grovel before you in abject intellectual humility and gladly buy you the lunch of your choice.

I couldn't find an anthropologist who said that. Actually, I never even bothered looking. Anthropologists define marriage by its cultural function, and "abiding love" isn't really their angle. But I did find this: "The inner and essential *raison d'etre* of marriage is not simply eventual transformation into a family but above all the creation of a lasting personal union between a man and a woman based on love."[54]

What radical, "fluttery" activist wrote these words? In fact, it was Pope John Paul II.

Of course the late pope says that marriage is "between a man and a woman"—no surprise there. But the interesting thing is that he defines it as "above all...a lasting personal union...based on love." Perhaps he was distracted when he wrote this. Perhaps the Radical Gay Agenda had begun to infiltrate the Vatican. Or perhaps the pope realized what most people know: marriage is indeed a lasting personal union based on love—which is not to say that it is *only* that. As I said above—and it bears repeating—any pithy definition of marriage will be partial and imperfect. The theologian's perspective will be different from the anthropologist's, which in turn will be different from the philosopher's, the lawyer's, the historian's, the family therapist's, and so on. There are counterexamples to the pope's characterization, ways in which it is both too broad and too narrow. But "marriage" is not definable in the way "triangle" or "bachelor" is. And when marriage-equality opponents feel compelled to repudiate characterizations of marriage that strike me, the late pope, and most married couples as perfectly reasonable, something is clearly amiss.

The problem stems largely from the different senses of "love." Do we mean love as a fluttery feeling? Then no, that doesn't tell us much about what marriage is. Do we mean love as an abiding, exclusive, lifelong interpersonal commitment?[55] Then that tells us a lot about what marriage is. More important, it also tells us why marriage is so good at doing what it does: providing for the needs of children, for example. Blankenhorn and Gallagher keep insisting on a false dilemma: Either marriage is about providing for children, or else it is "merely" an adult expression of love. Actually, marriage is both of these things—in interconnected ways—and then some.

3. CHILDREN AND CONSEQUENCES

Which brings us to what is probably the core objection to same-sex marriage, and certainly the one most often cited in contemporary public debates: that extending marriage to same-sex couples would be bad for children.

This is a serious charge. If you want to smear an individual or a group of people, a good way to do it is to accuse them of threatening children. I mention this not to stifle whatever sincere concerns marriage-equality opponents have. I understand that they're worried about future generations, as all of us should be. I mention it, rather, because, whether we like it or not, this discussion is fraught with emotion from the start, and it's important to acknowledge that challenge if we want to start generating more light than heat. When the issue of children comes up, one side feels that they're being smeared as predators or family-haters and the other side feels that their children are at risk. Actually, *both* sides feel that their children are at risk: lesbian and gay people have children too, and all of us started out as children. We must proceed with candor, but we must also proceed with care.

The "bad for children" argument comes in various forms, and I won't address them all here. For example, some have argued that extending marriage to gays will cause more children to become gay, a claim that is not only unsubstantiated, but also ultimately question-begging (since it assumes that it's bad for people to turn out gay). Others argue that gays can't be trusted with children because they're likely to harm them intentionally—for example, by molesting them. Fortunately, even social conservatives are beginning to acknowledge this latter argument for the slander that it is.

Still others argue that children whose parents are openly gay or lesbian will be teased by their peers. This is almost certainly true—just like children whose parents are too short or too tall, too fat or too thin, too poor or too rich; or who have funny accents, wear outdated clothing, or give them names like "Moonbeam." Children will get teased about all kinds of things, no matter who their parents are. This fact should often affect how parents prepare children to face the world, but should seldom affect whether they choose to have children in the first place.

What I want to do is to examine the strongest forms of the "bad for children" argument, including the one that Maggie Gallagher offers, in the hopes of making some progress.

Most of the more plausible "bad for children" arguments rest on the claim that the best setting for raising children involves a mother and father, and more specifically, their own biological mother and father. (Even more specifically, their own married biological mother and father in a low-conflict relationship.) This claim is widespread, and many who offer it do so with no apparent antigay bias. For example, the nonpartisan Center for Law and Social Policy (CLASP), after reviewing research on how family structure affects children's well-being, concludes that

> Research indicates that, on average, children who grow up in
> families with both their biological parents in a low-conflict

marriage are better off in a number of ways than children who grow up in single-, step- or cohabiting-parent households. Compared to children who are raised by their married parents, children in other family types are more likely to achieve lower levels of education, to become teen parents, and to experience health, behavior, and mental health problems. And children in single- and cohabiting-parent families are more likely to be poor. This being said, most children not living with married, biological parents grow up without serious problems.[56]

Opponents of same-sex marriage often cite such statements to show that their opposition to same-sex marriage is not right-wing bigotry, but instead a considered judgment based on scientific research. But here's an interesting thing about such research: when it says "biological mothers and fathers" it doesn't really mean biological mothers and fathers. As CLASP explains in a footnote, "The reference to biological parents is to distinguish between biological/adoptive parents and step-parents. Most studies that include data on adoptive parents include them in the biological-parent category."[57] In other words, "biological parents" really means two biological or adoptive parents, *as opposed to single parents or stepparents.*

But if the contrast class is single parents or stepparents, what can such research tell us about *same-sex* parents? Answer: very little.

At most, such research can tell us something about expected differences between gay *single* parents and gay two-parent families, or between same-sex *stepfamilies* and same-sex intact families. It is not surprising that two-parent, intact families have better child-welfare outcomes on average than single-parent families or stepfamilies, since the latter two kinds of families often involve the loss of a parent through death, abandonment, and divorce: things known to be traumatic for children. But to lump such situations together with *planned* same-sex two-parent families—ones begun by adoption, insemination, or surrogacy—is to mix apples and oranges.

What happens when we control for these other variables and directly compare children raised by same-sex parents to children raised by different-sex parents? Although the research (like all research) has its limitations, its conclusions are consistent: children raised in same-sex households fare just as well as their peers on standard measurements of health and well-being.[58] But don't take my word for it. According to the American Academy of Pediatrics, the nation's premier child-welfare organization:

> The American Academy of Pediatrics recognizes that a considerable body of professional literature provides evidence that children with parents who are homosexual can have the same advantages and the same expectations for health, adjustment, and development, as can children whose parents are heterosexual.[59]

And here's the American Psychological Association:

> There is no scientific basis for concluding that lesbian mothers or gay fathers are unfit parents on the basis of their sexual orientation. On the contrary, results of research suggest that lesbian and gay parents are as likely as heterosexual parents to provide supportive and healthy environments for their children.... Overall, results of research suggest that the development, adjustment, and well-being of children with lesbian and gay parents do not differ markedly from that of children with heterosexual parents.[60]

So too says the Child Welfare League of America, the National Association of Social Workers, the American Academy of Child and Adolescent Psychiatry—indeed, every major health and welfare organization that has examined the data.[61] These are not gay-rights organizations; they are not advocacy groups (unlike, say, the American College of Pediatricians, which was founded specifically to promote "traditional" families and is frequently cited by social conservatives).[62] While I don't want to play the game of "my sources can beat up your sources," mainstream professional opinion resoundingly supports the conclusion that, on average, children in same-sex households fare as well as children in heterosexual households.

So the claim that children do best on average with their own married biological mothers and fathers is at best misleading. It conflates a number of distinct variables, including parental number, parental gender(s), marital status, and biological relatedness. One could isolate any of these characteristics and make meaningful comparisons, claiming, for example, that children with two parents do better on average than children with single parents (true), or that children of married parents do better on average than children of cohabiting or divorced parents (also true, keeping in mind that what's true on average is not necessarily true in each individual case). But to the extent that researchers have isolated parental *gender*, comparing same-sex to different-sex parents, they have found that the children fare just as well in each case.

Let's suppose, however—just for the sake of argument—that CLASP's claim is right, and that children, on average, do best with their own married biological parents. What would follow?

To put it bluntly, what would follow is that gay and lesbian couples should not kidnap children from their own married biological parents.

Back on Planet Earth, where gay men and lesbians are not involved in a mass-kidnapping scheme, it's less clear what would follow. Same-sex marriage never—and I mean *never*—takes children away from competent biological parents who want them.[63] I don't mean to be glib, but from the premise

Children on average do best with their own married biological parents

to the conclusion

We should not allow same-sex couples to marry

there are a lot of missing steps. Indeed, more like entire missing staircases. I have yet to see any marriage-equality opponents fill in those missing staircases. Most do not even bother to try.

One immediate problem is that allowing people to marry is different from declaring that it would be ideal for them to raise children. Most same-sex couples don't have children. Those who do have children usually put a great deal of thought into this decision: they do not wake up one day and say "Oops, we're pregnant." In that sense, they are not like the "average" parent, who may or may not have planned for the child and may or may not be prepared for its arrival.

What's more, we allow many couples to marry who fall short of the alleged parenting ideal—as we should. Notably, we allow stepfamilies to form, even though the very same premise that opponents cite against same-sex marriage applies to them: children do best on average with their own married biological parents. We allow poor people to marry, people without college degrees to marry, people in rural areas to marry, and so on, even though research shows that children in these environments do less well on a number of factors than in the alternatives.[64]

We even allow convicted felons serving prison sentences to marry; in fact, we allow it as a matter of constitutional right. The U.S. Supreme Court in *Turner v. Safley* unanimously affirmed that right, noting that "inmate marriages, like others, are expressions of emotional support and public commitment," even given the obvious limitations of prison life.[65] In reaching this decision the Court drew on *Zablocki v. Redhail*, which held that persons delinquent on child support retain the fundamental right to marry.[66]

So a convicted murderer serving a life sentence may marry, but Boyd and Josh may not, because "Children do best on average with their own married biological parents." Do you see what I mean about missing staircases?

Indeed, there's something quite backward about this argument. For if one really believes (against the evidence) that children in same-sex households are disadvantaged, isn't that even *more* reason to provide them the support, stability, and security of marriage—especially in light of what we know about cohabiting parents versus married parents?

By what route can marriage-equality opponents get from the premise "Children do best on average with their own married biological parents," to the conclusion "We should not allow same-sex couples to marry"? Let me here consider two, which I'll call the Emboldening Argument and the Message Argument. (A third, related argument, "The Stretching Argument," is considered in Part 4.)

The Emboldening Argument

The Emboldening Argument asserts that extending marriage to same-sex couples would encourage (or "embolden") more of them to have children. The problem with the Emboldening Argument—aside from the fact that it's speculative—is that it runs up against the "no kidnapping" point: remember, same-sex couples who have children never take them away from competent biological parents who want them. When we consider whether a same-sex household would be a good environment for a child, we must always ask, "Compared to what?"

Putting aside the cases where gay and lesbian individuals have children from prior heterosexual relationships, there are two ways in which same-sex couples usually acquire children. The first is adoption. In most of these cases, the couple is taking the child, not from its biological parents, but from the state, and almost no one—including Gallagher—argues that it would be better for children to languish in foster care than to be raised by loving same-sex couples. There are more than one hundred thousand foster children in the United States alone, waiting to be adopted. If marriage would "embolden" some same-sex couples to provide homes for such children, then that is a reason *for* letting them marry, not against it.

The other way in which same-sex couples acquire children is by insemination, such as when lesbians use sperm banks. Is this bad for the children? Again we must ask: "Compared to what?" In such cases, the realistic alternative is not for the child to live with both biological parents, but for the child not to exist at all. Public-policy decisions must be evaluated by real-world results, and in the real world, lesbians who visit sperm banks are generally not contemplating marrying the father. Since every child is a unique genetic individual (as pro-lifers often remind us), these particular children either exist in same-sex households or don't exist, period.

Would it be better for such children not to exist? It's a difficult question to answer. Better for whom? Not for the children themselves, obviously. The best one could argue is that it would be better for the world at large, somehow, if such children didn't exist, although I'm not sure what such an argument would look like. My point is this: whether or not it would be better for such children to be raised by both biological parents, that's not an option on the table—at least not one that marriage policy will affect. At the risk of belaboring the obvious: banning same-sex marriage does not cause lesbians to marry their sperm donors and form traditional heterosexual families.

I do not wish to downplay the moral issues raised by donor conception. In our public debates over marriage equality, Glenn Stanton often holds up a picture of a small child wearing a T-shirt emblazoned with the words "My Daddy's Name is Donor." The line usually elicits a laugh from the audience, prompting Glenn to launch into his "Except it isn't funny" speech. I'm inclined to agree with him: the creation of life is a weighty matter, about as weighty as matters get. I take seriously the accounts of people who have grown up not knowing one or more of their biological parents and experience a genuine sense of loss as a result. I agree that there's something special about biological bonds, something that I have felt personally: the fact that I am literally flesh of my parents' flesh moves me.

At the same time, to say that the biological bond is special is not to say that it's the only significant bond, or that those who lack it are deprived of something necessary, much less sufficient, for a healthy parent-child relationship. As my own father once told me (in more colorful language): Getting someone pregnant makes you a father; it does not make you a Dad. We should support the many Dads and Moms, biological and nonbiological, straight and gay, who have sacrificed to provide good homes for their children.

What we shouldn't do is conflate the donor-conception issue with the same-sex marriage issue. By substantial margins, most people who use sperm banks are heterosexual; most same-sex couples never use sperm banks; and most sperm banks don't restrict usage to married persons. Activists concerned about the proliferation of donor conception should fight to regulate donor conception, not to deny the personal and social benefits of marriage to same-sex couples. That denial doesn't seem well tailored to their goal; more important, it's unjust: gay men and lesbians should not bear the weight of the donor-conception debate.

One last point on the Emboldening Argument: while I would welcome a thoughtful conversation about the moral dimensions of having children via various technologies, I don't think that conversation should proceed independently of a conversation about the moral dimensions of having children, period—including straight people's doing it the old-fashioned way. Just because heterosexual couples have the right-shaped body parts for having children, it doesn't automatically follow that they should. I would love to see this debate transformed into a more general discussion about whether, when, and why to bring children into the world, rather than just another opportunity for scapegoating gays—which is precisely what Stanton is doing when he holds up the picture of that T-shirt.

The Message Argument

Thus far I've argued that the Emboldening Argument won't connect the dots between the premise "Children do best on average with their own married biological parents"—which I've been granting for the sake of argument—and the conclusion "We should not allow same-sex couples to marry." I want to turn to a second, related argument, and one that, I think, captures Maggie Gallagher's central concern. Let's call it the Message Argument.

The idea is as follows: Children do best on average with their own married biological parents, but parents—and specifically, fathers—are not always naturally inclined to stick around for their children. As my 95-year-old Sicilian grandfather once put it, expressing concern about an unwed mother in our family, "A man pulls up his pants and walks away." So one of society's important functions is to pressure people to take responsibility for their offspring. We do this mainly via the institution of marriage, with all its complex and interrelated elements. We discourage sex outside of marriage because it might create babies for parents who are not bound together for the long haul. We nudge people to get married and stay married. We stigmatize divorce and illegitimacy (though far more mildly than we once did). All of these elements work toward promoting a message. In Gallagher's words: "The marriage idea is that children need mothers and fathers, that societies need babies, and that adults have an obligation to shape their sexual behavior so as to give their children stable families in which to grow up."[67]

Great, you might say, but what's the problem with same-sex marriage? How would it make mothers and fathers any less connected to their children?

The problem, in Gallagher's view, is that endorsing same-sex marriage means endorsing same-sex families, and you cannot do that while simultaneously insisting that children need their own mothers and fathers: "Same-sex marriage would enshrine in law a public judgment that the desire of adults for families of choice outweighs the need of children for mothers and fathers. It would give sanction and approval to the creation of a motherless or fatherless family as a deliberately chosen "good." It would mean the law was neutral as to whether children had mothers and fathers. Motherless and fatherless families would be deemed just fine."[68]

The central premise of the marriage-equality movement is that John and Jim's marriage is just as legitimate, qua marriage, as Jack and Jill's. (That's the whole point of calling it "marriage equality.") But if we make that equivalence, we cannot also insist that children—some of whom John and Jim may be raising—need their mothers and fathers. That insistence would now seem insensitive, even insulting. So Gallagher's argument poses a dilemma: either maintain the message that children need their mothers and fathers, and thus oppose marriage equality; or else embrace marriage equality, and thus relinquish the message. You can't have both.

The Message Argument has several noteworthy strengths. It's based on a premise that seems well motivated, at least on the surface: children need their mothers and fathers. Not in the same sense in which they "need" oxygen, obviously, but in the sense that, on average, that's an environment in which they tend to excel. This is a premise that has personal resonance for Gallagher, who speaks candidly of her own past struggles as a young single mother. Moreover, the Message Argument appears impervious to some standard rebuttals. Two of these rebuttals are worth noting.

First, it does not appear vulnerable to the "sterile couples" rebuttal, at least not at first glance. (There will be a second glance a few paragraphs down, so stay tuned.) Yes, we extend marriage to my elderly neighbor Walter and his lady-friend, but doing so doesn't seem to dilute the message that children need mothers and fathers in the same way that treating Boyd and Josh as married does. Walter and his wife won't have children, but if somehow they did, those children would have a mother and a father. Not so for Boyd and Josh.

Second, it's not vulnerable to the "Compared to what?" rebuttal, the idea that it's unfair to compare same-sex parents to heterosexual biological parents, since gays aren't snatching children away from straights. Of course they're not, but that's beside the point: Gallagher would likely concede that it's better for children to be adopted by a loving same-sex couple than to languish in foster care. But if we call that couple "married," if the law sanctions and approves them as "just fine," then it becomes harder to maintain the message that children need their own biological mothers and fathers. (She has other concerns too: see the "Stretching Argument" discussed in the next section.) In a sense, same-sex couples are a kind of "collateral damage" in Gallagher's culture war: her express aim is not to attack gays, but to maintain a message about children's needs, and she can't do that while also endorsing same-sex couples.

The Message Argument may be the best argument the other side has. Even so, it is pretty weak.

Return to Walter and his postmenopausal bride. If they were to have children, it would most likely be by the same means Boyd and Josh would likely have children: adoption. Then they, unlike Boyd and Josh, would provide those children with a mother and father. But they would not provide them with *their own biological* mother and father, which is how the ideal is typically expressed.[69] So, in fact, the sterile-couples problem looms again.[70] It's true that, as I've already noted, "biological" in the literature doesn't necessarily mean biological: it can also include adoptive parents. The problem for Gallagher is that there's absolutely no data showing that different-sex adoptive parents do better at parenting than same-sex adoptive parents. Again, once we isolate the gender of parents from other variables (such as biological relatedness, or number, or marital history), the evidence is clear: children raised by same-sex parents do just as well as children raised by different-sex parents.[71]

Admittedly, the vast majority of this research has been done on lesbians rather than on gay men like Boyd and Josh. But to the limited extent gay male couples have been studied, the conclusions are similar.[72] And the research on lesbian couples includes some surprising results. For example, in one recent twenty-five-year longitudinal study, children of lesbian couples scored significantly higher than their peers in different-sex households on social and academic competence, and significantly lower in social problems, rule-breaking, and aggressive behavior.[73] Such findings are not entirely surprising, given that mothers tend to be more involved in children's lives than fathers, and that people in same-sex relationships generally plan carefully for children. In any event, while I'm sure that Walter and his wife would make fine adoptive parents—albeit elderly ones—there is no evidence predicting that they are likely to make better adoptive parents than Boyd and Josh.

To put all of this another way: If the Message Argument is about sending the message that fathers shouldn't abandon their children, or that people with children should treat divorce as a last resort, that would be one thing. But if the message is that children with a male and female parent do better than children with two male or two female parents, then the argument is based on a false and unsupported premise.

This problem points to a second, and related, flaw in the Message Argument: namely, that it confuses what's (allegedly) ideal with what's mandatory. As CLASP acknowledges, "most children not living with married, biological parents grow up without serious problems." And even if one believes that being raised by a biologically related mother and father is significant for children's welfare, it's not nearly as significant as other factors that marriage-equality opponents routinely overlook, such as economic class, parental education, urban versus rural environments, race, and the number of other children already in a family.[74] The reasons why these factors correlate with children's welfare are complex, and sometimes obscure, but no one who has reviewed the literature denies the correlations. Take economic class, for example. Compared to their more affluent counterparts, poor children show significantly worse outcomes in terms of physical health, cognitive development, academic achievement, behavioral adjustment, crime, graduation rates, mortality, and eventual adult income.[75] And yet we allow poor couples to marry, as long as they're different-sex. How do we do this, without undermining the message that children "need" economic security and declaring that its absence is "just fine"? Marriage-equality opponents are strikingly inconsistent in their willingness to make the ideal the enemy of the good.

Which brings me to a third problem. Suppose you were interested in promoting children's well-being, and in particular, in addressing the problem of fatherlessness. What could you do? You could work on comprehensive sex-education programs, including accurate information about both abstinence and contraception. You could aim at some of the purported root causes, including poverty, lack of educational and employment opportunities, and incarceration policy. You could tighten up divorce laws, given the documented effect of divorce on children's well-being. You could promote relationship counseling. You could do all of these things, and a hundred more.

Or you could do what the National Organization for Marriage does. The National Organization for Marriage (NOM), which Maggie Gallagher founded, styles itself as

America's premier organization to protect marriage. Of the various ways just mentioned to address the problem of fatherlessness, how many do you think that NOM pursues? If you guessed "zero," you are correct. *Not a single one.* The National Organization for Marriage focuses on fighting same-sex marriage, and that alone. Which makes it very hard to believe that gays are just collateral damage in their effort to promote children's welfare.

There is a fourth problem. Gallagher claims that marriage's message is that children need mothers and fathers. That's certainly a message of marriage, but it's scarcely the only one. Marriage also sends the message that it's good for people to have a special someone to care for them and vice versa—to have and to hold, for better or worse, until death do they part. It sends a message about the importance of forming family, even when those families don't include children; about making the transition from being a child in one's family of origin to being an adult in one's family of choice. It sends the message that commitment matters—to individuals, couples, and the community at large. All of these messages are important, and none of them is unique to straight people.

Meanwhile, to deny marriage to a group of people also sends a message. When we consider other groups who were once excluded from marriage—notably, slaves and prisoners—that message is pretty clear: you are less than a full citizen. Your relationships aren't "real"; your families don't matter. Gallagher claims that she loves and respects gay people, and I want to believe her. But how can she sustain that message while also opposing marriage equality? How is she not telling couples like Boyd and Josh, along with thousands of same-sex families with children, that they are unworthy of equal dignity and respect? Gallagher's dilemma has a flip side: Either gay people are full-fledged members of our society—in which case they too deserve the rights and responsibilities of marriage—or else they are second-class citizens, people whose relationships and families aren't "real." You can't have both.

Real Children

My partner Mark and I neither have nor plan to have children. Although we have a large circle of friends, we have no close gay friends with children, except for some whose children are grown or nearly so. Our lack of experience with gay parents probably stems from the fact that people with kids tend to hang around other people with kids, with whom they share common interests (such as sofas that don't show jam stains). The only children routinely in our lives are our infant nieces, whom we thoroughly adore—although not to the point of wanting babies of our own.

So my direct experience of gay couples with children has mostly been through acquaintances. Among these are Dennis and Tom, who live on a farm just outside Ann Arbor, about forty-five minutes from where I live in Detroit. While working on this book, I visited them. I share their story in order to put a face on an issue that too often gets discussed only in abstractions, with vague assertions about an unspecified threat to unidentified children.

Dennis and Tom have four adopted sons: Josh, 14; Joey, 11; Paul, 11; and Raul, 9, who is Joey's half-brother. A fifth boy—Zack, 9—is a foster son, and they are hoping to adopt him as well. They live in a Victorian farmhouse on five acres, with chickens, pigs, goats, a bird, a turtle, some fish, a dog named Scout, and a cat named Milkshake. I met Tom some years ago when we both served on the selection committee for a local gay and lesbian film festival. The family came back on my radar when the local LGBT newspaper profiled them around the time of Michigan's 2004 marriage amendment, which prohibits same-sex marriage "or similar union[s] for any purpose." In order to devote more attention to the boys, Tom—a high-school math teacher—had decided to work only part-time, and he was getting his health-insurance benefits through Dennis, a university communications professor. The amendment's wording threatened those benefits, potentially forcing Tom to choose between having affordable health insurance and spending days with his boys.

As we sit in the large screened porch behind their house, I ask Dennis about this problem. "Yes, it's unfair, but the main problem isn't the benefits," he explains. "It's the lack of protections for the boys." Because Michigan forbids same-sex couples from marrying, and because it doesn't have a clear policy on second-parent adoption by unmarried partners, typically only one partner in a gay couple can be the adoptive parent. Let's suppose that parent is Dennis. If Dennis were to die, Tom—the man these boys know as "Papa"—might lose the children: it all depends on whether they find a sympathetic judge. Even while they're both living, there are challenges related to hospital visitation, family leave, school access, and so on. And there's also the more general sense of permanence that marriage helps provide, and that this family is denied.

Dennis has always wanted children. Tom needed some convincing, but now he's hooked. I can see why. The boys, who greet me at various points during my tour of the property, are charming. As Dennis and I chat, two of them come running in. "Dad, can I use my allowance to buy a movie on demand?" one asks. Before he finishes his sentence, the other interrupts, "Dad, can I buy something on eBay?" They both give me a curious glance. Dennis specializes in family communication, and he speaks with the calm, assured demeanor one might associate with a family therapist. "Okay, but can we talk about that later?" he responds patiently. "We have a guest right now." "Oh, okay!" they shout in unison, running off.

A rooster crows nearby, and I'm reminded that this is a real farm. It's a nice setting for raising children—downtown

Ann Arbor is only fifteen minutes away—and the boys strike me as happy and well-adjusted. Given what I know of Tom and Dennis, this doesn't surprise me, although I'm also aware that these children, like many adopted by same-sex couples, were difficult to place. One has a seizure disorder and cognitive disabilities. One is hearing-disabled. Two have ADHD. Two have been sexually abused or have witnessed sexual abuse by their "natural" (biological) fathers. At least three have had parents who have been incarcerated. One wasn't speaking when Tom and Dennis first met him. He was 5 at the time. Dennis's professional training is doubtless a strong asset here.

Zack, the foster child the couple is trying to adopt, is in his sixth placement. Two previous families had told him that they would adopt him, but didn't. Needless to say, he has serious "trust issues."

I ask Dennis whether the kids expressed any concern about living in a same-sex household. He smiles. "No. Their concerns were much more practical. Like, 'What kind of video-game system do they have?' Or, 'Do they have a dog?' Only recently have they come to realize that this is at all controversial." Last year the family participated in an episode of *Thirty Days*, Morgan Spurlock's reality series where participants spend a month in an unfamiliar setting in order to explore cultural divides. The family hosted a conservative Mormon mother who vocally opposed homosexuality. While she acknowledged that Tom and Dennis are loving parents, she was resolute in her conviction that such adoptions should be forbidden. Her cited reason was God's law.

The porch door swings open again, and another boy appears. This one seems more hesitant and shy. "Dad, what are you doing?" he asks quietly. "I'm having an interview with my friend John," Dennis answers. "He's asking about our family. Why don't you go get your brothers so he can talk to you guys too?" As the boy runs off, Dennis and I continue our conversation. Tom, meanwhile, is preparing dinner in the kitchen, and he sends us a delicious tray of fried vegetables. The vegetables are from their garden, and Dennis warns me that some of the peppers are quite hot. "The boys like to play a version of 'Russian Roulette' with them, mixing one hot pepper with a bunch of mild ones and then daring their friends to taste them," he informs me with a chuckle.

"Do you ever worry about the absence of a mother?" I ask pointedly. Dennis pauses. "It depends on what you mean by 'mother.' When I think 'mother,' I think of things like *nurturing, caring, unconditional love.*[76] The boys have all of that. And they certainly have female influences in their lives. One of their biological mothers visits regularly. They also have grandmothers, aunts, and the women who dote on them at church." (Tom and Dennis are active in the United Church of Christ.)

I wince when I learn that one of the boys ended up in foster care because his mother was selling his ADHD meds to support her drug habit. Dennis continues, "We may not be 'mothers' in the technical sense, but we're certainly giving them a loving, safe home, which they desperately needed."

The boys return, and I become slightly uneasy. I'm not accustomed to being around children, and I'm certainly not used to interviewing them about their personal lives. Dennis, a communication expert, senses my discomfort. "Guys, John was just asking about what it's like living here without a mom." Several of them shrug: "It's fine." I realize that their point of comparison is rather different from mine: group homes or foster care, not a stable mother-father environment from birth. I'm reminded, again: Same-sex marriage never takes children away from competent biological parents who want them.

One of the boys pipes up, "Sometimes kids at school ask if my mom died. She's not dead!" The other boys laugh: "We saw her last month!"

I decide I should ask them something directly. "What would it be like if your Dad and Papa could get married?" I offer.

At first, more shrugs. Then, after some prompting from Dennis, they start opening up. Before I know it, they're all talking at once, interrupting and elbowing and teasing each other the way brothers do: "It would be fun...I would wear a tuxedo...You would wear a wedding dress! [giggling]...I would not! You be quiet!...No, you be quiet!...He would be the flower boy! [more giggling]...There is no flower boy, silly..."

Two things strike me as I hear this cacophony. One is that, same-sex parents or not, boys will be boys. The other is that, in kids' minds, it's hard to separate "marriage" from "wedding." Josh, Joey, Paul, Raul, and Zack don't understand legal reality, and their personal reality already looks to them like "family"—because that's what it is. I can only hope that they never experience the devastating problems that often arise when the legal and personal realities don't align.

It's not just the absence of legal protections that concerns me, however. It's also the less tangible—but undeniable—social support, stability, and security that marriage brings. And it's the message that we're sending them, and society at large, when we deny it to their "Dad" and "Papa": this family isn't worthy.

There are some who will dismiss this case as anecdotal, or as a fallacious appeal to emotion. It is true that not all same-sex households look like that of Tom and Dennis: a family-communication professor and a high-school math teacher raising adopted special-needs children on an idyllic farm near Ann Arbor. But it's equally true that not all different-sex households look like the "ideal" family that traditionalists invoke when they insist that "children need their own biological mother and father"—a point that is painfully underscored by these kids' family histories.

In any case, allowing gays to marry will not take children away from such "ideal" families. This is where the rubber meets the road in the marriage debate: same-sex marriage does not take children away from competent biological mothers and fathers who want them, but its absence denies the security of marriage to real children—children like Josh, Joey, Raul, Paul, and Zack.

4. THE SLIPPERY-SLOPE ARGUMENT AND THE BEYOND-MARRIAGE ARGUMENT

There are other objections to marriage for gays and lesbians. In this section I'd like to discuss two which, though loosely related, come from sharply different quarters: the "right-wing" argument that if we accept same-sex marriage, we must also accept polygamy, incest, bestiality, and so on, and the "left-wing" argument that we should embrace family forms beyond the traditional narrow confines of two-person marriage.

The first of these I'll label the slippery-slope argument, although it comes in two rather different versions, and it's not clear whether the label is properly applied to both.[77] The general idea is that there is some connection between same-sex marriage, on the one hand, and various objectionable relationships, on the other. Since polygamy, incest, and bestiality are the most commonly cited, I've sometimes called this the PIB argument.[78] As former U.S. Senator Rick Santorum (a Republican presidential candidate at the time of writing) infamously put it, "if the Supreme Court says that you have the right to consensual sex within your home, then you have the right to bigamy, you have the right to polygamy, you have the right to incest, you have the right to adultery. You have the right to anything." Later in the same interview he compared same-sex marriage to "man on child, man on dog, or whatever the case may be."[79]

Why are these other kinds of relationships any more connected to homosexuality than to heterosexuality? After all, polygamy can be heterosexual or homosexual, and the societies that practice it tend to be the *least* accepting of same-sex relationships. Incest can be heterosexual or homosexual. Bestiality, I suppose, can be heterosexual or homosexual, although like most people I prefer not to think about it too carefully. In short, what does one thing have to do with the other?

There are two possible answers to this question, and they give us the two broad versions of the PIB argument: a *logical* version and a *causal* version. (Note: calling one the *logical* version does not mean that the other one is illogical; it just means that it's based on logical, *a priori* connections rather than empirical ones.) Let's take each in turn.

The logical version states that the reasons for accepting same-sex marriage are equally good reasons for accepting polygamy, incest, or bestiality, so that if you embrace the one you have no principled reason for rejecting the others. In other words, the pro-gay position logically entails the pro-PIB position. Why would anyone think this? The answer, I suspect, is that opponents misread the pro-gay position as claiming that "People should be able to marry anyone they love." It does indeed follow from the "anyone they love" premise that people should be able to marry multiple partners, their children, their pets, their kitchen appliances, and so on. But I know of no one in the marriage-equality movement who really accepts this premise, despite pithy bumper-sticker slogans suggesting otherwise. It's a straw man.

When we look at the actual pro-gay (or pro-equality) argument, what do we find? I've already explained the "mutual-lifelong-caregiving" case: Society should embrace marriage equality because it's good for gay and straight people alike to have a "special someone" to have and to hold, and so on, for life. Such partnerships are good, not only for the individuals who have them, but also for the community around them. Does the same apply to PIB?

I think it's pretty obvious that bestiality doesn't qualify. Actually, I thought it was pretty obvious until I had a student push the point in one of my classes. "What about a really intelligent chimpanzee?" he asked with apparent seriousness. But Jonathan Rauch, who was visiting the class via audio conference at the time, settled the question nicely: "And when the spouse is in the hospital on life support," Rauch responded, "and the doctor calls and asks what to do, what does the really intelligent chimpanzee say?"

Most serious arguments for marriage equality rest on the premise that marriage (between human beings) achieves important goods, for gays as well as straights. Marriage to pets does not, and the case against "bestial marriage"—which, among other problems, lacks full and equal voluntary participation—is the same across the board.

So too is the case against marrying relatives. The reason why straight people should not marry relatives is not just because their offspring might have birth defects (a problem which can be anticipated via genetic testing, and which doesn't apply past childbearing age), but also because of the ways in which sex changes the dynamics of family life. As Rauch vividly puts it,

> Imagine being a fourteen-year-old girl and suspecting that your sixteen-year-old brother or thirty-four-year-old father had ideas about courting you in a few years. Imagine being the sixteen-year-old boy and developing what you think is a crush on your younger sister and being able to fantasize and talk about marrying her someday. Imagine being the parent and telling your son he can marry his sister someday, but right now he needs to keep his hands off her...I cannot fathom all of the effects which the prospect of child-parent or sibling-sibling marriage might have on the dynamics of family life, but I can't imagine the effects would be good, and I can't imagine why anyone would want to try the experiment and see.[80]

There is another important disanalogy between banning incestuous marriage and banning same-sex marriage. The incest ban means that every person is forbidden to marry *some* people—a relatively small group—with whom he might fall in love: his relatives. By contrast, the same-sex marriage ban means that gay people are forbidden to marry *anyone* with whom they might fall in love. Unlike the incest ban, it reduces their pool of available marriage partners to zero—an infinitely greater restriction.[81]

The alleged slippery slope to polygamy is harder to address for several reasons. The "mutual lifelong caregiving" case does seem to apply here, at least at first glance (but stay tuned again for a second glance). Polygamy is the most common form of marriage historically,[82] and there are people who practice it today even in the United States—in states that adopt a "don't ask, don't tell" policy for Fundamentalist Mormons and other religious communities. Moreover, there are serious people, including some prominent pro-gay academics, advocating for polygamy and other family forms. Does my position logically commit me to accepting polygamy as well?

I don't think so. Remember, the "mutual-lifelong-caregiving" case is a prima facie case, one that can be revised after examining the relative costs and benefits. After examining most of the major arguments, we have yet to see any serious costs from extending marriage to same-sex couples. By contrast, we have thousands of years of human history demonstrating the typical costs of polygamy. Polygamy tends almost always to be polygyny, where one man has multiple wives. (By contrast, polyandry—one wife with multiple husbands—is quite rare.) The usual result is a sexist and classist society where high-status males acquire multiple wives while lower-status males become virtually unmarriageable. In that sense, examined from the social-policy point of view, polygamy actually undermines our "mutual-lifelong-caregiving" goal: if we want to ensure that as many people as possible form stable family units, we should be wary of allowing any one individual to take multiple spouses.

Could polygamy be structured in such a way as to avoid these typical effects—perhaps via "polyamory," a more egalitarian form of "group love"? Maybe. I leave it to those who want to advocate for other family forms to make their case. My point is that there's no logical connection between the case for polygamy (which must include consideration of its likely social effects) and the case for same-sex marriage (ditto). Each issue must be judged on its own merits.

I've expressed this point before, which usually elicits a "Gotcha!" response from my critics: "Aha! So you're saying that *if* polygamy actually promoted individual well-being and community flourishing, you wouldn't oppose it?" Yes—that is precisely what I'm saying.

From this admission, opponents gleefully conclude that I have no principled objection to polygamy after all, and that I've thus conceded the logical version of the PIB argument. For example, here's Robert George, responding to an essay by Rauch:

> Rauch and the authors he cites (John Corvino, Dale Carpenter, and Paul Varnell) do not make a serious effort to show that, as a matter of principle, marriage is an exclusive union of the sort that is incompatible with polygamy (much less polyamory). Corvino doesn't even join Rauch in asserting that there is anything wrong with polygamy—much less that polygamy is incompatible in principle with true marriage. Putting it in the hypothetical, he says, "If there's a good argument against polygamy, it's likely to be a fairly complex public-policy argument having to do with marriage patterns, sexism, economics, and the like."[83]

George thus sees my position as further evidence for his conclusion that marriage-equality advocates must abandon "*any principled basis* for understanding marriage as the union of two and only two persons" (italics mine).[84] Aha!

Aha nothing. George is simply confused here about what it means to have a "principled" objection to something. More specifically, he confuses having "a principled objection" with having "an objection in principle." The distinction is subtle but important. To have a principled objection is to base one's opposition on moral principles, rather than simply to assert it arbitrarily. In considering the potential social costs of polygamy, Rauch, other marriage-equality advocates, and I surely do this. By contrast, to have an "objection in principle" is to object to a thing *in itself*, not on the basis of extrinsic reasons or consequences. Rauch and I don't object to polygamy "in principle:" we object to it for its expected social costs. (To her credit, Maggie Gallagher agrees, siding with Rauch against George in the debate over whether polygamy is wrong "in principle."[85]) The distinction is crucial, because once one moves from "no objection in principle" to "no principled objection," it's a short slide to "no serious objection"—and thus a bad misrepresentation of our position.[86]

George's mistake is especially egregious because, as far as I can tell, he doesn't have any compelling "objection in principle" to polygamy either. (Aha, yourself!) As I explained earlier, George's position depends on the new-natural-law understanding of biological unity: "Marriage...can be achieved by two and only two because no single act can organically unite three or more people at the bodily level or, therefore, seal a comprehensive union of three or more lives at other levels."[87] It is startling that any view rooted in reproductive biology should claim exclusivity as one of its characteristic features. Although human sexual reproduction requires two and only two persons, it doesn't follow that those persons cannot each form reproductive pairs with multiple others: they can, and many do. So the argument for monogamy will have to come from somewhere other than the biological complementarity of the sexes. Insofar as that argument depends on the mutual commitment between the partners, there is no reason why it wouldn't be equally available to marriage-equality advocates: only one person can be your "Number One Person."

The Causal Slippery-Slope Argument

Thus far I've been arguing that there's no *logical* connection between same-sex marriage and PIB. But there's another way of understanding the slippery-slope argument. Perhaps the connection is not logical, but causal. That is, perhaps extending marriage to gays *will* result in PIB, whether or not it logically should. For example, maybe it will embolden polygamists' rights groups and make it harder for everyone else to resist their advocacy.

The most prominent proponent of the causal PIB argument is Stanley Kurtz, who claims that the slippery slope to polygamy is "[a]mong the likeliest effects of gay marriage."[88] (The causal version generally ignores incest and bestiality, and from here on so shall we.) Kurtz has been predicting this pro-polygamy effect since the mid-1990s. But his evidence for it is slim, and his evidence for its connection with same-sex marriage is even slimmer.

Kurtz writes,

> It's getting tougher to laugh off the "slippery slope" argument—the claim that gay marriage will lead to polygamy, polyamory, and ultimately to the replacement of marriage itself by an infinitely flexible partnership system. We've now got a movement for legalized polyamory and the abolition of marriage in Sweden. The Netherlands has given legal, political, and public approval to a cohabitation contract for a polyamorous bisexual triad. Two out of four reports on polygamy commissioned by the Canadian government recommended decriminalization and regulation of the practice. And now comes *Big Love*, HBO's domestic drama about an American polygamous family.[89]

This paragraph nicely encapsulates the kinds of exaggerations and outright falsehoods that typify Kurtz's discussion of this issue.

First, at the time Kurtz wrote the above paragraph (in 2006), Sweden didn't have "gay marriage": it had "registered partnerships," the kind of "separate-but-equal" status most marriage-equality advocates ultimately oppose—as should anyone worried about an "infinitely flexible partnership system." Second, the case of the "polyamorous bisexual triad" was not a marriage, but a private cohabitation contract signed by a Dutch notary public: the relationship was neither registered with, nor sanctioned by, the state. It was no more a legal polygamous marriage than a three-person lease agreement is a legal polygamous marriage. Third, the fact that some Canadian studies of polygamy recommended decriminalization and regulation is hardly evidence of widespread support for the practice: compare, for example, U.S. studies recommending decriminalization and regulation of currently illegal drugs. Fourth, Europe is culturally different from the United States in a variety of ways. And fifth, the success of the HBO series *Big Love* signaled a wave of support for polygamy about as much as the success of *The Sopranos* signaled a wave of support for the Mafia.

The deeper problem is that Kurtz fails to show any causal connection between this supposed pro-polygamy shift and same-sex marriage. He has tried to establish one by looking at marriage trends in Scandinavia, but his analysis falters on the fact that these trends substantially pre-dated marriage equality there. (See William Eskridge and Darren Spedale's *Gay Marriage for Better or for Worse?: What We've Learned from the Evidence* for a book-length refutation.)

He has also tried to establish the connection by arguing that some of the same people who endorse polygamy also endorse same-sex marriage, and that they invoke the same "civil rights" language in both cases. This is true but entirely inconclusive.

Some of the same people who oppose abortion also oppose capital punishment and invoke the same "sanctity of life" language, but that's no reason to conclude that one movement leads to the other. Recall that the vast majority of the world's polygamy supporters are religious fundamentalists who strenuously *oppose* gay rights, and that the practice tends to appear in U.S. states (like Utah, Nevada, and Texas) with the *lowest* support for marriage equality. Kurtz can link the two movements only by selective myopia.

Kurtz has also tried to connect the two via the issue of infidelity. He claims that polygamous societies tend to have high rates of infidelity, because they promote the idea that men "need" multiple women. Such infidelity is problematic because it causes instability for both wives and children, many of whom are born "illegitimate." (Notice again the theme that children need their fathers.) How does Kurtz then connect this problem with homosexuality? His "logic" seems to go like this: polygamous societies have high rates of infidelity; gay men have high rates of infidelity; therefore, the gay-marriage movement will lead to polygamy—presumably by weakening the norms of fidelity that hitherto kept polygamy at bay (as if Americans were just itching to become polygamous if only they could get away with it).

It thus appears that polygamy isn't Kurtz's ultimate target: his real concern is infidelity, with its consequent out-of-wedlock births, jealousy, and general instability. The resulting argument is similar to another which has been more recently formulated by *New York Times* columnist Ross Douthat, blogger Eve Tushnet, and other conservative writers. Call it the *Stretching Argument.* The idea is that heterosexual relationships differ in important ways from both gay male relationships and lesbian relationships, and that stretching marriage to cover all three kinds of pairings (male-female, male-male, female-female) would dilute its purposes. As Tushnet explains,

"If you have a unisex model of marriage, which is what gay marriage requires, you are no longer able to talk about marriage as regulating heterosexuality and therefore you're not able to say: Look, there are things that are different about heterosexual and homosexual relationships. There are different dangers, there are different challenges, and, therefore, there are probably going to be different rules."[90]

There are many striking features of this argument. One is the way it overlooks the great extent to which same-sex couples face the same challenges—of commitment, care, childrearing, intimacy, security, and so on—as their heterosexual neighbors. (We gays are not a different species, despite some conservatives' efforts to paint us as such.) Even more striking, though, is the way the argument glosses over the diversity of heterosexual relationships, with their "different dangers...different challenges, and...different rules." To take just one example, consider a pair of elderly widowed heterosexuals—like my neighbor Walter and his fiancée—who marry. Does anyone imagine that their challenges are quite like those of young newlyweds? Does anyone presume that, by treating them as married, we lose the ability to acknowledge that the stakes are different for them (and for society) than they were in the case of their first marriages? Or that they might respond to those differences by incorporating "different rules"?

Of course, the "different rules" that most concern Tushnet, Douthat, Gallagher, Kurtz, and others have mostly to do with sexual exclusivity (or "monogamy" or "fidelity," words that mean somewhat different things even though they are often used interchangeably[91]). Although these authors rarely make the argument explicit, it is not hard to put two and two together and come up with the following on their behalf:

(1) Sexual exclusivity is challenging, and people are unlikely to achieve it unless given good reason to do so.

(2) Same-sex couples have less reason for sexual exclusivity than (most) heterosexual couples do, because gay sex doesn't make babies. (Note: "less reason" does not mean "no reason.")

(3) And gay men in particular have less reason for sexual exclusivity, because sexual openness/promiscuity doesn't correlate with male unhappiness the way it correlates with female unhappiness (according to research cited by Douthat, among others).[92] So, for example, if Walter fools around on the side, that might not bother him, but it would almost certainly bother his new wife.

(4) Therefore, we should expect gay couples—especially gay male couples—to be less sexually exclusive than straight couples. And indeed, social science research and anecdotal evidence confirms this expectation: men who have sex with men appear to have a higher tolerance for open relationships.[93]

(5) Letting gays marry would thus undermine the norm of sexual exclusivity for everyone.

(6) This effect would be bad for society generally, because of more out-of wedlock births, unhappy women, and so on.

There's more than one place to attack this argument, but the weakest point, in my view, is at (5): *Letting gays marry would undermine the norm of monogamy for everyone.*

It should go without saying, but letting gays marry will not change the fact that straight sex makes babies or that straight relationships contain women. It also won't change the fact that at least half of same-sex couples *are* women. (Even Kurtz admits that "Lesbians, for their part, do value monogamy."[94]) Finally, it won't change straight people's ability to think for themselves, notwithstanding social conservatives' apparent pessimism on this point.

While sexual exclusivity may be hard, it's not so hard that a sexually exclusive couple (straight or gay) can't look at a sexually open couple (straight or gay) and conclude, "Nope, that's not right for us." After all, people read the Bible without deciding to acquire concubines. More realistically, they encounter neighbors with different cultural mores while still preferring—and sometimes having good reason to prefer—their own. As marriage-equality opponents often remind us, gay men and lesbians make up a relatively small minority of the general population.[95] Same-sex *couples* make up a smaller minority, *coupled gay males* an even smaller minority, and *coupled gay males in open relationships* a smaller minority still. In Rauch's words, "We might as well regard nudists as the trendsetters for fashion."[96]

I conclude that letting the gay couple next door marry is no more likely to create a wave of open relationships than letting the swinging straight couple next door marry: there are still compelling reasons to encourage monogamy, especially (but not only) for those whose sex can result in pregnancy. It is also worth pointing out where the causal version of the slippery-slope argument has taken us: Gay men and lesbians should not be permitted to marry, Kurtz and others seem to be arguing, because if they do, straight people will misbehave. (The argument is similar to what law professor Kenji Yoshino has identified as the "reckless procreation" rationale: only straight people should be allowed to marry because only straight couples ever say "Whoops, we're pregnant."[97]) Maybe proponents don't make the Stretching Argument explicit because it ultimately sounds so silly.

Things that Hang Together

Perhaps asking for a causal link between same-sex marriage and various social ills was too much. David Blankenhorn seems to think so. He writes, "Neither Kurtz nor anyone else can scientifically prove that allowing gay marriage causes the institution of marriage to get weaker. Correlation does not imply causation."[98] This is a refreshing concession. Unfortunately, Blankenhorn proceeds as if it makes no difference: "Scholars and commentators have expended much effort trying in vain to wring proof of causation from the data," he writes, "all the while ignoring the meaning of some simple correlations that the numbers do indubitably show." But what can these correlations mean, if not that same-sex marriage is causally responsible for the alleged problems? What do the numbers "indubitably show"? Blankenhorn's answer provides a textbook example of a circular argument:

> Certain trends in values and attitudes tend to cluster with each
> other and with certain trends in behavior....The legal endorse-
> ment of gay marriage occurs where the belief prevails that marriage
> itself should be redefined as a private personal relationship. And all
> of these marriage-weakening attitudes and behaviors are linked.
> Around the world, the surveys show, these things go together.[99]

In other words, what the correlations show is that these things are correlated. Not very helpful.

From there, Blankenhorn argues that if things "go together," opposition to one is good reason for opposition to all. He attempts to illustrate by analogy: "Find some teenagers who smoke, and you can confidently predict that they are more likely to drink than their nonsmoking peers. Why? Because teen smoking and drinking tend to hang together."[100] So if you oppose teenage drinking, you ought to oppose teenage smoking, because of the correlation between the two. In a similar way, Blankenhorn argues, if you oppose nonmarital cohabitation, single-parent childrearing, or other "marriage-weakening behaviors," you ought to oppose same-sex marriage, since they too "tend to hang together."

This is breathtakingly bad logic. The analogy sounds initially plausible because teen drinking and teen smoking are both bad things. But the things that correlate with bad things are not necessarily bad. Consider: find some teenagers who have tried cocaine, and you can confidently predict that they are more likely to have gone to top-notch public schools than their non-cocaine-using peers. This is true. But it's not because superior education causes cocaine use. It's because cocaine is expensive, and expensive drugs tend to show up in affluent communities, and affluent communities tend to have better public schools than their poor counterparts. Yet it would be ridiculous to conclude that, if you oppose teen cocaine use, you ought to oppose top-notch public education.

The whole point of noting that "correlation does not equal cause" is to acknowledge that things that "tend to hang together" are not necessarily mutually reinforcing. They are sometimes the result of third-party causes, and often the result of a complex web of causes that we haven't quite figured out yet. Which brings me to another problem with Blankenhorn's "correlation" argument. Even if we grant that support for marriage equality correlates with certain negative factors, it also correlates with positive factors such as higher education, higher incomes, greater support for religious freedom, and greater respect for women's rights. On Blankenhorn's logic, we ought to oppose those things as well, since they "tend to hang together" with the negative trends. Or we could go in the other direction, and argue that since these positive factors correlate with support for marriage equality, we ought to support such equality.

In fact, if we confine our focus to the United States, it's not clear that the correlations that Blankenhorn alleges actually hold. On the contrary, states with the highest support for marriage equality (such as Massachusetts) also tend to have the lowest rates of divorce, teen pregnancy, and single motherhood.[101] How can that be?

The problem is that Blankenhorn—like Kurtz, Douthat, and most marriage-equality opponents—is setting up a false choice between sexual worldviews. As they see it, there's the procreation-centered worldview and the pleasure-centered worldview. The procreation-centered worldview values the begetting and rearing of children, and thus rejects same-sex marriage, premarital sex, extramarital sex, cohabitation, divorce, and even (sometimes) contraception. The pleasure-centered worldview values self-fulfillment—in new-natural-law theorist John Finnis's colorful words, "the getting of orgasmic sexual pleasure in whatever friendly touch or welcoming orifice (human or otherwise) one may opportunely find it"[102]—and thus rejects sexual restraint of any sort. The procreation-centered worldview promotes children's welfare, whereas the pleasure-centered worldview undermines it—or so the story goes. But the story is wrong. It falsely asserts that there are only two options on the table: 1950s Peoria or 1960s Haight-Ashbury. What's more, among the genuinely available options, it picks the wrong one for promoting children's welfare.

Naomi Cahn and June Carbone, in their book *Red Families v. Blue Families*, have argued that there is an emerging family model in the United States.[103] This model tends to separate sex from procreation through the widespread use of contraception. Unlike the traditional model, which encouraged early marriage and parenting, this new model favors delaying marriage—but not sex—until after one has completed more education. It emphasizes emotional and financial maturity, rather than family form, as the hallmark of responsible parenting. Because its exemplars are more mature when they marry, they have lower divorce rates. They also tend to restrict the number of their children to those they can comfortably support. The result is that their children, on average, have better-educated parents, more material advantages, and more family stability: in other words, more of the factors that most dramatically improve child welfare.

If Cahn and Carbone are right, then sexual freedom is not the enemy of child well-being. Sexual freedom, particularly the ability to separate sex from procreation and to choose when and whether to have children, promotes the kind of environments in which children excel. But the corollary of this kind of sexual freedom, with its separation of sex from procreation, is greater acceptance for homosexuality—which may explain why American demographic groups with the highest support for gay rights tend to have not only higher education levels but also lower rates of divorce, illegitimacy, and single parenthood. In the United States, at least, these things tend to hang together.

Beyond Marriage

And speaking of sexual freedom, it's time to address my critics on the left. I'm referring to those who are deeply skeptical of marriage. For them, the important question is not "Why gay marriage?"; the important question is "Why marriage at all?" Marriage involves the state and society discriminating between different types of relationships, privileging some (the married) at the expense of others (the unmarried). What's more, it tends to do so coercively, pressuring people to get married and stay married and stigmatizing those who choose differently. At times marriage has been deeply oppressive to women. The marriage-equality debate could be an opportunity for serious critical reflection on these problems. But instead I've proceeded blithely along, these critics might argue, as if marriage were all sweetness and light.

These critics may have a point. To the extent that this book is able to move the ball down the field at all, it's because Gallagher and I begin with at least a few shared assumptions. Key among those assumptions is that marriage, for all its flaws, is a fundamentally good institution. Not perfect, but good. Because I want to move the ball down the field, I don't want to spend a lot of time debating whether we should even be on this particular field in the first place. A longer work of the same title could have a third contributor arguing against both Gallagher and me from this marriage-critical standpoint. For those who want to expand the debate in this way, I recommend Michael Warner's book *The Trouble with Normal*, or more briefly, Claudia Card's article "Against Marriage and Motherhood."[104] Their arguments deserve serious discussion, but I'm not going to provide that discussion here. Instead, let me offer a few general words about why I ultimately disagree with them on marriage.

Card, Warner, and similar critics object to marriage for a variety of reasons, but a core theme is the fact that marriage involves the state's privileging certain relationships above others. It pressures people in subtle and not-so-subtle ways, including economic incentives such as health care, employment, and tax benefits. It grants status. Those who remain single tend to be stigmatized, or at least pitied, as are those who pursue alternative family forms. Card is also especially concerned about the legal access marriage gives spouses to each other, access which can make partners—especially women—vulnerable to abuse.

There is much of value in such critiques. There was a time—mostly past, but not entirely or by long—when married women could not defend themselves against rape by their husbands, because of a legal system that treated wives as their husband's property. Marriage does grant status, and married people sometimes flaunt it obnoxiously. And it's unfortunate that single people have a harder time getting affordable healthcare than their married counterparts, although that is more because we attach health insurance to employment than a problem with marriage per se.

But I don't see how solving these problems requires dismantling marriage entirely. Yes, marriage puts pressure on people: that's part of what makes it work as a social institution. Yes, sometimes that pressure goes too far. Yes, there are other valuable ways in which people organize their lives, and many of these deserve more attention than they get. From where I stand, however, these points just indicate that we ought to correct the injustices, not do away with marriage.

Consider an analogy to another valuable social institution: higher education. One could make many of the same critiques of college that my fellow professors Card and Warner make of marriage: it privileges some life choices over others; it grants status; it unlocks a variety of economic and social benefits. We pressure young people to attend college and (perhaps unwittingly) stigmatize those who don't. We claim to recognize that college isn't right for everyone, and yet we do very little to support alternatives. Now suppose that gay men and lesbians were excluded from college. The appropriate response would not be to insist that, because of college's problems, we ought to dismantle it altogether. The appropriate response would be to address the injustices, including the exclusion of gay men and lesbians.

Anticipating a similar argument, Card responds with a counter-analogy: suppose there were a slave-owning society that prohibited women from owning slaves, on the grounds that women are somehow inferior to men. Of course the grounds of their denial would be unjustly discriminatory. But the appropriate response would not be to allow women to own slaves! "Likewise," she argues, "if marriage is a deeply flawed institution, even though it is a special injustice to exclude lesbians and gay men arbitrarily from participating in it, it would not necessarily advance the cause of justice on the whole to remove the special injustice of discrimination."[105] So my disagreement with Card and Warner boils down to whether marriage is more like college—a flawed but basically good thing—or more like slavery, which is irredeemably morally flawed. To me it seems patently obvious that marriage is more like college.

That's my quick response to the antimarriage critics. I would add a pragmatic point: Marriage is not going to go away, despite its radical critics' hopes and Stanley Kurtz's fears. As long as it exists, we are all better off if it includes gay and lesbian couples.

Interestingly, many of the people who once sounded the antimarriage call have come around to the latter point. Where they once saw same-sex marriage as "selling out" to an oppressive patriarchal institution, they now see it as potentially transformative. In 2006, a group of progressive scholars and activists circulated the statement "Beyond Same-Sex Marriage: A New Strategic Vision for All Our Families and Relationships." (Warner is among the signatories.) Noting that U.S. Census findings show a majority of people living outside of traditional nuclear families, the authors announced that "The struggle for same-sex marriage rights is only one part of a larger effort to strengthen the security and stability of diverse households and families."[106] They sought to "honor the diverse ways in which people find and practice love, form relationships, create communities and networks of caring and support, establish households, bring families into being, and build innovative structures to support and sustain community."

Again, there is much here to admire. The authors ask "who among us seriously will argue that the following kinds of households are less socially, economically, and spiritually worthy?" and include such noncontroversial family forms as "Adult children living with and caring for their parents," "Grandparents and other family members raising their children's (and/or a relative's) children," blended families, extended families, and "Close friends and siblings who live together in long-term, committed, nonconjugal relationships, serving as each other's primary support and caregivers." Who among us, indeed, would want to deny such families support?

Unfortunately, marriage-equality opponents tend to single out the most controversial family form on the list—"committed, loving households in which there is more than one conjugal partner"—and use the statement as evidence that the marriage-equality movement is really a Trojan horse for a sexual free-for-all. Aha! The slope is slippery after all! Robert George wasted no time in gloating: "they let the cat out of the bag," George gleefully announced when the statement was published. "What lies 'beyond gay marriage' are multiple sex partners."[107]

Let's take a deep breath and remain calm, shall we? Polygamy has been around for as long as marriage has been around, and it should surprise no one that when a group of progressive scholars consider the panoply of worthy family forms, they include it. Need I remind social conservatives that the Bible they tout as an infallible moral guide unselfconsciously portrays the patriarchs as having multiple wives? Or would they deny that Abraham's household was "socially, economically, and spiritually worthy"?

It of course does not follow that we will or should legalize polygamy, or that the mainstream marriage-equality movement is on some kind of stealth mission. Some marriage-equality advocates endorse polygamy, but most do not; some polygamy advocates endorse marriage equality, but most do not. (Remember, most are religious fundamentalists.) As always, each proposal must be evaluated on its own merits. As much as George and others would love to change the subject, we shouldn't indulge them in this ploy.

5. MARRIAGE, FREEDOM, AND EQUALITY

A prominent figure in the marriage-equality debate once wrote, "I believe that today the principle of equal dignity must apply to gay and lesbian persons. In that sense, insofar as we are a nation founded on this principle, we would be more American on the day we permitted same-sex marriage than we were the day before."[108] Can you guess who that figure was? Evan Wolfson, the founder and president of Freedom to Marry? Jonathan Rauch?

Ted Olson or David Boies, lead attorneys fighting for marriage equality in the California Proposition 8 case? Not even close. It was David Blankenhorn, one of same-sex marriage's strongest opponents.

To his credit, Blankenhorn sees this debate not as a debate of good against evil, but as a debate about competing goods. "One good," he writes, "is the equal dignity of all persons. Another good is a mother and father as every child's birthright."[109] In previous sections, I argued that letting gays marry never deprives a child of its mother or father, and that there are entire "missing staircases" between the premise that children need their own biological parents and the conclusion that we should forbid gays to marry. In this final section, I'll turn to Blankenhorn's positive theme—that marriage equality makes us "more American"—by focusing on the fundamental American values of freedom and equality. I'll begin with freedom.

One would think that the connection between freedom generally, and the freedom of gays to pursue happiness as they see fit, would be obvious. If only it were so. Just this morning someone sent me a link to the Texas State Republican Party Platform. In large capital letters on the first page appear the words "PRESERVING AMERICAN FREEDOM." Yet just a few pages later, the same document supports making it a felony for gays to have consensual sex and for any civil official to perform a same-sex wedding service. In other words, these folks are in favor of freedom...unless you're going to do things with it that they don't like.

Sadly, this warped sense of freedom is not an anomaly. To the contrary, it is becoming a familiar theme in the fight against marriage equality. Consider the now-infamous "Gathering Storm" ad put out by Gallagher's National Organization for Marriage (NOM). (Google it: it has been immortalized on YouTube, along with dozens of hilarious parodies.) The ad was part of NOM's 2009 "religious-liberty campaign" following marriage-equality victories in Vermont and Iowa. In it, various characters warn that their fundamental liberties are under threat: "There's a storm gathering. The clouds are dark, and the winds are strong, and I am afraid. Some who advocate for same-sex marriage have taken the issue far beyond same-sex couples. They want to bring the issue into my life. My freedom will be taken away.... [S]ome who advocate same-sex marriage have not been content with same-sex couples living as they wish. Those advocates want to change the way I live. I will have no choice...."

If you didn't know better, you would think that some states had just made same-sex marriage mandatory for everyone. But of course they didn't. Heterosexual marriage is, and will remain, an option in all fifty states. Marriage licenses are not a finite resource, where giving them to gays means taking them away from straights. There is, in Evan Wolfson's apt phrase, "enough marriage to share."[110]

How does marriage for gays take liberty away from heterosexuals? The ad mentions three cases—presumably the most compelling available examples at the time—to illustrate the alleged danger:

(1) "I'm a California doctor who must choose between my faith and my job."

Not exactly. The case in question involved a doctor who declined to perform artificial insemination for an (unmarried) lesbian, thus violating California antidiscrimination law.[111] I can appreciate the argument that a liberal society protects religious freedom, and that we should thus allow doctors in non-emergency cases to refer patients to a colleague for procedures that violate their consciences. But what are the limits of such exemptions? What if a doctor opposed divorce, and thus refused to perform insemination for a heterosexual woman in her second marriage? What if she opposed interfaith marriage, and refused to perform insemination for a Christian married to a Jew, or even for a Catholic married to a Methodist? Or what if a doctor refused to perform insemination for anyone except Muslims, on the grounds that children ought only to be raised in Muslim households? These are questions that marriage-equality opponents never bother to consider when playing the religious-liberty card. I'm not saying that the answers are obvious, but the tension between professional responsibility and personal religious conviction is hardly unique to the gay case.

The main problem, however, is that this case is a red herring. The real objection here is not to marriage, but to antidiscrimination laws, which pre-dated marriage equality in California. California law prohibits healthcare providers from discriminating on the basis of both sexual orientation and marital status, among other factors. Whether this doctor's patient was married (or could or should be married) was not at issue. (In fact, at the time of the incident, marriage was not available for same-sex couples in California.)

Gallagher makes the same mistake later in this book, when she discusses the "most egregious case" of Illinois, which no longer grants to Catholic Charities state contracts for adoption services. As the *State Journal-Register* explained, in a passage quoted by Gallagher herself, "This case had less to do with any religious organization's acceptance or recognition of civil unions than it did with reinforcing the antidiscrimination element of the law that created civil unions in Illinois."[112] In other words, it was the fact that Illinois prohibits discrimination on the basis of sexual orientation, not its stance on marriage or civil unions, that created the conflict for Catholic Charities. Antidiscrimination law and marriage law are not the same thing.

(2) "I'm part of a New Jersey church group punished by the government because we can't support same-sex marriage."

No, you're (an actor playing) part of a New Jersey church group that operates Ocean Grove Camp. Ocean Grove Camp received a property-tax exemption by promising to make its grounds open to the public; it also received substantial tax dollars to support the facility's maintenance. It then chose to exclude some of those taxpayers—in this case, a lesbian couple wishing to use the camp's allegedly "public" pavilion for their civil-union ceremony. So New Jersey did the right thing and revoked the pavilion's (though not the whole camp's) property-tax exemption. Once again, the issue here is not marriage—which New Jersey did not and still does not have for same-sex couples—it's nondiscrimination law related to public accommodations.

(3) "I am a Massachusetts parent helplessly watching public schools teach my son that gay marriage is OK."

Sort of. As long as marriage is legal for same-sex couples in Massachusetts, public schools will naturally teach that it's legal. That's part of educating students about the world around them. But at home Massachusetts parents can add whatever evaluative judgments they'd like, on this or any issue. What they cannot do is censor public-school curriculum so that it mentions only the families they like. After all, Massachusetts parents—like all states' parents and taxpayers—include same-sex households.

What these complaints make clear is that by "freedom," marriage-equality opponents mean the freedom to live in a world where they never have to confront the fact that others choose to exercise their freedom differently. In other words, they intend the very opposite of a free society.

The grain of truth in the NOM ad is this: marriage is a public institution. That means that everyone is required to respect the legal boundaries of marriages that they might not condone. But that has always been true. My mother-in-law believes that "real" marriages must originate in a Catholic church, preferably in the context of a nuptial mass. She was horrified when her daughter chose to marry on a beach at a tropical resort with a justice of the peace officiating. But her daughter did so, and the law now requires my mother-in-law—and everyone else—to treat the couple as legally married. Now imagine that my mother-in-law demanded that the law prohibit such marriages on the grounds that they interfere with her freedom. This is exactly what Gallagher and NOM are doing when they argue that same-sex marriage restricts their religious liberty. Religious liberty does not include the liberty to live in a world where the law enforces your particular religion's conception of marriage. Just the opposite.

Notice, too, how those who cite religion to justify their opposition to legal same-sex marriage are remarkably selective. The Christian Bible forcefully condemns divorce, with Jesus himself repeating the Genesis teaching that no one may separate what God has joined, and adding that those who divorce are tantamount to adulterers.[113] (Note also that the common secular rationale for opposing marriage equality—that children need mothers and fathers—seems far more relevant to divorce.) Yet there is no significant movement, religious or otherwise, for banning divorce. In other words, marriage-equality opponents are quite willing to subject the gay and lesbian minority to a far more restrictive standard than they would ever tolerate for themselves.

At the beginning of this book, I wrote that the marriage-equality debate affects "everyone who has a stake in what family means." That is true. But it does not affect everyone equally. When marriage-equality opponents complain about gay-rights advocates "changing the definition of marriage for everyone," their wording misleads. No one is trying to take heterosexual marriage away from straight people. Whatever happens in this debate, Maggie Gallagher and other heterosexuals will retain the full legal right to marry the partners of their choosing.

The question is whether they will have that right in a world where their gay and lesbian fellow citizens enjoy the same right. The question is one of equal treatment under the law.

Marriage-equality opponents sometimes retort that gay and lesbian citizens already enjoy the equal right to marry, because they, like everyone else, can marry someone of the opposite sex. But this response is specious. Formally speaking, it has the same structure as a long-discredited argument supporting antimiscegenation laws: whites can marry within their race; nonwhites can marry within their race; therefore everyone has equal marriage rights. The problem with this antimiscegenation argument is not merely that the white/nonwhite distinction is arbitrary—which it is, in the same way that the male/female distinction is arbitrary for virtually all of marriage's purposes besides biological procreation. The problem is that the argument treats "equality" as a purely formal notion, rather than a substantive one. As long as gay and lesbian *couples* lack the right to marry, gay and lesbian individuals do not enjoy the right to marry in any substantive sense.

This point is relevant for those making a Constitutional argument for marriage equality, something I do not intend to do here, beyond these brief closing words. The Fourteenth Amendment of the U.S. Constitution guarantees the "equal protection of the laws." By itself, I don't believe that this guarantee automatically gives anyone—gay or straight—the right to marry, at least not in the sense of a particular kind of state recognition. As Martha Nussbaum (among others) has argued, there are various ways in which the state might consistently and fairly treat its citizens, including getting out of the marriage business altogether.[114] But once the state provides marriage as an option for different-sex partners, even if they cannot or choose not to have children; even if they are elderly; even if they are divorced; even if they are incapable of coitus, and thus what the new-natural-law theorists consider "real marriage"—once the state provides marriage in all these diverse cases and more, but then denies it to same-sex couples, it is treating citizens unequally.

We can do better. As a just society, premised on ideals of freedom and equality, we ought to do better. There is enough marriage to share.

3

The Case Against Same-Sex Marriage

MAGGIE GALLAGHER

■ □ ■

HOW SHOULD WE DEBATE same-sex marriage?

Millions of words at this point have been splattered over print or lit up in pixels or printed in ink in newspaper articles, legal briefs, blog postings, and scholarly essays.

The prospect of achieving agreement on marriage appears further than ever.

Worse than the failure to "achieve agreement" is the abject failure to "achieve disagreement." Achieving disagreement is the process whereby both sides understand the others' arguments and understand why they disagree.

I believe this failure to achieve disagreement is mostly one-sided. People who oppose gay marriage and support retaining our traditional understanding of marriage understand the arguments for gay marriage very well. But advocates for gay marriage, with but very few exceptions, literally do not understand the arguments opposing it.

The prevailing argument for gay marriage is not just that gay marriage is the better idea. (Everyone by definition believes their own position is the better one.) Gay marriage advocates promulgate the strange and peculiar idea that there is no possible rational argument against same-sex marriage.

In one sense, they do this because it serves their core myth and purpose: opposition to gay marriage is based on bigotry—irrational hatred—that will disappear once determinedly exposed to the disinfectant of sunlight.

For those of us who support our marriage tradition, this is the most peculiar feature of the public debate on same-sex marriage. An idea about marriage that has been incarnated over and over again in diverse human societies—marriage is a sexual union of male and female oriented toward connecting fathers to mothers and their children—is now apparently unintelligible, especially to many in the intelligentsia.

Gay marriage advocates argue there are no relevant differences between gay and straight when it comes to marriage, and therefore gay couples can do "the work of marriage" just as well as opposite-sex couples.[1] Evan Wolfson even claims that gay marriage is not a change to marriage at all: "The truth is that ending the exclusion of gay people from marriage does not change the 'definition' of marriage any more than allowing women to vote changed the 'definition' of voting," he wrote in the pages of *The Economist* in 2011.[2]

My goals in this debate are threefold: First to lay out the case for marriage as the union of husband and wife that millions of Americans, and others around the world, believe in, in a way that makes this argument visible to those who disagree. Second, to identify the reasons achieving "disagreement" has been particularly difficult in this debate: What are the assumptions from which support for our marriage traditions appear not only mistaken, but lacking any rational basis at all? Third, to lay out the deepest reasons why people who fully embrace respect for gay people in civil society nonetheless stubbornly resist the idea that same-sex unions are marriages.

Here I am making an argument for the sociology of truth that is worth underscoring: The fact that people do not believe that same-sex unions are marriages does not fully explain why they care enough about this issue to organize against it—to form organizations,[3] donate money, collect signatures, speak publicly—not to mention withstand the charges of hatred, hostility, unreason, and bigotry that are routinely hurled at us.[4]

Gay marriage advocates consistently misunderstand the opposition to gay marriage in part because they genuinely believe that support for our marriage tradition is irrational, and therefore persistent opposition must be rooted in something dark and deeply irrational, most likely fear or hatred of gay people.

So *Salon* asked David Boies, lead lawyer (with Ted Olson) in the pending federal legal case against Proposition 8 in California this question: "[W]hat exactly is your opponent's argument?"

Boies was speaking for far too many when he responded, "Well, a good lawyer has got to understand his opponent's argument to the extent that there is one. I think that this case is probably the case in which my opponent has had less of an argument than in any case that I can think of. They have essentially a slogan, a bumper sticker, a tautology: They say 'marriage is between a man and a woman.' That's the question. That's not the answer. And they don't have any reasons why that ought to be the answer."[5]

Really? For generations not only in this culture but in virtually every known human society, human beings have separated out a certain kind of union of male and female for special attention and status—for no reason at all?

But it is the related question, "Why do you care?" that is perhaps most insistently thrust at me as someone who has not only made an intellectual case but founded an activist organization to fight for our marriage tradition.

It is a perfectly legitimate question. "What is true?" and "Why do you care?" are related but distinct inquiries. If in this book I am to make an advance toward achieving disagreement—that is, toward showing why resistance to same-sex marriage persists even in the face of a manifest desire to express tolerance and compassion to gay people—the second question must be addressed as explicitly as the first.

For gay marriage advocates, the ultimate end is equality: the recognition of gay unions as marriages in all fifty states and ultimately around the world as part of the process of creating a world in which sexual orientation is treated like race.

For opponents of gay marriage, stopping gay marriage is not victory, it is only a necessary step to the ultimate victory: the strengthening of a culture of marriage that successfully connects sex, love, children, and mothers and fathers.

Core assumptions that same-sex marriage advocates make about the nature of marriage, about the reason for the government's involvement in marriage, about how legal classifications affect culture, and about the relationship between civil marriage as a legal institution and marriage as a social institution, must be disinterred and addressed.

The fact that ordinary voters continue to grasp the losses same-sex marriage entails more deeply than many intellectuals is part of the paradox of this debate. Very few intelligent gay-marriage advocates appear to even grasp what they are asking of those of us who disagree with their core assumptions about sex and marriage.

If in the course of reading the next few thousand words, we come to understand one another better across the great gulf of our moral and intellectual assumptions, even if we continue to passionately disagree, my essay will achieve its core goal.

A side note: When I first read John Corvino's essay, I realized how different our essays are. Corvino lays out a fairly brief case for gay marriage and devotes the bulk of his essay to rebutting the arguments of others (including in brief form a version of my argument I have made elsewhere). This essay by contrast strives to lay out in greater detail why our marriage tradition is just and reasonable and how same-sex marriage will change marriage. Before responding in depth to Corvino's argument, I intend to make fully the case for the reasonableness of our marriage tradition, that is, its grounding in human nature and in real and enduring differences between same-sex and opposite-sex unions.

What is marriage? Why is government involved in marriage? By what right does government insist that third parties view a relationship as a marriage? What will happen to marital rules and norms if government insists that both same-sex and opposite-sex unions are equally marriage?

These are the questions I address primarily in this essay.

Achieving agreement is important where possible, but in a pluralistic society, achieving disagreement can be even more crucial.

The sound bites of the David Boies of this world suggest that only the ignorant or irrational could possibly oppose same-sex marriage. The reality is that in the modern context it is the argument for our marriage tradition that requires far more intellectual sophistication to grasp.

Once you have entered the world of genderless marriage,[6] same-sex marriage "makes sense."

What is lost once you enter that world is the subject of this essay.

WHY IS MARRIAGE A UNION OF HUSBAND AND WIFE?

Here is the view of marriage that many elites now find literally incomprehensible:

> Marriage is intrinsically a sexual union of husband and wife, because these are the only unions that can make new life and connect those children in love to their co-creators, their mother and their father.

Marital unions are those capable of uniting goods that otherwise tend to fragment, with high social and personal costs: sex, love, caretaking, babies, and mothers and fathers.

Not every marriage realizes the ideal of uniting these goods. But only a union of husband and wife can ever do so.

This is why the law has historically been involved in marriage and why we have social norms about marriage. These unions are socially necessary in a way that other kinds of unions, however valuable they may be to the people in them, are not.

Friendships are not regulated by government, even though very few of us would consider life worth living without a single friend to call our own.

To say a relationship is not a marriage is not to say that it is unimportant (much less "worthless" as Dale Carpenter suggested when I debated him this October at the University of St. Thomas).[7] Many fine and valuable relationships are not marriages.

The critical public or "civil" task of marriage is to regulate sexual relationships between men and women in order to reduce the likelihood that children (and their mothers, and society) will face the burdens of fatherlessness, and increase the likelihood that there will be a next generation that will be raised by their mothers and fathers in one family, where both parents are committed to each other and to their children.

By "regulation," I do not mean only the direct legal incidents of marriage. Marriage as a public social institution regulates not only those who marry but also those who are not married. Because marriage is a public institution, we know who is committing adultery—and we can teach our children, our friends, and our families that this behavior is wrong.

Because marriage is a public institution, we know who is having an out-of-wedlock child;[8] unmarried people can be motivated—by the culture, by their family, by religious figures, and even by policy makers—to avoid creating children in unmarried relationships (through abstinence, contraception, or shotgun weddings) only because we have a socially shared understanding of what marriage is and who is married.

Not every married couple intends or realizes all the social goods toward which the public institution of marriage aims.

This is almost certainly a feature of institutions generally. One might argue the whole point of institutions is that they substitute for (or at least supplement) individual thought and intention.[9]

To put it another way, none of these individual elements—sex, love, intimacy, caretaking, babies, mothers and fathers—defines marriage, or is necessarily an entry requirement to marriage imposed by the state. There are marriages that are not loving or not particularly intimate, marriages that are not faithful, marriages where the spouses do not have sex, marriages where spouses withhold money and other worldly goods, marriages that fail to include children, marriages in which one or both partners fail at parenting.

On this one point Corvino and I agree: a man can (and often does) love his mistress and hate his wife, but that does not mean his mistress *is* his wife. It means that a particular marriage has failed—for the moment, and perhaps forever—to unite the goods that marriage as a civil and social institution aims to unite.

The classification system at work in marriage—sexual union of male and female—which sets apart certain kinds of unions for special care and attention, is based on deep human realities, which were not created by government and cannot be changed by government fiat.

Here is the fundamental case for the rationality—the morality—of our marriage tradition:

> Sexual unions of male and female are the only unions that create new life. When they do, these unions will either connect these babies to their mothers and fathers or fragment that child's family life.

These unions are freighted with a significance unlike any other, a significance that the law and the society will either recognize, direct, and support, or fail to recognize, direct, and support as uniquely significant.

Marital unions are necessary in a way that other unions (however morally good or individually beneficial) are not.

Because my argument is often misunderstood as "merely" consequentialist, let me make it clear that the first reason to oppose treating same-sex unions as marriages is that it is not true. Same-sex unions are not marriages.

Statements of this form are typically rejected by gay marriage advocates as inherently circular. If gay marriages are not marriages because marriage is the union of male and female, they ask, why can't we change the definition of marriage?

In some sense words can be assigned any meaning we choose. The use of words and symbols to capture reality is an ongoing, interactive process. But in the same breath, let's acknowledge that in choosing to accept or reject same-sex marriage, we are not choosing merely whether some class of applicants can enter marriage, we are choosing between two contradictory truth claims about what marriage is, and why the law is involved with marriage.

Here is one of the more recent formal statement of these competing claims in the *Harvard Journal of Law and Public Policy* article, "What is Marriage?" by Sherif Girgis, Robert George, and Ryan T. Anderson:

> Conjugal View: Marriage is the union of a man and a woman who make a permanent and exclusive commitment to each other of the type that is naturally fulfilled by bearing and rearing children together. The spouses seal (consummate) and renew their union by conjugal acts—acts that constitute the behavioral part of the process of reproduction, thus uniting them as a reproductive unit. Marriage is valuable in itself, but its natural

orientation to the bearing and rearing of children contributes to its distinctive structure, including norms of monogamy and fidelity. This link to the welfare of children also helps explain why marriage is important to the common good and why the state should recognize and regulate it.

Revisionist View: Marriage is the union of two people (whether of the same sex or of opposite sexes) who commit to romantically loving and caring for each other and to sharing the burdens and benefits of domestic life. It is essentially a union of hearts and minds, enhanced by whatever forms of sexual intimacy the partners both find agreeable. The state should recognize and regulate marriage because it has an interest in stable romantic partnerships and in the concrete needs of spouses and any children they may choose to rear.[10]

(Note in pointing to these two functional definitions of marriage—one that leads to support for our marriage tradition and one that leads directly to the idea that same-sex unions are marriages—in order to highlight the idea that same-sex marriage requires a different understanding of marriage—I am not necessarily embracing all of Girgis and colleagues' natural-law philosophical super-structure.)

Alternatively, I would substitute two simpler functional definitions.

The traditional understanding of marriage:

Marriage is the exclusive, enduring sexual union of husband and wife, where the couple promises to care for each other and any children their union produces.

The revisionist view is that:

Marriage is the loving, caring union of any two people.[11]

"What is marriage?" is not a closed circular argument but an open debate. It is a meaningful question, indeed the core question in the marriage debate,[12] but if and only if it refers to something outside of the word itself: is there a basic human reality, captured by this word, that deserves to be named as distinct and unique compared to other human realities?

Definition in this sense is not merely nominal and therefore not merely circular.

As Corvino notes, Abraham Lincoln once famously asked "If we call the tail of a dog a leg, how many legs does a dog have?" Lincoln's answer was "four," because a tail is not a leg.

Of course we can choose to redefine the sound combination "leg" to mean "any appendage capable of independent movement that hangs off a body," in which case a tail is a leg.

But when we redefine "leg" in this way, what is lost are the specific characteristics of what we now understand as a leg. Sure, "weight-bearing leg" could be used to make sure when you want a leg and not a tail; formal communication is still possible. But still, once the core features of what counts as a leg changes, the core meaning of the word "leg" will be changed as well.

In this precise spirit the question we need to ask first is "What is marriage?' and therefore the question "Are same-sex unions marriages?" becomes intelligible.

To reject this question as irrelevant or unanswerable, as many same-sex marriage advocates do, is to trivialize marriage and to make the equal protection claims that underlie the case for same-sex marriage similarly meaningless. If marriage is a word that means whatever the individuals decide it means, then marriage cannot be a subject of shared social concern or shared social definition. The statement that "same-sex unions have an equal right to be considered marriages" means little if the content of the term "marriage" has no outside referent.

The debate about gay marriage, if it is to be rational, must be a debate about truth claims; the core questions become not "what do we think about gay and lesbian people?" but "what is marriage?" and (for so-called "civil marriage") "why do we have laws surrounding it?"

The historic understanding of marriage described above and embraced by our civil law until quite recently produces corollaries. Many of these are clear and obvious to those of us who embrace the view that marriage is the union of husband and wife, but seem to be virtually unintelligible to many of those who do not, such as:

> It is not discrimination to treat different things differently. The sexual love of two men or two women for each other does not further the same interests that marital unions do. Because same-sex unions are not the same as marriages, it is unjust to insist that law or society designate and treat them as marriages.

Furthermore, for those of us who accept the truth claims of our marriage tradition, the consequences of same-sex marriage are clear and visible: including same-sex unions in the legal category of "marriage" will necessarily change the public meaning of marriage for the entire society in ways that must make it harder for marriage to perform its core civil functions over time.

Can we at least agree that gay marriage is a profound change to the meaning of the word "marriage"? Why? Because it disconnects marriage from its grounding in the human reality that male-female sexual relationships are different from other kinds of relationships, sexual and non-sexual. If so, if we can acknowledge that profound change, we will have made a serious advance over the current state of public argument.

This is not primarily a consequentialist argument. The deepest reason for continuing to protect our conjugal vision of marriage in law and culture is *not* that failing to do so will do harm. It is that our traditional vision of marriage is true, good, and just—that marriage understood in that way deserves its unique legal and cultural status because it is rooted in real and enduring differences between marriage and other relationships.

A law that insists the word "dog" will now mean "either dogs or cats" (in order to point out their deep similarities) may not in fact do any harm. We could say "dogs that bark" if we want someone to buy us a dog and not a cat. (Just as Corvino proposes we say "heterosexual marriage" when we mean a husband and wife).

Nevertheless, to require people to call cats "dogs" would be unjust because the statement is untrue.

A law that insists we call all cohabitations "marriage" might do no harm. Still, the law would be unjust because it required us to say something untrue.

The negative consequences of gay marriage are not the premise of the argument against it, but the natural corollary.[13]

WHAT KIND OF A WORD IS MARRIAGE?

There are a number of typologies that can help illuminate the kind of debate over meaning we are having.

Let me offer four possibilities that bring out some core differences between supporters and opponents of gay marriage: is the word "marriage" more like "red," more like "dog," more like "mother," or more like "corporation?"

Let's start with "red." Redness is an immediate sensory perception; we know we are speaking of redness because we can immediately experience it. (Those who cannot, as those who have red-green colorblindness, cannot really know what are talking about, nor can we understand what they are talking about.)

"Dog" is an intermediary case, because it combines certain perceptions with a certain cognitive way of classifying the world. Is a wolf a dog? Is a cat a dog? Those are meaningful questions that cannot be answered with the same simple clarity with which we can say "that is red or not red." Nonetheless, the definition of "dog" is bounded by a real phenomenon outside the definitions created by law or assigned in the dictionary.

"Mother" falls into yet a third category. While the word clearly has a natural meaning outside of its legal definition, we have also agreed to use the law to transfer the natural meaning of "mother" to a class of people who would not immediately fit that meaning.

Through adoption, a woman who does not give birth to the child can become the child's mother. And yet if natural motherhood did not exist, the legal transfer of meaning would have little relevance. The mother is the person who bears the child with her body. The natural, ordinarily observed consequence is a particular kind of relationship between mother and child and also a set of social obligations imposed on mother and child by others (law, family, friends, religion, and society). When the natural mother cannot or will not perform the maternal function for the child, we give a motherless child a mother through the legal process. Still the referent category of "mother" the law makes use of refers to a natural phenomenon that the law does not create or control.

If the law were to define "mother" to mean "either the mother, or the nanny," we would object to this not only because it would have negative consequences, but because it is not true. Nannies perform many of the tasks of mothers but they are not mothers. To create a world in which this difference between mothers and nannies cannot be seen (or can only be seen with difficulty) because it is linguistically masked by the law would be unjust, regardless of the consequences.

Some words have greater consequences than others. Redefining "mother" to mean "mother or nanny" matters to us with much greater emotional intensity because the word "mother" is not just another word, but a word that constitutes an important social identity and contains important norms about behavior. Because "mother" is such a word, we would reasonably predict that over time the mere linguistic redefinition of "mother" to include "nannies" would likely have negative real-world consequences. The legal definition would interfere with the cultural process of socially communicating what a mother is; this linguistic interference would be in addition to the perhaps obvious practical problems created by legally redefining "mother."

The final possibility is that the word "marriage" is like the word "corporation." Corporations are real things, but they do not exist in nature. They come into being by and through the law's definition and can be redefined by the law at will to serve the original purposes for which the law constitutes them. If the law of corporations changes, the meaning of "corporation" changes as well. In this sense the legal definition of "corporation" can be either better or worse, more or less economically productive. But it cannot really be true or false. If "marriage" is a word like "corporation," we are launched into a purely consequentialist argument, in which truth claims do not arise.

Many gay marriage advocates argue as if, and even appear to believe, that marriage is a word like "corporation"—it means what the law says. When the Massachusetts high court set about analyzing Massachusetts' marriage laws, the justices cut through the mystique that so fascinated the Warren Court in *Griswold v. Connecticut*—"Marriage is a coming together for better or for worse, hopefully enduring, and intimate to the degree of being sacred. It is an association that promotes a way of life, not causes; a harmony in living, not political faiths; a bilateral loyalty, not commercial or social projects. Yet it is an association for as noble a purpose as any involved in our prior decisions."[14] Instead, the court baldly asserted as key to its analysis, "In short, for all the joy and solemnity that normally attend a marriage, G.L. c. 207, governing entrance to marriage, is a licensing law."[15]

Not all gay marriage advocates adopt this "legal constructionist" view, and many switch back and forth between views, holding changing the meaning of a word all-important when it comes to gays' and lesbians' self-understanding of their relationships, but not at all important when it comes to affecting how others understand their own or others' marriages.[16]

By contrast, for most supporters of our historic understanding of marriage, the word "marriage" is most similar to "mother"; it refers not primarily to the law, but to a phenomenon outside the law, that the law either recognizes or fails to recognize, supports or fails to support, with real-world consequences. The law is an important player in sustaining marriage, but the law alone cannot create marriage in a socially meaningful way.[17]

If the law creates marriage, then the only question in this marriage debate is consequentialist: what harms can there be to recognizing gay unions as marriages? And the burden of proof is transferred onto advocates of our marriage norms to prove a harm.

But if "marriage" is like "mother" rather than like "corporation"; if the question "what is marriage?" has meaning prior to and outside a current legal definition, then the question "are same-sex unions marriages?" becomes not only intelligible, but key.

If the natural basis for our marriage traditions can be made clear, then the burden of proof that the civil definition of marriage can be changed without harm falls on advocates for this fundamental change in public meaning.

If our traditional conception of marriage is reasonable and true, and captures important differences between unions of husband and wife and other sorts of unions, then our current understanding of "civil" marriage is reasonable and just; for the government to insist that nonmarital unions must be considered marriages would be fundamentally unjust.

Moreover, if this is the case then the emotional harms experienced by gay people from being excluded from marriage are self-inflicted. The exclusion of same-sex couples is not "harsh."[18] It is a reflection of the reality that these individuals do not want to marry, they want a different kind of relationship. A gay man does not want to be a husband in the sense of taking sexual responsibility for a woman and the children their sexual union produces. He wants something else.

Under this view, the question of practical benefits for same-sex couples and also the proper vehicle to demonstrate social respect for gay relationships would remain an important "live" social, moral, and legal question. But marriage would be off the table.

On the other hand, if gay marriage advocates wish to assert that gay unions *are* marriages, they need to explain how their understanding of marriage can explain the core features marriage has had—or to acknowledge that after gay marriage, these once core features will no longer be considered key to marriage. After gay marriage: Why a sexual union? Why just two? Why not sisters? Why automatic coparenting? Why fidelity?

They need to acknowledge that reshaping the public understanding of marriage so that gay unions can fit requires decentering and downgrading once-core features of marriage.

They need to come to terms with what redefining marriage to include same-sex unions means for the institution of marriage.

WHAT IS MARRIAGE: THE CASE FOR OUR HISTORIC, CROSS-CULTURAL UNDERSTANDING

Let's begin with this fact: Marriage is a virtually universal human social institution. It exists in virtually every known human society.[19]

THE CASE AGAINST SAME-SEX MARRIAGE | 107

Marriage is not static. It changes, adapts, and evolves. The forms that marriage takes, the norms that custom and law assign to it, vary considerably across time and place in history and culture. Many of the deepest assumptions of our own marriage culture have roots that are specific to our society—to Christian culture, in particular.

For example, the idea that sexual fidelity is required of both spouses is not a human universal. Disapproval of female infidelity is far more common anthropologically than male adultery. (Ancient Jewish law defines adultery as sex with a married woman by a man not her husband; a husband who has sex with a single woman commits fornication, not adultery. Early American law mirrored that understanding.[20])

Our culture's affirmation that husbands are as bound as wives to sexual fidelity appears to be a product of a specifically Christian conception of marriage:

St. Paul:	"The wife hath not power of her own body, but the husband: and likewise also the husband hath not power of his own body, but the wife."[21]
Jesus:	"But I say unto you, That whosoever looketh on a woman to lust after her hath committed adultery with her already in his heart."[22]

Nevertheless, with all its admitted cultural variations, adaptations, and evolutions, marriage emerges again and again across time and in diverse cultures with a certain basic, recognizable shape:

Marriage is a public union, not just a private and personal union.
Marriage is a sexual union, not some other kind of union.

As Girgis, Anderson and George put it "They pledge to play tennis with each other, and only with each other, until death do them part. Are they thereby married? No."[23]

Marriage is a public, sexual union between at least one man and woman,[24] in which the rights and responsibilities of the man and the woman toward each other, and toward any children their sexual union produces, are publicly defined and supported.

Society does not leave it up to adolescents and young adults in the midst of erotic, romantic, and emotional drama to work out on their own the meaning of this dimension of human experience.

Why does this cross-cultural truth matter? I am not arguing that because marriage has always had this shape, we cannot change it. I raise this historical fact for a different purpose, to ask "why?" Why does this basic shape of the marriage idea occur over and over again in diverse societies?

There are not many human universals. Why is it in the jungle of the Amazon, in the steppes of Asia, in the deserts of Africa, and the forests of Europe or America, why is that over and over again, human beings come up with this core institution?

Institutions arise to solve social problems. When problems are merely individual, individuals find or fail to find solutions. When individual problems become social problems, institutions develop to direct and guide individual behavior. When a social institution is universal, or nearly so, it must be addressing some persistent and pervasive human problem.

When a basic institution such as marriage emerges over and over again in diverse human societies, then it is probably responding to some basic and universal problem that human societies need to address.

What is the human problem out of which marriage emerges, again and again, as a civil and social solution? What is its core organizing principle?

If the question is taken seriously, the answer is not hard to find. Marriage arises over and over again because it addresses three persistent truths about human beings everywhere.

The first is that the overwhelming majority of us are powerfully attracted, and not by reason, to an act that makes new human life. Sex between men and women makes babies.

The second persistent truth: society needs babies.

Reproduction is optional for the individual. But only those cultures that successfully manage the procreative implications of male-female sexual attraction survive to become one of the human possibilities.

Marriage is often only one way a culture manages this challenge. Infanticide and/or child neglect are among the less attractive solutions human beings have come up with to the problem of babies. A culture that believes in the equal dignity of every human life has a much more difficult "problem" to solve than a culture which is content to designate some women and some children, as of lesser or no value. Our strong form of marriage has evolved in a culture that proposes the idea that every child is a child of God with an intrinsic dignity and worth.[25]

The third truth on which marriage is based is that children ought to have a father as well as a mother.[26]

For the first twenty years of my career, I was deeply involved in the debates over family structure. In the 1970s, many credentialed elites embraced the view that high rates of divorce and unmarried childbearing were actually good, liberating women from archaic moral norms in ways that would make adults, children, and society better off. People who claimed that marriage protected children were often dismissed as religious zealots who hated single mothers.[27]

We now know that these credentialed elites were wrong. An enormous amount of social science affirms that children do better when they are raised by their mothers and fathers in decent, loving, average, good-enough marriages.[28]

Twelve leading family scholars recently summarized the research literature this way: "Marriage is an important social good associated with an impressively broad array of positive outcomes for children and adults alike."[29]

A Child Trends research brief summed up the scholarly consensus on family structures that have been well studied:[30] "Research clearly demonstrates that family structure matters for children, and the family structure that helps the most is a family headed by two biological parents in a low-conflict marriage. Children in single-parent families, children born to unmarried mothers, and children in stepfamilies or cohabiting relationships face higher risks of poor outcomes.... There is thus value for children in promoting strong, stable marriages between biological parents."[31]

A Center for Law and Social Policy Brief concludes, "Research indicates that, on average, children who grow up in families with both their biological parents in a low-conflict marriage are better off in a number of ways than children who grow up in single-, step-, or cohabiting-parent households."[32]

An impressive array of professional services organizations have waded into the public debate of late to claim that scientific evidence proves that children raised by same-sex couples fare just as well, on average, as children raised by their married mother and father. In these reports, however, there is usually a fleeting reference somewhere noting the actual gaps in the scientific evidence.[33]

These gaps are not small and technical, they are large and obvious. For example, when it comes to evaluating gay parenting, very few studies rely on probability samples.

Without a probability sample, we simply do not know how representative the children of gay parents in these studies are of children with gay parents generally, as Meezan and Rauch acknowledge in their journal *Future of Children*: "What the evidence does not provide, because of the methodological difficulties we outlined, is much knowledge about whether those studied are typical or atypical of the general population of children raised by gay and lesbian couples. We do not know how the *normative* child in a same-sex family compares with other children. To make the same point a little differently, those who say the evidence shows that many same-sex parents do an excellent job of parenting are right. Those who say the evidence falls short of showing that same-sex parenting is equivalent to opposite-sex parenting (or better, or worse) are also right."[34]

The potential for selection bias in nonprobability samples is quite large. Gay parents participating in these studies know they are being studied in the context of an effort to affirm the status and rights of gay people in society. How likely, under these circumstances, would gay parents whose children are having serious difficulties be to volunteer or remain in a study of gay parenting? I wouldn't do it, if I were a gay parent. Given these and other potential selection biases, strong reliance on the conclusions of this small body of research is hard to justify.

An even bigger hole in the scientific literature on child well-being and gay parenting is that almost none of it has been conducted on children raised by gay men. This gaping hole was acknowledged by leading gay-parenting scholars Biblarz and Stacey. In a 2010 review of the literature purporting to show that children do not benefit from having moms and dads, these pro–gay marriage scholars had to acknowledge, "We located no studies of planned gay fathers that included child outcome measures and only one that compared gay male with lesbian or heterosexual adoptive parenting."[35]

No studies, not one. We have not a single study of "planned motherless families." We have zero scientific information on how children fare raised by single gay dads, or two gay dads.

(There is, as far as I have been able to discern, only one study that looks at a child outcome measure of children with gay fathers.[36] This study found that adult daughters with gay fathers are considerably worse off on measures of "attachment styles" [i.e., adult romantic relationships], but the author then suggestively attributes this to the young women's mothers' anger as a result of the divorce process, not their gay fathers.)

I cannot explain why the very large data gaps—including the virtual absence of data on motherless children raised by gay men—has not given the APA or other professional organizations more pause, or led to more measured pronouncements about what we know and do not know about same-sex couples and child well-being.

The fact remains a broad and deep body of scientific literature suggests that the family structure that best protects children is a married mom and dad. The scientific information we have on how the average child fares when raised by a same-sex couple is weak for lesbians and nonexistent for gay men.

Of course children can be raised to be responsible, loving adults in a variety of family forms. Marriage is not the only institution directed at protecting children or families.

But the challenges for children and society rapidly multiply when men and women do not form the faithful, exclusive sexual unions called "marriages" that protect children.

HOW MARRIAGE PROTECTS CHILD WELL-BEING

It is fatherhood, far more than motherhood, that is at stake in our current marriage debate.

Many culturally consequential voices now contest this idea. Gender doesn't matter anymore, they say, and Judge Walker ruled.[37]

I am always puzzled when the claim we have transcended gender in the name of equality is used to endorse same-sex marriage. If men and women are just the same, why shouldn't a gay man just marry a woman? Sexual orientation presumes that gender is a real, significant, and important feature of human society. If a gay man answers that he responds in a primal and pre-rational way to men differently from the way he responds to women, perhaps we ought to entertain the possibility that children do as well?

The passionate desire of the child for his mother and father is not based on sex roles, or tasks performed, but on a desire to experience both male and female love, and to experience his own creation as an act of love by both his parents.

When it comes to sex, marriage, and family, a genderless theoretical ideal can produce highly gendered consequences: 100 percent of the people who get pregnant as a result of acts of sexual passion are women. Zero percent of them are men.

Put it another way: when a baby is born there is bound to be a mother somewhere close by. If we want fathers to be there for the children their bodies create, and for the mothers of their children, biology alone is not going to take us very far. Nor will assertions that gender does not matter.

We need a cultural mechanism for attaching fathers to the mother-child bond, and for communicating to young adults in the middle of erotic, romantic, psychological, and emotional dramas, that they need to act with restraint and even self-sacrifice if they are to obtain this great good for their children.

Preventing the creation of children except when both natural parents are willing and committed to caring for that child together turns out to be enormously difficult for people attracted to the opposite sex. It requires not only a powerful normative commitment but consistent discipline of one's sexual life both before and after marriage.

Heterosexuality, unregulated by marriage as a public institution, produces immense human suffering: dead children, damaged children, gendered inequality, and inequality of opportunity.[38]

This remains true even though children created outside of marriage are more advantaged now than ever before in human history. The Supreme Court struck down legitimacy laws as a violation of equal protection in the 1970s. The formal legal obligations of fathers to their biological children are exactly the same inside and outside of marriage. Today's unwed mothers have the capacity to generate more economic resources on their own than just about any women in history. Even the poorest children get indoor plumbing, heat, vaccinations, clean water, and free basic public education. Obesity is one of the most pressing health problems of our poor.

And yet, although children conceived outside of marriage are as legally entitled to fathers as the children of married couples, they almost never get them. Mothers may get a child-support check; they do not get the kind of practical and economic support that wives get from husbands. The sociobiological underpinnings of effective fathering are still tied to marriage in a unique way because they are so tied by gendered human nature.

We know this by hard experience. Only by getting the 98 percent of men attracted to the opposite sex to pledge fidelity to a woman, to offer her "all his worldly goods," and to accept her children as his own can we create effective fathers in any systematic way.

The default position of unregulated male-female sexuality is now too well known to be seriously contested: even in a society that has raised contraception and abortion to the quasi-sacred status of constitutional rights, children are created on an irregular but frequent basis as the result of sexual relationships in which they are neither planned, nor anticipated, nor welcomed by one or perhaps either parent.

We live in a society where "planned parenthood" is a powerfully endorsed ideal, and where Constitutional law has been used to assure the absolute means of planning. And yet even today, three-quarters of all births are unintended by at least one of the parents.[39]

How does marriage protect children? Not primarily by offering a set of legal benefits that the law can transfer to other

family forms. If the civil, legal benefits of marriage were critical, children in remarried families would fare better on average
than children raised by solo mothers. They do not.[40]

Here is the key way marriage protects children: Whether
or not his parents intended to create him (or her!), almost
every child born to a married couple at least begins life with
his mother and father committed to caring for him in one family, together. Virtually no child from any other type of union
receives this gift.[41]

Marriage serves this purpose even when a married couple
does not intend to have children because intention is not what
creates children. Any time a man and a woman marry, society
has dodged a bullet: any child created by this couple's sexual
acts will begin life with a mother and father precommitted to
his or her care. If the husband lives up to his marriage vows, he
will not be creating fatherless children in other households.

(Corvino pokes a little fun of this as the purpose of marriage in elderly couples. I will only say: if you have seen the pain
of children abandoned by their fathers, you would not ridicule
this part of the public purpose of every marriage.)

Marriage not only solves a problem, it promotes an ideal: it
increases the likelihood the couple will have children, increasing the proportion of the next generation who are raised in the
optimal situation.

Simply by being married, a husband and wife reduce the
likelihood that either will create a child out of wedlock who will
face significant disadvantages and hardships and who will also
incur public costs.

This is not why individuals marry. It is why we all have a
stake in marriage; it is in particular the key reason why government is in the marriage business.

To put it another way, marriage arises, like all social institutions, to answer a set of social problems. In the case of marriage, the institution emerges in every human society because

the problems it addresses are rooted in human nature. If this is the reason that marriage exists and in particular the reason that societies employ law as well as custom to support marriage, then same-sex unions do not fit. They are neither part of the problem marriage seeks to solve, nor part of the solution.

Gay sexual unions, either temporary or enduring, may entail their own unique goods and difficulties, but they have nothing to do with babies. No same-sex union produces a child. And no same-sex union can give any child the gift of a mother and father in the same family. A gay man is not "banned" from marriage. He quite reasonably does not want to become a husband, and do the full work of marriage. Marriage does not fit him or his needs.

To reorient marriage to the needs of same-sex couples is necessarily to orient it away from its core public and civic mission of channeling sexual passion so that children do not get hurt and so that society gets the next generation it needs.

WHY DID THE LAW REGULATE MARRIAGE?

These three ideas—sex makes babies, society needs babies, children need mothers and fathers—do help explain the most peculiar thing about marriage at all: Why is the law involved? Why does civil marriage exist?

The answer cannot be: because marriage is a sacred, important, and intimate human relationship.

The way we demonstrate the importance of our adult relationships is not to surround them with legal regulation. Quite the opposite: in general, the more sacred, intimate, and important an adult personal relationship is, the less likely the law is involved. Generally speaking it is commercial, not personal relationships that the law regulates. I am a godmother, an adult daughter of a beloved mother, a best friend, a mentor, an aunt—the law impinges on these relationships imperceptibly if at all. Not even filial devotion—one of the Ten Commandments—is actually required of me under the law. If I want to ignore my sick and ailing mom, the law will not intervene to compel or regulate our relationship. Nor are my relationships with my adult children regulated by law. The only person a man can't disinherit under the common law is his wife.[42]

Marriage is the great exception to the rule that adult personal relationships are personal, not civil or legal. The question is, why?

We do not have to debate this question, because there is a clear historical answer to the key public purpose of marriage, which explains its basic shape: responsible procreation.

Here I want to insist on a fact. (We are all entitled to our opinions but not our own facts.) Repeatedly the law has explained why government was involved in marriage by pointing to the urgency of responsible procreation. Long before the law even imagined the existence of gay marriage, and even as old people and infertile people were allowed to marry, judicial authorities reiterated again and again that a key public purpose of marriage was regulating procreation so that children do not get hurt and so that society has the next generation it needs.

- "Marriage and procreation are fundamental to the very existence and survival of the race."[43]
- "[Marriage] is the foundation of the family and of society, without which there would be neither civilization nor progress."[44]
- "Marriage is one of the 'basic civil rights of man,' fundamental to our very existence and survival."[45]
- "All of the cases infer that the right to marry enjoys its fundamental status due to the male-female nature of the

relationship and/or the attendant link to fostering procreation of our species.... Thus, virtually every Supreme Court case recognizing as fundamental the right to marry indicates as the basis for the conclusion the institution's inextricable link to procreation, which necessarily and biologically involves participation (in ways either intimate or remote) by a man and a woman."[46]

- "Nearly all United States Supreme Court decisions declaring marriage to be a fundamental right expressly link marriage to fundamental rights of procreation, childbirth, abortion, and childrearing."[47]
- "[T]he first purpose of matrimony, by the laws of nature and society, is procreation."[48]
- "[T]he procreation of children under the shield and sanction of the law" is one of the "two principal ends of marriage."[49]
- "The family is the basic unit of our society, the center of the personal affections that ennoble and enrich human life. It channels biological drives that might otherwise become socially destructive; it ensures the care and education of children in a stable environment; it establishes continuity from one generation to another; it nurtures and develops the individual initiative that distinguishes a free people. Since the family is the core of our society, the law seeks to foster and preserve marriage."[50]
- Procreation is "[o]ne of the prime purposes of matrimony."[51]
- "[P]rocreation of offspring could be considered one of the major purposes of marriage"[52]
- "[M]arriage exists as a protected legal institution primarily because of societal values associated with the propagation of the human race."[53]
- "The institution of marriage as a union of man and woman, uniquely involving the procreation and

rearing of children within a family, is as old as the book of Genesis."[54]

- "Having children is a primary purpose of marriage."[55]
- "One of the primary purposes of matrimony is procreation."[56]
- "[P]rocreation of children is one of the important ends of matrimony"[57]
- "It has been said in many of the cases cited that one of the great purposes of marriage is procreation."[58]
- "One of the most important functions of wedlock is the procreation of children."[59]
- A "state has a compelling interest in encouraging and fostering procreation of the race."[60]
- This "central purpose...provides the kind of rational basis...permitting limitation of marriage to heterosexual couples."[61]

The judges who wrote these words knew that not all married people had children, and that marriage was not necessary to produce children. They knew that procreation was not an entry requirement to marriage, that infertile and elderly people could marry, though sexually impotent men could not. They could not have possibly been disguising homophobia when they repeatedly asserted that nonetheless the public institution of marriage is crucially bound with regulating sex in the interests of procreation.

As one legal observer has noted, "This concern with illegitimacy was rarely spelled out, but discerning it clarifies why courts were so concerned with sex within marriage and renders logical the traditional belief that marriage is intimately connected with procreation even as it does not always result in procreation."[62]

Something important to the civic order was obviously at stake in marriage: regulating the sexual behavior of men and women toward each other so that the next generation would be created in the only context where they would be cared for by a mother and father.

Marriage regulates not only the people in a marriage. The categories of "illegitimacy" or "adultery" (or even, for the very religious, "fornication") have meaning only because we have a shared social understanding of who is married.

Historically, in law and culture, the fact that sex produces children is the reason the law was involved in helping craft, identify, and sustain the marriage bond while ignoring most other close personal and even sacred intimacies.

EXCEPTIONS THAT POINT TO THE CROSS-CULTURAL RULE OF MARRIAGE

Advocates for same-sex marriage sometimes point to three historical examples to rebut the idea that marriage has always been about regulating male-female relationships in the interest of procreation. (And yes, Corvino raises two of them in his essay.) Each of the examples, however, is an exception that points to the general rule. These examples of same-gender marriage are not examples of gay marriage, and they each serve to underline the main organizing principles of marriage—they are a very rare adaption to the norm that marriage arises in every society because every society has to find an answer to the gendered problem of procreation.

The "berdache" (a Western term for what some now dub a "two-spirit" man or woman) was an institution in a variety of North American tribes, wherein a person born male could, upon the call and consent of the gods, assume a female identity and therefore marry a man. (Female berdaches have also been documented but were less common.) The man who married a berdache was not considered homosexual or abnormal in any way and would also typically have other wives able to bear children, as North Americans tribes permitted polygyny.[63]

Berdache marriages were therefore not considered same-sex marriages at all but rather more akin to the current legal practice of permitting those who have legally changed their gender to marry; under a polygamous marriage system, berdache marriage did not interfere with the core purposes of marriage.

On rare occasions, the Nuers of Sudan would permit an older childless woman to "marry" another woman. Occasionally an older woman would inherit or build sufficient wealth in cattle that she could support children. The only way for such an older childless and mate-less woman to have heirs capable of inheriting her wealth (thus keeping it in the lineage) would be to "marry" a woman, whose children would then belong to her lineage. The woman in these cases was seen to be acting as a man; the children would address her as "father." The women did not have sex with one another. Gay sex would have defeated the whole purpose of this unusual adaptive use of Nuer marriage system. The point was to create legitimate children who could remain in the wealthy woman's family system. Thus Nuer had rare instances of same-gender marriages, but they were not gay marriages at all.

The Nayars of India are presented as a possible example of a people without a real marriage system that is oriented toward procreation. The Nayars did marry, and the children of the wife addressed her husband as "father." But the marriage obligations consisted of three days of cohabitation, to be followed only by ritual mourning obligations on the part of the wife and children. The husband took no further responsibility for his wife or her children. The men went off to perpetual war, and the women remained and had temporary sexual unions with other men of suitable caste. The mother's brother assumed most paternal responsibilities. Among the Nayars, marriage rituals common to Southern India were practiced but their content was mostly eviscerated. The form of marriage remained but its substance was drained of meaning.

The purpose of this unusual mating system was to free Nayar men up for nearly constant warfare. As one sixteenth-century scribe put it, the Nayar mating system "springs from the wish of a certain king to relieve the men of the burden of maintaining sons, and leave them ready for warlike services whensoever the kings calls upon them."[64]

Notice that the Nayars are not a people or a culture: they are a specialized military caste of a larger social and cultural system, which did have a substantive marriage system to manage procreation and its responsibilities. Nayar men were relieved not only of the responsibility of husbanding and fathering but of economic duties generally, which were assumed by the larger tribe. In this sense, to say the Nayars had no real marriage system, is more like saying that Catholic priests have no real marriage system. Catholic priests are ritually married to the Church, and that ritual, as among the Nayars, no longer serves the purpose of managing procreation between men and women so children have a father. In both cases, the language and ritual of marriage have been adapted for the purpose of a caste with particular responsibilities, which is supported by a larger society with a functioning marriage system oriented toward managing responsible procreation.[65]

The Nayar mating system lasted only as long as the military caste system that sustained it. After the British took over Kerala and disbanded the Nayar armies, the system rapidly died out. The Nayars reverted to a norm of monogamous marriage in which mothers and fathers raised children together.

What can we learn from such exceptional practices? For a time, with sustained cultural energy and effort, marriage rituals for a particular group can be diverted from the core public purposes of marriage to serve other social or political purposes (provided these core public purposes of marriage are sustained by some third parties in the culture). Nevertheless, because sex between men and women makes babies, marriage, as a public sexual union of male and female giving children both fathers and mothers, recurs again and again across time and history.[66]

These three exceptions are repeatedly cited by many gay marriage theorists precisely because exceptions are so rare. The great obvious fact is that cross-culturally and historically, marriage emerges as an attempt to grapple with underlying biological reality. Marriage emerges as a cultural mechanism to assign fathers to children deemed valuable enough to protect, and to ensure that socially valued women have help in raising them.

The historical record in our own culture, and the cross-cultural record, is emphatically crystal clear. The question is not whether same-sex unions have ever been included in the public institution of marriage or have been understood to fulfill the core purposes that make marriage a public institution. They haven't.

The question before us is whether marriage can be redefined in law to include same-sex unions without damaging or diminishing the core public purpose of marriage of managing procreation in the interests of children and society. Will gay marriage function like the berdache or the Nuer, as a minor feature of a system that preserves the capacity of marriage to manage procreation?

That is the question we take up next. What's the harm of same-sex marriage?

CONSEQUENCES: HOW WILL SAME-SEX MARRIAGE CHANGE MARRIAGE?

Privatizing and Stigmatizing Traditional Conceptions of Marriage

What changes when, in order to further the brand-new concept dubbed "marriage equality," the law insists that two men are a marriage? Two big ideas about marriage must necessarily change if same-sex couples are to be considered in law and by society as just as married as anyone else.

The first is the idea that marriage has something centrally to do with regulating "responsible procreation." If two men are a marriage, marriage is obviously not about getting mothers and fathers for children. Period. The law itself repudiates that as a core feature of marriage.

Moreover, same-sex marriage also necessarily calls into question related marital norms: Why sex? Why fidelity? Why permanence? Why not sisters? Why only two?

In the marriage system we have inherited, the answers to these questions are quite clear: They rest in two great principles the society endorses: marriage is oriented toward protecting children by giving them a mother and father—and every child is equally worthy of protection.

These two great principles together explain and undergird most of our core features of marriage.

A marriage requires sexual fidelity, because without it marriage cannot protect children or give these children their own mother and father. Marriage is presumptively sexual, because only a sexual union can create new life. By pledging and practicing fidelity, the partners guarantee no children will be born outside of marriage into fatherless households. Marriage presumes joint parenting because, by pledging sexual union and sexual fidelity, the husband and wife promise that any child the wife bears will be their child jointly. Sisters cannot marry because they cannot form a sexual union, however much caretaking and joint child-raising they engage in together.

After same-sex marriage, all of these norms surrounding marriage become vulnerable. Norms rooted in realities that apply only to opposite-sex unions would have to be justified as equally applicable to same-sex unions. These formerly core marital norms may survive as influential personal preferences, but their persistence as public norms will become harder and harder to justify.

Marriage does not protect children by providing a set of legal benefits that can be transferred by legislative or judicial fiat to other family forms. Marriage protects children primarily by increasing the likelihood that children will be born to and raised by their own mother and father.[67]

Over time, the institutionalization in law and the embrace by society of the core ideas driving same-sex marriage will make the key social tasks of marriage (aka "civil marriage") more difficult. The inclusion by law of same-sex unions in the classification "marriage" will necessarily dilute and almost certainly repudiate responsible procreation as a key civil purpose of marriage.

As many advocates of gay marriage have recognized, gay marriage severs the link between sex and diapers. It institutionalizes the preexisting and increasing disconnect between marriage and procreation and family structure. Gay marriage advocate E. J. Graff made this claim: "Marriage is an institution that towers on our social horizon, defining how we think about one another, formalizing contact with our families, neighborhoods, employers, insurers, hospitals, governments. Allowing two people of the same sex to marry shifts that institution's message.... If same-sex marriage becomes legal, that venerable institution will ever after stand for sexual choice, for cutting the link between sex and diapers." Same-sex marriage, she argues, "does more than just fit; it announces that marriage has changed shape."[68]

If two men are a marriage then marriage no longer represents, encodes, or promotes the ideal that children ought to have a mother and father. If marriage is no longer the social institution which incarnates the ideal that children should have a mother and father, there will no longer be any social institution that represents or institutionalizes that ideal.

Individuals may still use marriage for this purpose. But after same-sex marriage, it is a newly privatized purpose, no longer part of the core or animating purposes of marriage in the public square.

Gay marriage, however, does more than merely privatize the once-key aspects of "civil" marriage. It will almost certainly lead to new efforts to stigmatize and repress the traditional view of marriage, both in law and in culture.

The heart of the gay marriage idea is this: when it comes to marriage there is no publicly relevant or morally acceptable distinction to be made between same-sex and opposite-sex unions. If you see a difference between these two kinds of unions, there is something wrong with you. In the strong and increasingly common form of this claim, people who see marriage as the union of husband and wife are like bigots who oppose inter-racial marriage.[69]

The emerging conflicts between religion and gay equality have been raised in other venues.[70] Here I want to raise the church-state conflicts created by same-sex marriage not to defend religious liberty, but to point to the ways in which new legal pressures will interfere with the private transmission of our marriage culture after same-sex marriage.

Gay marriage will not only create a new public definition of marriage, it will lead to the stigmatization of traditional views of marriage. The resulting negative effects on traditional faith communities will make it harder for private actors to sustain the core marriage norms once government and "civil marriage" have stigmatized these ideas as "anti-equality."

The best way to see this is to take gay marriage advocates seriously: if opposition to gay marriage is the moral equivalent of opposition to interracial marriage, then we need to ask: how does the law treat people who oppose interracial marriage?

Here's the good news: you can be a racist in American society without being thrown in jail. The First Amendment applies to racists too.

That's the end of the good news. Because the law powerfully intervenes (properly in the case of racism) to marginalize, stigmatize, and repress racist people and especially racist institutions.

Consider for example professional licenses: Can you be a teacher, a social worker, an attorney, a psychiatrist, marriage counselor, or obstetrician if you are openly racist? Probably not, and certainly not if you attempt to import your racist views into your professional practice.

Or consider employment generally. In America, if you voice racist views, you will almost certainly face consequences from your employer, and if they become publicly known you will likely be fired. Americans are typically employed "at will" and can be fired any time an employer wants to for any reasons, except certain prohibited categories like race, religion, gender, and in some states sexual orientation.

The biggest weapon, other than the criminal law, in the government's arsenal is the decision to withhold tax-exempt status to racist charities and educational institutions. This is true even if the racist institutions are religious organizations citing a religious-liberty right to their beliefs, as the Supreme Court held when it took away Bob Jones University's tax-exempt status by an eight to one vote.

Equality is the state's religion in America. Ideas and people who are perceived as "anti-equality" do not get to play on a level playing field, but one decidedly tilted against their views by government, law, and society. Equality arguments do not lead to pluralism but to the use of government and social power to suppress dissent, dissenters, and dissenting institutions.[71]

Could the government really use weapons meant to fight racism against traditional, religious organizations and institutions that promote the idea that marriage is intrinsically a union of male and female, or that kids need moms and dads? Yes. The marginalization, stigmatization, and repression of traditional understandings of marriage is what the phrase "marriage equality" *means.*

If affirming traditional marriage is an act of bigotry, then the government can require you to offer marital benefits to gay couples, even within your religious schools, summer camps, and charitable agencies. The government may require you to hire or retain as teachers or other professionals people who publicly flout your group's religious views on marriage, making it difficult for these institutions to transmit within their own private communities the idea of marriage as a union of husband and wife.

Adoption and foster agencies may be refused licenses, or shut out of public funding streams, if they refuse to personally endorse adoption by gay couples. (And the public status of gay couples as united by civil marriage makes the older "don't ask, don't tell" kludges used by these agencies untenable.)

These things are now happening, in this country or in our close sister democracies. By and large the organized, institutionalized same-sex-marriage movement applauds these steps, because this is what "marriage equality" means.

If John Corvino thinks it's wrong to force Christian adoption agencies to act against their beliefs (or be shut down), wrong to exclude Christian marriage counselors who do not counsel gay couples, wrong to fire Christian public high school teachers who accept biblical understandings of sex or marriage, then he is the exception to a gay rights establishment that increasingly applauds and promotes the exclusion of "discriminators" in some or all of these domains.

But more importantly, if Corvino disagrees, he also needs to explain why he believes his personal objections will become normative, once "marriage equality" is institutionalized in law by government.

Dale Carpenter, Andrew Sullivan, and several other "conservative" gay marriage advocates have said they do not believe Christian foster care agencies should be excluded from helping to place children (so long as other agencies accept gay parents), but that opinion has not prevented the logic of "marriage equality" from operating in Massachusetts, the District of Columbia, and Illinois.

CONSEQUENCES: THE DIFFICULTY OF CREATING MARITAL NORMS AND RULES THAT FIT BOTH SAME-SEX AND OPPOSITE-SEX RELATIONSHIPS EQUALLY

"Marriage equality" means that same-sex and opposite-sex unions will be regarded equally as marriages.

What if the foundational idea of "marriage equality"—that a union of two men or two women is just the same as a union of husband and wife—isn't true? We've discussed the biggest way in which it is not true: the creation of new life that connects children to moms and dads. But there are other ways in which key marital norms do not fit same-sex and opposite-sex unions equally—most likely not because orientation matters, but because gender does.

In some ways, all close personal relationships are similar, as much literature on gay relationships points out.[72] Close personal relationships involve good communication, trust, loyalty, care-taking and the ability to manage conflict in ways that allow the friends, family members, or lovers in a close personal relationship to repair problems and limit damage to the relationship.[73]

But are unions of two men or two women, substantially or typically the same as opposite-sex unions, especially? The evidence suggests not, and for reasons that may have more to do with gender than orientation. Consider two key marital norms: permanence and sexual fidelity.

Marriage in our culture means a permanent exclusive sexual union. This is a public norm that retains a strong hold on the public imagination and is reflected in various state laws as well.[74]

A May 31, 2011, Gallup poll found that 91 percent of Americans morally disapprove of adultery and 86 percent of Americans disapprove of polygamy.[75]

For opposite-sex couples, a fairly strong body of evidence shows that these marital norms of fidelity and permanence are mutually supportive: open marriage has not survived the test of time and experience. Fidelity is important to both the survival of a marriage, and to the satisfaction of husband and wife. In 2009, one marriage scholar noted that "[e]xtramarital affairs are the leading cause of divorce across 160 cultures and are one of the most frequent reasons that couples seek marital therapy."[76]

Evolutionary psychologists offer a possible explanation for this strong relationship between sexual fidelity and marital success. Because sexual relationships between men and women regularly give rise to children, the cost to men of their mate's sexual infidelity includes investing time and resources in offspring not their own. For women, male infidelity threatens to divert their mate's resources to a competing second woman and her family.[77]

Regardless of whether the evolutionary explanation holds, very few marriages between husband and wife can tolerate ongoing, open extramarital relationships.

As Alfred DeMaris pointed out in a 2009 study of infidelity, "The expectation of sexual fidelity in marriage is nearly universal in our culture. Treas and Giesen for example, found that 99 percent of respondents in their national sample expected their spouse to have sex only with them, and 99 percent assumed that their spouse subscribed to the same creed."[78]

DeMaris goes on, "the revelation of infidelity tends to have a devastating impact on the course of a marriage. Atwood and Seifer reported that affairs are given as a reason for marital separation by 31 percent of men and 45 percent of women." In fact, "[w]ork by Amato and his colleagues found infidelity to be the most commonly reported reason for divorce, as well as the single strongest proximal determinant of divorce in a hazard analysis."[79]

Even cyber infidelity, or pornography use, negatively affects marital satisfaction, according to one recent study of 433 couples: "A partner effect emerges for marital infidelity, suggesting that a spouse's infidelity is costly for sexual satisfaction. Finally, some evidence suggests that pornography consumption is costly for one's own and spouse's sexual satisfaction, especially when pornography is used by only one spouse."[80]

Even when opposite-sex partners are not actually married, sexual infidelity causes intense distress, even for those who choose to engage in infidelity. One study of unmarried romantic partners in short-term relationships concluded, "The present findings replicate and extend the existing literature on infidelity, suggesting that individuals who have been unfaithful to their romantic partners report significantly more psychological distress than those who have not engaged in infidelity. In terms of general distress, perpetrators of infidelity reported greater depressive symptoms and lower general well-being than other individuals."[81]

Another fascinating piece of recent research looks into the effect of gender. Men in couple relationships in one recent study were only half as likely to say they would break up the relationship if their girlfriend had sex with another woman than if she had sex with another man.[82]

For unions of husband and wife, the social norms and legal rules that connect sex, fidelity, monogamy, and marriage make sense. They are mutually reinforcing. Without fidelity, marriages are unlikely to last or to be happy, just as without sexual fidelity, children conceived will not necessarily enjoy the security of being raised by their own mother and father in one home. Polygamy dilutes the access of children to their fathers, creating unequal relationships between mothers, fathers, and their children.

Does sexual fidelity play the same role in same-sex unions?

The radical challenge to marriage from gay marriage is not that gay men are by nature promiscuous, as some have argued. The challenge gay male unions pose to marital norms is not (or not just) that two men in a domestic union are far less likely to expect, require, or achieve sexual fidelity than opposite-sex couples—although a great deal of evidence now shows that they are.

The more fundamental and radical challenge to the notion of "marriage equality" is that for the majority of gay men, sexual fidelity may not point to or support permanence or relationship satisfaction in the same way it does for opposite-sex relationships.

Consider first the evidence for this proposition: Gay men in committed unions are far less likely than married opposite-sex couples to require or expect or achieve sexual fidelity of one another.

The evidence for this is now so powerful that it is difficult for any honest observer to avoid. I personally avoided making this argument for most of a decade, until Proposition 8 witnesses who supported gay marriage testified under oath it was true,[83] and stories affirming it began appearing on the front pages of the *New York Times*:

> A study to be released next month is offering a rare glimpse inside gay relationships and reveals that monogamy is not a central feature for many. Some gay men and lesbians argue that, as a result, they have stronger, longer-lasting and more honest relationships. And while that may sound counterintuitive, some experts say boundary-challenging gay relationships represent an evolution in marriage—one that might point the way for the survival of the institution.
>
> The Gay Couples Study has followed 556 male couples for three years—about 50 percent of those surveyed have sex outside their relationships, with the knowledge and approval of their partners...

The study also found open gay couples just as happy in their relationships as pairs in sexually exclusive unions, Dr. Hoff said. A different study, published in 1985, concluded that open gay relationships actually lasted longer.[84]

Scholarly literature directed to clinicians is emphatic about the dangers of importing hetero-normative assumptions about sexual fidelity into relationship counseling for gay male couples. For example,

> It is often assumed that sexual relationships among gay and heterosexual men are similar, and therefore, understandings of gay sexual relationships are fit into preexisting frameworks of heterosexual relationships. However, there appear to be significant differences in the ways that gay and heterosexual males conceptualize relationships. Compared to heterosexual couples, gay couples may hold more diverse definitions of monogamy. Specifically, some gay men may form emotionally monogamous relationships which are sexually non-monogamous, or "open." In a qualitative study of 65 coupled gay men, 28 (43.1 percent) reported that both partners agreed to permit sex outside the primary relationship. This subset of gay men explained that they did not necessarily associate sex with emotional intimacy and commitment, and believed that an open relationship allowed each partner to experience personal freedom. Further, they stressed the importance of emotional fidelity and did not believe that emotional fidelity was compromised by their open sexual relationship. In another study of 121 gay male couples, 48 couples (39.6 percent) reported that they were in non-monogamous sexual relationships.[85]

Another study of a convenience sample of 142 gay male couples in Seattle and Portland found that "less than half of the couples had a sexual agreement and far fewer chose their agreement to be monogamous."[86]

The largest and most recent such convenience sample was gathered in the San Francisco area—566 gay male couples, about half of whom were either in gay marriages or civil unions: "A majority reported explicitly discussing their agreements and nearly equal numbers reported being in monogamous and open relationships. A small number (8 percent) reported discrepant agreements." [87] An expert who testified in the trial of the Proposition 8 case, *Perry v. Schwarzenegger*, found that the majority of men in "closed" relationships had in fact had sex with an outside partner, making the proportion of gay couples who achieved monogamy less than 25 percent.[88]

Because many monogamous gay couples open up their relationships sexually as time goes on, it is also relevant to note that 40 percent of this sample had been together two years or less.

Not only are many gay male relationships sexually open, even more strikingly, social science has failed to find any evidence that agreeing to be sexually faithful affects relationship satisfaction for male same-sex couples. "Similar to the findings of the previous study, no differences were found between couples who were sexually monogamous and non-monogamous on measures of relationship satisfaction and relationship agreement. Shernoff (2006) posits that, despite the fact that non-monogamy is an accepted part of gay culture, many therapists regard it as problematic as a result of heterosexual norms. Thus, therapists must be aware of their own attitudes regarding sexuality and monogamy in order to effectively work with this population."[89]

An Australian study of 170 gay men found that monogamy played no role in relationship satisfaction for gay men: "We found no significant difference between open or closed relationships in levels of satisfaction or attachment styles"[90] In the Bay Area study, "there was no difference in relationship satisfaction between couples with monogamous and open agreements."[91]

In a 1982 interview in *Canadian Family Physician*, David Kessler, a professor of clinical psychiatry at University of California School of Medicine in San Francisco, explained that "[t]he prohibition against 'open' relationships is much more important for heterosexuals, and perhaps lesbians, whereas for gay men, happy and stable long-term partnerships are characterized by 'openness.'" He cited a study of 156 gay male couples who had been together for 18 months to 30 years which showed that the men were more likely to be monogamous in the early stages of their relationship than later on. None of the couples who had been together for more than 5 years had maintained a "sexually exclusive partnership," the researchers found. "Successful couples found that as time went on, sexual exclusivity didn't work, and outside sexual relationships seemed to enhance the quality of their mutual sexual attraction," Kessler said. "Far from destroying relationships, sexual infidelity seemed actually to be a necessary ingredient of keeping relationships together."[92]

Letitia Peplau, an expert witness testifying for gay marriage (i.e., against Proposition 8) in *Perry v. Schwarzenegger* confirmed this fundamental disjunction. It is not just that gay men are less monogamous—it is that sexual fidelity does not appear to be clearly related to any other measure of the success of their relationships. "I think that's why researchers have found that whereas monogamy is correlated with relationship satisfaction for heterosexuals and lesbians—that is, having monogamy is associated with being in a happy relationship—for gay men there's no association between sexual exclusivity and the satisfaction of the relationship."[93]

In an earlier study, Peplau studied gay men in Los Angeles and concluded: "All men in relationships identified as having been closed and lasting three years or longer had engaged in sex with at least one person other than their primary partner."[94]

A study by Blasband and Peplau in the *Archives of Sexual Behavior* looks at forty gay male couples, twenty-three of who were sexually open and seventeen who agreed their relationship was sexually closed. "No significant differences were found in the quality of open versus closed relationships. Almost all the men (93 percent) said they were in love with their partner." The authors concluded that it "appears that sexually open and closed relationships can be equally satisfying."[95]

Even when partners agreed the relationships should be closed, "Most men in closed relationships had had at least one outside sexual liaison, although they reported having many fewer sex partners than men in open relationships."[96]

A study of gay male Christian couples concludes, "The majority of couples were expectationally and behaviorally nonexclusive." However, like other studies this one found no relationship between sexual fidelity and couple success: "Couples in all the three categories did not demonstrate significant differences in terms of their level of relationship satisfaction and commitment."[97] A 1979 study found that for gay men, open relationships were more likely to lead to permanent unions: "The data were also consistent with the proposition that the open marriage is the more viable and enduring form of gay male liaisons."[98]

In sum, the stability and happiness of caretaking affectionate relationships between two men do not appear to turn on sexual fidelity and may even benefit from infidelity, while for unions of husband and wife, fidelity serves both the private and public purposes of marriage.

Let's pause to digest this finding. On the one hand, men in general (not just gay men) are more likely to value sexual novelty and variety. On the other hand, men in relationships with women typically have great trouble tolerating outside sexual relationships, while the men in sexual relationships with other men frequently find outside sexual relationships have no affect on relationship satisfaction.

Fidelity emerges as a marital rule because it represents a compromise, or a bridge between the sexes. Women in general

find less value in sex that has no romantic or affectional component. The idea of having sex with lots of different strange men
who don't really care about them is far less appealing, on average, to women. Women like sex, but they like sex when it means
love in the context of a committed relationship. Casual sex is
just not as erotic for the typical woman, and for many the idea
of random sexual couplings is often positively unappealing.[99]

Men are more often strongly physically excited by the idea
of casual sexual encounters, and more often value the idea of
sexual variety for themselves.[100] So why do men commit to the
rule of monogamy and fidelity? Of course religion and culture
play a role. Men often view fidelity as a sacrifice good men make
to protect and please the woman they love. But it's clear there is
also a great good that men get from marriage and its norm of
fidelity and permanence. The great good men get from fidelity,
in addition to paternity certainty, is a reduction in the intense
sexual anxiety and tormenting jealousy and rage produced by
the possible competition of other men. They trade variety in
sexual partners for the certainty that one woman who loves
them is willing to have sex with them and no other competitor.

In *Enemies of Eros*, I noted the phenomenon of heterosexual
men who believed they could tolerate open relationships only
to find their wives' infidelity very painful:

> Such a man may seek an "open relationships" as a resolution to
> the problem of combining domestic affection and sexual pas-
> sion—and resolving his own guilt over his extramarital affairs—
> but such a husband often dramatically underestimates his own
> negative reaction when another man has sex with his wife.[101]

During the sexual revolution of the 1970s, open marriage was
heralded as the future of the institution in a widely touted book
by the same name. Within a decade, almost every "open marriage" the authors wrote about had either ended in divorce or

been "closed." Sexual infidelity doesn't work very well for opposite-sex unions because male sexual jealousy is a powerfully disruptive force, because women tend to fall in love with ongoing sex partners, and of course because children regularly result. To permit an outside sexual relationship is to surrender the boundaries of the nuclear family to third parties' fertility intentions.

Men in same-sex relationships, by contrast, frequently find that sexual novelty with outside partners helps them sustain their core domestic affection.

This fact alone is a powerful signal that in fact same-sex and opposite-sex relationships are dramatically different kinds of sexual unions. Putting both sorts of relationships under the same marriage rules is likely to cause problems in sustaining marital norms.

The norms surrounding marriage grow out of experience in sustaining opposite-sex unions. If under the "marriage equality" paradigm, they are applied now to all marriages, including same-sex ones, they may be dysfunctional for same-sex couples (as many hard-Left opponents of gay marriage once feared). The greater danger, however, is the capacity of a tiny proportion of same-sex couples in the marriage pool to disrupt existing marriage norms in the pursuit of the promises government and society make in embracing "marriage equality."

"Marriage equality," institutionalized in law and culture, will exert continuous ongoing pressure to sideline marital norms that do not work for both kinds of couples equally—to demote them from marital norms to marital preferences, to privatize once-public standards.

Fidelity, while very important to successful marriages of husband and wife, is also difficult, requiring discipline, long-term insight, and the capacity to delay and sometimes sacrifice gratification in pursuit of a larger goal. Marital fidelity is a classic case of an individual good that requires intense social support in order for that good to be realized in individual lives.

Even modest undermining of that social support is likely to make achieving faithful marriages more challenging.

Will marriage "tame" gay men, as some gay men fear?[102] Or will including same-sex couples into our public understanding of marriage lead to renewed challenges to the necessary connection of marriage and sexual fidelity?

If gay people were really a marginalized and culturally powerless minority, perhaps their inclusion in the marriage pool would pass unnoticed, a tiny statistical anomaly of no cultural consequence, as Eugene Volokh among others has argued.[103] The "marriage equality" paradigm makes this difficult to believe. If the goal is a society in which gay unions are understood to be just as much a marriage as the union of husband of wife, then the powerful cultural tools of the media, law, and the arts used to push for gay rights generally will be used to ensure that marriage equality is not a technical legal status, but a cultural rule.

(As testimony to the weight gay people now pull in the public imagination, consider a 2011 Gallup poll in which Americans on average estimated that 25 percent of the population is gay or lesbian, an order of magnitude approximately ten times larger than the actual number.[104])

People who dissent from new "marriage equality" norms will likely find themselves cut off from access to powerful institutions and levers of cultural influence. "Marriage equality" advocates, having won this public fight, will make sure that every culturally influential venue includes gay married couples and displays their values and practices as equally valid norms for marriage.

Just days after passage of a bill authorizing same-sex marriage in New York, the *New York Times* published an essay questioning sexual fidelity in marriage, featuring a strenuous argument by the now-influential sex columnist Dan Savage that monogamy, not adultery, is damaging to marriage.

> The mistake that straight people made was imposing the monogamous expectation on men. Men were never expected to be monogamous.
>
> Men had concubines, mistresses and access to prostitutes, until everybody decided marriage had to be egalitarian and fairsey.
>
> [Rather than granting women] the same latitude and license and pressure-release valve that men had always enjoyed, we extended to men the confines women had always endured.
>
> And it's been a disaster for marriage.[105]

As the *Times* essayist observes, "In *Savage Love*, his weekly column, he inveighs against the American obsession with strict fidelity. In its place he proposes a sensibility that we might call American Gay Male, after that community's tolerance for pornography, fetishes and a variety of partnered arrangements, from strict monogamy to wide openness."

> Savage believes monogamy is right for many couples. But he believes that our discourse about it, and about sexuality more generally, is dishonest. Some people need more than one partner, he writes, just as some people need flirting, others need to be whipped, others need lovers of both sexes. We can't help our urges, and we should not lie to our partners about them. In some marriages, talking honestly about our needs will forestall or obviate affairs; in other marriages, the conversation may lead to an affair, but with permission. In both cases, honesty is the best policy.[106]

In the past, gay marriage advocates shied away from advocating sexually nonexclusive marriages, but with increasing confidence, voices are emerging to champion the gay sexual ethic of marriage for both orientations.

Other advocates for gay marriage besides Dan Savage now argue that straight people can learn from gay couples how to do marriage differently—and better. Gay couples are already being held out in culturally influential venues as examples for other married couples to follow:

"When Rio and Ray married in 2008, the Bay Area women omitted two words from their wedding vows: fidelity and monogamy." "'I take it as a gift that someone will be that open and honest and sharing with me,' said Rio, using the word 'open' to describe their marriage," reports a prominent story in the *New York Times*, "A study to be released next month is offering a rare glimpse inside gay relationships and reveals that monogamy is not a central feature for many. Some gay men and lesbians argue that, as a result, they have stronger, longer lasting, and more honest relationships. And while that may sound counterintuitive, some experts say boundary-challenging gay relationships represent an evolution in marriage—one that might point the way for the survival of the institution."[107]

The *New York Times* quotes Joe Quirk, "'The traditional American marriage is in crisis, and we need insight,' says Quirk citing the fresh perspective gay couples bring to matrimony. 'If innovation in marriage is going to occur, it will be spearheaded by homosexual marriages.'"[108]

If gay unions are really marriages, just as much as anyone else's, and if "adultery" helps many gay men sustain long-term relationships, what will happen—or should happen—to our public commitment to the idea that sexual fidelity is core to marriage?

If the promise of marriage equality is to come true, fidelity must cease to be a public marital norm and become merely a private one, subordinated to the moral imperative of viewing same-sex marriages as just as much marriages as those between men and women.

As the economics professor Douglas Allen has argued,[109] to put same-sex and opposite-sex couples into the same legal framework, as if they were identically situated, means the legal rules and social norms that evolve around marriage will favor or disfavor one of these two groups. If our drive for "marriage equality" trumps our concern for marriage as a regulator of opposite-sex relationships that give rise to children, then the same taste for equality will prevent the adoption of rules that maximize the well-being of opposite-sex couples when they disadvantage gay couples.

And yet the public and private goods at stake in marriage as the union of male and female are far more critical to social well-being than the goods at stake in same-sex marriage. Sexual relationships that give rise to children intrinsically have a greater potential impact on the public good than other sexual relationships.

If gay marriage prevails, the law—and the society it helps form—will be premised on a falsehood. Same-sex and opposite-sex couples are not the same, or even very similar with respect to the core public norms of marriage. The basic rules of marriage—many but not all of which are currently encoded in law—stem from centuries of experience in the always-evolving, ever-adapting task of reconciling male and female in a way that is satisfying to both and most likely to protect the children they create.

To add on to this difficult task the task of figuring out the best social norms and legal rules for gay couples is to complicate, at a minimum, an already-urgent social problem.

The main message of "marriage equality" is fundamentally misleading. To claim that two very different kinds of relationship are the same does an injustice to both sorts. Grounding the law in a lie about human nature is not a small accommodation but a grave mistake. It would certainly be unjust to require third parties to assent to the claim that both types of unions are marriages if they differ profoundly with respect to key marital rules or norms. Yet that's what civil "marriage equality" means.

If these very different types of unions differ in the norms that ought to govern them (because they guide the relationships to lasting success), "marriage equality" will require subordinating one set of norms to the other not only in law but in the culture. At best, certain norms now attached to marriage generally will have to be treated as options within marriage, not integral to marriage itself.

Social institutions affect behavior by creating habitual patterns that govern the way people think, that is, the way they perceive reality.[110] When norms become "optional" for marriage in the public mind—then practically speaking, they cease to be norms: they become marital options.

Douglas Allen lays out the theory in the language of law and economics in a 2010 essay on the "negative externalities" of same-sex marriage:

> There are two types of proposed same-sex marriage externalities in the law and economics literature. The first is that same-sex marriage changes the cultural meaning of marriage. This different meaning of marriage transcends borders and can influence every marriage and family decision. Call this the general externality effect. The second type of externality comes from a cost of redefining marriage to include same sex couples. This cost results from different types of unions being regulated by a single law. Allowing different types of couples to marry, necessarily requires elements of marriage to be redefined. The more different the new marriage type, the greater the chance traditional marriage law will be further altered to accommodate the new type. These changes must necessarily be sub-optimal for traditional marriages, and the sub-optimal regulation can lead to more divorce, fewer marriages, etcetera, depending on the specific changes to the law. Call this the specific externality effect.[111]

Allen points out, "The introduction of same-sex marriage is logistically more complicated than a simple decree. Often hundreds of legislative acts are required to be updated, but more importantly, many definitions are required to be changed as well." These changes include changes to the definition of parent, the legal presumption of paternity, and

> over time other changes are likely for divorce grounds, child support payments, and property rules, given the different needs between same-sex and opposite sex couples.
>
> Any one of these changes can lead to externality effects within a given state because all marriages are regulated by the same laws. Laws that change to accommodate a new type of family, necessarily are not appropriate for the first type of family. How large this impact is, remains to be seen, but the effect will likely take time to emerge.[112]

Allen concentrates on legal rules, but the same insight can be applied to the effect of the law's understanding on social norms surrounding marriage. Marriage is not, as the *Goodridge* court ruled, a licensing scheme.[113] The law does not create marriage so much as recognize and support marriage (or fail to do so).

In "Marriage and the Law: A Statement of Principles," a group of more than a hundred legal and family scholars (some of whom support gay marriage), pointed out,

> The law's understanding of marriage is powerful. Legal meanings have unusually powerful social impacts. People who care about the common good, therefore, need to take seriously the potential consequences of dramatic legal changes in marriage and family law. "Neutrality" is rarely an option.
>
> When government intervenes in important social debates, from no-fault divorce to same-sex marriage, the law privileges its own viewpoint and has the power to affect the culture of marriage as a whole, often in ways few intend or foresee...
>
> Marriage is first and foremost a social institution, created and sustained by civil society. Law sometimes creates institutions (the corporation is a prime modern example). But sometimes the law

recognizes an institution that it does not and cannot meaning-fully create. No laws, and no set of lawyers, legislators, or judges, can summon a social institution like marriage into being merely by legal fiat. Marriage and family therefore can never be reduced to a legal construct, a mere creature of the state. Faith communi-ties play a particularly powerful role in sustaining marriage as a social institution. The attempt to cut off "civil marriage" from "religious marriage"—to sever our understanding of the law of marriage from the traditions, norms, images, and aspirations of civil society that give marriage real power and meaning—is in itself destructive to marriage as a social institution.[114]

If the law teaches an idea about marriage that is not true, it will become harder for other actors in society to sustain mar-riage as a social institution.

Marriage is rooted in sex difference. Our strong ideas of gender roles have shifted over time. Nevertheless, the structure of marriage has been worked out over many millennia to recon-cile men and women in their differing sexual natures, in such a way that the children they make will also be protected.

Sexual exclusivity has been a core organizing principle of marriage for exactly this reason. The sexual fidelity of the wife is necessary to ensure that her children are also her husband's children. To permit a third party to have sex with the wife is to confuse the unity of the family.

Male sexual fidelity in marriage, while not a human univer-sal, serves the public purposes of marriage because husbands who stray may produce children with women who are not part of the wife's family. The dilution of resources—financial and emotional—hurts the marital children. Ultimately neither men nor women in opposite-sex relationships can tolerate or cham-pion adultery.

The relative unavailability of the father hurts the extramari-tal child as well. All the children are hurt as well by the loss of their siblings, who will be raised in different family systems, difficult to combine.

If managing procreation is no longer the public purpose of marriage, the purpose of sexual fidelity in "civil marriage" norms becomes less clear.

Why is sexual infidelity wrong for gay men? Of course it is always wrong to break a promise, but why should marriage necessarily entail such a promise for gay men or women?

Not surprisingly, gay marriage does not necessarily include such a commitment. Just a few years after gay marriage became a reality in Massachusetts, a front page story in the *New York Times* on young gay married couple casually mentioned that sexual fidelity is not typically required.

> Eric Erbelding and his husband, Michael Peck, both 44, see each other only every other weekend because Mr. Peck works in Pittsburgh. So, Mr. Erbelding said, "Our rule is you can play around because, you know, you have to be practical."
>
> Mr. Erbelding, a decorative painter in Boston, said: "I think men view sex very differently than women. Men are pigs, they know that each other are pigs, so they can operate accordingly. It doesn't mean anything."
>
> Still, Mr. Erbelding said, most married gay couples he knows are "for the most part monogamous, but for maybe a casual three-way."[115]

Except for maybe the casual three-way?

No man in a sexual relationship involving a woman could casually speak in this way (even if, in a very small number of instances, it accepted this practical rule).

If extramarital sex helps some or many gay men maintain the relationship, by what criterion can we say the adultery is wrong or that sexual fidelity is intrinsically part of civil marriage norms?

Same-sex marriage attacks the underlying logic of marriage, which is rooted in the experience of reconciling two genders.

In the absence of this human reality, the logic of every feature of marriage is going to become harder to explain or justify.

Why sex?

The role of sex in marriage as it has been understood historically or cross-culturally is clear: sex between husbands and wives generates the next generation, and ensures those children are connected to both a mother and a father. If two men or two women are equally a marriage, what is the role of sex in marriage? Why does the government or the wider society care if the couple's union is sexual or not?

If not sex or babies, why not sisters?

If "civil marriage" is no longer intrinsically oriented toward procreation or sex, then why the bar against close relatives marrying?

After all, two sisters can love and care for each other and even raise their children together. Why deny them the public recognition of marriage?

Why just two?

If marriage is a sexual union of male and female oriented toward procreation and childrearing, the logic of "civil monogamy" is clear. Polygamy necessarily and intrinsically creates profound inequalities in the relationships between husband and wife and between mothers and their children's father; children are not raised in one family equally tied to mother and father but in a half-fragmented family, in which ties to their father are loosened by his multiple commitments to other wives and their children.[116]

If marriage is about love and caretaking, what right do we have to insist that people love and care only in twosomes? There may be some practical restrictions to the administration of benefits in polygamy or its trendier cousin, polyamory. But surely basic rights to have one's loving and caring relationships recognized as marriages can be separated from any administrative difficulties. Who is the government to tell a single person in love with a married one that he or she cannot marry the person she or he loves?

Why coparents?

A husband and wife, by pledging sexual fidelity, promise each other that any children they have they will have together. The husband accepts the children of his wife as his own. The wife acknowledges the husband's right to do so.

Under the common law, this presumption of paternity could only be challenged by the husband and only on the grounds that he could not possibly be the biological father of the child.

The default rule of coparenting was grounded in sexual reality, in real and enduring facts about human beings. In consenting to sex, a husband and wife consent to the possibility a child will arise, and precommit to raising the child together as coparents. In pledging sexual fidelity, they committed to having children only with and through each other.

With same-sex couples, these presumptions make little sense. Will one partner have a unilateral right to impose parenthood on the other, without the consent of the other? This would turn marriage into a form of personal bondage. Will some additional legal step (say a written agreement) be required before same-sex couples are considered coparents of a biological child of one of the others? Then marriage itself is irrelevant legally to parental status.

Courts are already coming to contradictory conclusions about how to reconcile biological and social parenthood for gay couples.[117] Under "marriage equality" presumptions, there is no natural or coherent reason to presume coparenting as part of marriage; this presumption arises from the deep relationship between marriage, sex, sexual fidelity, and the natural family.

This is not a slippery-slope argument. I do not believe that gay marriage will lead necessarily either to polygamy or to sexless sister-marriage. It appears equally likely that gay marriage could lead to the abandonment of "civil marriage" altogether, rather than its expansion to include many more claimants, especially if Christian conservatives decide to join with libertarians and the Left to get government out of the marriage business.[118]

The driving force behind the impulse to get the government out of marriage, however, would be precisely the sense that we no longer want the government involved in supporting the norms of marriage because those norms have been lost, become incoherent, or been reduced to merely private preferences. Gay marriage undermines the presuppositions that marriage is sexual, is sexually exclusive, presumes joint parenting, is therefore inappropriate for family members, and requires two and only two people. Redrawing the boundaries of marriage in order to make same-sex unions part of "marriage" makes these presumptions less intelligible, less coherent, and harder to defend.

An institution with deep roots in human nature and human necessity becomes contingent and arbitrary, a product of will and politics, as the rational connections between its component parts are severed because we cannot both affirm those connections and also proclaim "marriage equality" to be our highest marriage value.

I cannot say for certain which direction our public ideas of marriage will take after same-sex marriage. And whatever the changes, they will not happen overnight or instantaneously. The sky will not fall, because it never does. Inertia will carry us forward for some years, or even one generation. I do know that we cannot deny in law the presumptions that make marriage coherent and that give us the goods of families with mothers and fathers, and yet maintain those ideas as vital in the culture. We cannot legally stigmatize the premises, or promises, of marriage as a code of bigotry, and expect those promises to be fulfilled just as before.

HOW INSTITUTIONAL CHANGE HAPPENS

The threat gay marriage poses to marriage is not limited to states or jurisdictions that formally adopt gay marriage into law. Institutions are ideas.[119] A bank is not a set of brick and mortar, but a complex system of ideas, many of which are enforced by law, but much of which is simply assumed as part of the meaning of what a bank does.

A school is a place where children are taught things they need to know to become responsible adults. Say the word "school" and both the people we call students and the people we call teachers and the community surrounding them know many things: what kind of interactions are appropriate and inappropriate, what kind of resources approximately are needed, the relationship between the people in the room.

Psychology as an academic discipline is not a set of rules but a set of ideas about how in particular to approach the study of the human person. If you study how a human being's liver fails, you are not doing psychology. If you study how liver failure affects human emotions, you are. The defining idea of psychology channels human thought to a productive common end.

Institutions shape behaviors by constraining the way human beings think, making some truths easier to explore and some goals easier to achieve because these truths are highlighted. Institutions channel the behavior of individuals through the complex foundational webs of meaning they create. Institutions move human behavior by focusing our view of reality, by pointing to the thing that, for this endeavor, really matters.

Cultural power is the power to name reality.[120] The most important question in the marriage debate is not what benefits gay couples will get, but whether gay couples are marriages. Government has enormous power to credential reality. Once government says gay couples are part of marriage, the web of meaning that makes marriage a powerful institution will shift in obedience to the new norm.

When it comes to marriage, it is theoretically possible to maintain a view of reality that contradicts the law of the land, but it is extremely difficult. (Ask Catholics whom the law has civilly divorced how others respond if they assert they are still married to their original spouse, because the sacrament is more binding than the law.)

The founding idea of a social institution like marriage is not a side issue or a frill, or a mere matter of emotions, nor "merely" a word. How we understand the marriage idea is at the heart of how the institution operates. The public meaning, and not the incidental (and rather weak) benefits currently attached to the institution by law, is the primary force behind how marriage shapes behavior and protects children and the common good.

Let's pause to note that marriage once provided rather strong legal incidents, benefits, and corresponding punishments to discipline behavior. The only legal way to have sex was through marriage. The only legal way for men to claim fatherhood (or for women to have a legal claim on their child's father) was through marriage. Not only the carrots of marriage "benefits" but the sticks of tort law and even the criminal law were used to direct sexual behavior in the ways that keep men and women from hurting each other, and the children their bodies create.

This strong system of supports for marriage has been dismantled, partly by public opinion and partly by the Supreme Court in a series of decisions that took several key legal benefits of marriage (the right to sex and the right to fatherhood) and apportioned them to individuals regardless of marital status.

For constitutional law theorists this, I believe, is the true answer to the claim that "the right to marry" is a fundamental human right. As a liberty interest, the right to marry does not include same-sex marriage because the core personal liberty rights encoded in the phrase "the right to marry" (the right to have sex, to cohabit, to have natural children, and to the care and custody of your natural children) have already been given to every U.S. citizen including gay people.

An individual cannot have a liberty interest in having his relationships regulated by the government. It cannot make a couple more free to allow them to apply for a license to do what they are already free to do without a license.

So why does marriage in law matter anymore? Why is it worth fighting for? Precisely because institutions are ideas, because the ideas animating institutions govern, protect, and largely define a culture, and for that reason the phrase "merely a word" is all but meaningless.

The principal regulatory function of marriage is not in any legal incident or benefit, but in providing a bright line marker of who is married to whom. Without this marker, without a shared definition of who is married, it is virtually impossible, especially in a fluid and mobile society, for any other actors—families, friends, neighbors, faith communities—to teach, encourage, police, or enforce the more important substantive content of the marriage vow.

If we do not know for sure who is married, we do not know who is committing adultery. We may not even be sure ourselves if we are committing adultery. Without a clear marker for who is married, we cannot tell who is having an out-of-wedlock birth—or indeed even know if we ourselves are having an out-of-wedlock birth.

(One reason young women in cohabiting relationships are at such high risk of giving birth is that many believe they are "as good as married," i.e., in permanent sexual caretaking relations. Unfortunately men who cohabit with women [unless they are engaged] have the lowest level of commitment to their female partners, less even than men who are dating and sexually involved but not living with their female partners.[121])

Moreover, the vast majority of same-sex marriage advocates, including judges who have ruled in favor of "marriage equality," agree with me on this point. Gay marriage will change the idea of marriage. After "marriage equality," marriage cannot be about procreation and childrearing, and the ideal for children can no longer be to be raised by a mother and father.

These two ideas must go because they contradict "marriage equality." Once "marriage equality" becomes the foundational idea of marriage, any differences between gay and straight cannot be relevant to marriage per se. Any idea about marriage that suggests "things mothers and fathers do" but that male sexual partners do not do, must be false. Under "marriage equality," any person uttering such an opinion must be a liar.

Institutional change takes time—the old must die off before the new institution can fully dominate the public mind. But the die is clearly cast, the meaning of "marriage equality" crystal clear.

HOW DO WE KNOW INSTITUTIONAL CHANGE WILL HAPPEN?

How do we know that "marriage equality" requires replacing traditional understandings of marriage with a new idea disconnected from the public good of creating new life to be cared for by a mother and father? The process is already happening.

1. What gay marriage advocates say.

William Eskridge, in his early book making the case for same-sex marriage, argued that procreation is relatively unimportant to marriage, to people, and to society:

Post-Freudian society understands sexual expression as an important goal of personhood, the modern liberal state guarantees its citizens substantial liberty to make choices about their own sexuality, and an earth that struggles to feed its existing population is not an earth that should overemphasize procreation. Procreation is good and important, but procreation is no longer central to either relationships or to social welfare.[122]

He further argues, "in today's society the importance of marriage is relational and not procreational."[123]

Journalist E. J. Graff wrote a book endorsing same-sex marriage around the same time. Her book makes clear that she understands the power of marriage as a social institution to influence how people think and behave, and she understands the transforming power of same-sex marriage:

> Marriage is an institution that towers on our social horizon, defining how we think about one another, formalizing contact with our families, neighborhoods, employers, insurers, hospitals, governments. Allowing two people of the same sex to marry shifts that institution's message....If same-sex marriage becomes legal, that venerable institution will ever after stand for sexual choice, for cutting the link between sex and diapers.[124]

She recognizes that same-sex marriage does not merely constitute opening up an institution to a new group of participants. Same-sex marriage, she argues, "does more than just fit; it announces that marriage has changed shape."[125]

Another journalist, Andrew Sullivan, introduced a pro-con anthology about same-sex marriage with this admission:

> Because marriage is such a central institution in so many people's lives, because it forms such an integral part of our own self-understanding, any change in it opens up a host of questions about what the union of two people means, what it has become, and what it could stand for—for everybody....It is at moments like this that we realize that marriage itself has changed....From

being a means to bringing up children, it has become primarily a way in which two adults affirm their emotional commitment to one another.[126]

Notice his recognition that "any change" to marriage will trigger questioning about the institution's purpose and meaning. Specifically, he rejects the idea that marriage could still be "a means to bringing up children" rather than merely "a way in which two adults affirm their emotional commitment to one another."

Jonathan Rauch proposed a similar, and characteristically thoughtful, argument—that the essential purpose of marriage is to provide adults with caregivers:

> I hope I won't be accused of saying that children are a trivial reason for marriage. They just cannot be the only reason.... There is a lot of intellectual work to be done to sort the essential from the inessential purposes of marriage. It seems to me, however, the two strongest candidates are these: settling the young, particularly young men; and providing reliable caregivers. Both purposes are critical to the functioning of a humane, stable society, and both are better served by marriage—that is, by one-to-one lifelong commitment—than by any other institution.[127]

Mark Strasser, a tireless advocate of same-sex marriage in the law-review literature, downgrades both the importance of procreation and its relationship to marriage, and the significance of family structure:

> In *Skinner* [*v. Oklahoma*], the [U.S. Supreme] Court held that "marriage and procreation are fundamental to the very existence and survival of the race." Yet there is no reason to think that the very existence and survival of the human race should or will rest on the shoulders of only those individuals who are raised by both of their biological parents. Otherwise, the human

race would be in great danger indeed, given the number of individuals raised by single parents or by two parents, at least one of whom is not biologically related to the child.[128]

Thus, the mere possibility of childbearing outside of marriage, in Strasser's view, strips the institution of any link to a broader public purpose related to children.

Legal activist Evan Wolfson is entirely dismissive of the idea that marriage and procreation could be linked and that this linkage could have positive implications for children:

> There is no evidence to support the offensive proposition that only one size of family must fit all. Most studies—including ones that [Maggie] Gallagher relies on—reflect the common sense that what counts is not the family structure, but the quality of dedication, commitment, self-sacrifice, and love in the household.[129]

As this quotation indicates, he seems to believe that even the assertion that marriage is related to procreation (which he oddly modifies to "only one size of family must fit all") is "offensive."

Dr. Judith Stacey, who testified before Congress that social science evidence showed "what places children at risk is not fatherlessness, but the absence of economic and social resources that a qualified second parent can provide, whether male or female,"[130] also speculated with approval on the likelihood that gay marriage would inaugurate a new, more expansive embrace of family diversity:

> Legitimizing gay and lesbian marriages would promote a democratic, pluralist expansion of the meaning, practice, and politics of family life in the United States, helping to supplant the destructive sanctity of The Family with respect for diverse and vibrant families... Subjecting the conjugal institution to this sort

of heightened democratic scrutiny could help it to assume varied, creative and adaptive contours. If we begin to value the meaning and quality of intimate bonds over their customary forms, people might devise marriage and kinship patterns to serve diverse needs...Two friends might decide to "marry" without basing their bond on erotic or romantic attachment...Or, more radical still, perhaps some might dare to question the dyadic limitations of Western marriage and seek some of the benefits of extended family life through small group marriages arranged to share resources, nurturance, and labor. After all, if it is true that "The Two-Parent Family is Better" than a single-parent family, as family-values crusaders proclaim, might not three-, four-, or more-parent families be better yet, as many utopian communards have long believed?[131]

Notice that the preferred changes to marriage for Stacey include rejecting all the norms mentioned above: procreation, sexual union, exclusivity, and so on.

These advocates underscore the reality that, for same-sex marriage to make sense, marriage must be something different than it once was. Same-sex marriage is an expression of a powerful public commitment to the ideal that there are no important differences between gay and straight, between same-sex relationships and other kinds of relationships. Getting to that commitment necessarily requires us to consistently deny or downgrade the significance of the biggest, most obvious, and intractable difference between same-sex and opposite-sex unions: that only the latter are capable of producing children and uniting the child with its own mother and father.

2.   What courts have ruled.

Courts that have ruled same-sex marriage is constitutionally mandated have consistently affirmed that moving to same-sex marriage requires downgrading or eliminating the idea that mothers and fathers matter, or that the public purpose of marriage is related to procreation. Observing that "many opposite-sex couples marry for reasons unrelated to procreation, that some of these couples never intend to have children, and that others are incapable of having children," and again that "increasing numbers of same-sex couples are employing increasingly efficient assisted-reproductive techniques to conceive and raise children," the Vermont Supreme Court in 1999 rejected the state's assertion that marriage laws were intended to promote children, or a connection between children and their biological parents.[132] The Massachusetts Supreme Judicial Court was even more dismissive:

> It is hardly surprising that civil marriage developed historically as a means to regulate heterosexual conduct and to promote child rearing, because until very recently unassisted heterosexual relations were the only means short of adoption by which children could come into the world, and the absence of widely available and effective contraceptives made the link between heterosexual sex and procreation very strong indeed...But it is circular reasoning, not analysis, to maintain that marriage must remain a heterosexual institution because that is what it historically has been. As one dissent acknowledges, in "the modern age," "heterosexual intercourse, procreation, and child care are not necessarily conjoined."[133]

Similarly, every court decision moving us toward gay marriage downgrades procreation, explicitly and rigorously.

Take, as another example, this passage from the Ontario Court of Appeals' decision that the Canadian Charter of Rights and Freedoms required marriage licenses be issued to same-sex couples:

> Marriage is, without dispute, one of the most significant forms of personal relationships.... Through the institution of marriage,

individuals can publicly express their love and commitment to each other. Through this institution, society publicly recognizes expressions of love and commitment between individuals, granting them respect and legitimacy as a couple. This public recognition and sanction of marital relationships reflect society's approbation of the personal hopes, desires and aspirations that underlie loving, committed conjugal relationships. This can only enhance an individual's sense of self-worth and dignity.[134]

Marriage, to the court, is a "significant form" of a "personal relationship" that allows the public expression of adult commitment and also allows the government to approbate those personal commitments.

In a similar way, Judge Vaughn Walker's opinion in the Proposition 8 case proceeds under the assumption that marriage is the state's way of giving its stamp of approval to adult relationships. As the court says, "The state respects an individual's choice to build a family with another and protects the relationship because it is so central a part of an individual's life."[135]

Judge Walker also finds that there is no benefit to children from having a mom and a dad:

Children do not need to be raised by a male parent and a female parent to be well-adjusted, and having both a male and a female parent does not increase the likelihood that a child will be well-adjusted.

When the Connecticut Supreme Court ruled in favor of same-sex marriage, it addressed procreation in a footnote. It noted the state's attorney general had disavowed any argument based on marriage's procreative purpose and said: "even though procreative conduct plays an important role in many marriages, we do not believe that such conduct so defines the institution of marriage that the inability to engage in that conduct is determinative of whether same sex and opposite-sex couples are similarly situated for equal protection purposes, especially in view of the fact that some opposite-sex couples also are unable to procreate, and others choose not to do so."[136] Procreation here is an optional activity, fine for those who may choose it but not inherently connected to the public purpose of marriage.

The Iowa Supreme Court had very little to say about what marriage means when it ruled the state constitution mandated its redefinition. The unanimous opinion of the court did, however, disclose the court's operating assumption in a fleeting passage. The court avers same- and opposite-sex couples are similarly situated as to the purpose of marriage laws, "which are designed to bring a sense of order to the legal relationships of committed couples and their families in myriad ways."[137]

"A sense of order" in "myriad ways" replaces marriage's once crystal-clear connection with responsible procreation and protection of children.

What about those who believe and argue that marriage is intimately connected with the good of responsible procreation, of bringing together the mother and father with the child their bodies make? To the *Goodridge* court, this is just an example of homophobia. So the court argues:

> The "marriage is procreation" argument singles out the one unbridgeable difference between same-sex and opposite-sex couples, and transforms that difference into the essence of legal marriage. Like "Amendment 2" to the Constitution of Colorado, which effectively denied homosexual persons equality under the law and full access to the political process, the marriage restriction impermissibly "identifies persons by a single trait and then denies them protection across the board." In so doing, the State's action confers an official stamp of approval on the destructive stereotype that same-sex relationships are inherently unstable and inferior to opposite-sex relationships and are not worthy of respect.[138]

In order to make gay relationships fully equal, the state—through the courts—must repress from its own consciousness (and hopefully eventually from the private citizens in the state) the idea that the procreative potential of opposite-sex couples is worthy of special attention. It is a difference that ought to make no difference, when it comes to marriage.

3. Individual attitude surveys.

It may be theoretically possible to find someone who can say both "gay unions have a right to be considered marriages" and "marriage matters because children need a mom and a dad."

In point of actual practice, however, it is extremely difficult to embrace gay marriage and support anything like the traditional connection between marriage, children, and family structure, because that traditional connection repudiates the "marriage equality" paradigm. Polling data from around the world show as much. The more accepting a country becomes of gay marriage, the less likely people in that country are to accept the idea that children need a mom and a dad.

David Blankenhorn looked at responses to five poll questions assessing agreement with statements about marriage as a social institution and found: "By far the weakest support for marriage…is in the seven surveyed countries that have same-sex marriage." In some cases "the differences between the groups of countries are quite large" so that "people in countries with gay marriage" are "significantly less likely—37.8 percent compared with 60.3 percent—to say that people who want children ought to get married. They are also significantly more likely—83.1 percent compared with 49.7 percent—to say that cohabiting without intending to marry is all right, and are somewhat more likely to say that divorce is usually the best solution to marriage problems."[139] A broader international survey found the same result: "The weakest support for marriage as an institution is in those countries with same-sex marriage."[140]

The dramatic rise of out-of-wedlock births is testimony to the fact that the next generation—which has embraced gay marriage the most strongly—is losing touch with the idea that marriage has any strong relationship to having or raising children. The reason that young people easily embrace gay marriage is they have embraced "soul-mate" marriage.[141]

Soul-mate marriage and gay marriage reinforce one another. Together, they make extremely difficult doing what we need to do to address the marriage crisis: create a new respect for the truths on which a marriage culture is founded: sex makes babies, babies need moms and dads, and adults have a powerful obligation to make sacrifices, if necessary, to create the goods marriage for their children. These sacrifices may include (though not ideally), sacrificing the restless yearning for the next soul-mate.

Corvino is quite right to say the data on attitudes David Blankenhorn gathers is not "proof." It is something else. It is evidence: gay marriage is not just a minor add-on to a marriage system. Gay marriage is exactly what gay marriage advocates say it is when they are proclaiming its virtues rather than trying to hide its consequences. It is the final decision we are now making on whether to institutionalize a new idea of marriage to replace our existing one.

4. Traditional attitudes toward marriage then will be stigmatized in the public square as the moral (and possibly legal) equivalent of racism, and those who hold such views will be treated in the same manner as racists.

Once again, I am not (here) arguing gay marriage is wrong because it will lead to the stigmatization of advocates for the traditional understanding of marriage, or to threats to religious liberty. I am arguing that gay marriage will necessarily change the marriage culture because it will lead to the stigmatization

of the traditional view. The point, if you will, is not that stigmatizing people who advocate traditional marriage as bigots is
wrong (though of course I do believe that). The point is that it
will work.

The evidence is already persuasive. A variety of means, from
law, to elite power networks, to codes of employee behavior, to
public educational programs, are already being used to suppress
and marginalize those who disagree with same-sex marriage
and its premises.

This process, which has been happening behind the scenes
and out of the public eye for several years, burst into the public
sphere in 2011, most prominently when King and Spaulding,
a major law firm, dropped the House of Representatives as a
client after the Human Rights Campaign threatened to disrupt its recruiting and clients. As one anonymous blogger put
it: "Making a blue-chip law firm drop the federal government
as a client? Oppressed groups don't usually have that kind of
clout."[142]

Peter Vidmar, America's most decorated male Olympic
gymnast, abruptly resigned his position as chef de mission for
the 2012 U.S. Olympic team after the gay press objected to his
appointment because he had donated money to Proposition 8.
He said he did not want to distract attention from the athletes,
but he also makes a living as a corporate speaker. In any case, the
asymmetry was established. Athletes can come out for gay marriage, but if they oppose it their platforms are threatened.[143]

In Canada, a sportscaster named Damian Goddard made
a comment in Twitter in response to a professional hockey
player who had expressed support for same-sex marriage. Mr.
Goddard said, "I completely and whole-heartedly support Todd
Reynolds and his support for the traditional and TRUE meaning of marriage." For this, he was fired by his employer.[144]

Religious institutions are beginning to feel the legal heat
as well. In the wake of the *Goodridge v. Department of Public*

Health decision, Massachusetts Catholic Charities sought a religious exemption from state law requiring adoption agencies to make no distinctions on the basis of sexual orientation.[145] The legislature refused the exemption and Catholic Charities had to withdraw from the adoption business.[146] It is a felony to run an adoption agency without a license in Massachusetts, and to get a license you must pledge not to discriminate on the basis of sexual orientation. After all, same-sex marriage means married same-sex couples must be treated like any other married couples.

At the beginning of 2010, the Catholic Archdiocese of Washington, D.C., ceased its foster care placement program because, given the District's new same-sex marriage law, it would have been required to approve same-sex couples for placement.[147]

The most egregious case was in the state of Illinois.

Illinois passed a law creating civil unions in 2011. For four decades prior to that, Catholic Charities had contracted with the state to provide adoption and foster care services. The arrangement involved a series of successive one-year contracts between Catholic Charities and Illinois. After the passage of the civil union bill, same-sex couples deliberately went to three religious adoption agencies known not to do same-sex couples adoptions (the vast majority of foster and adoption agencies do). A formal investigation was launched in which the attorney general's office and the Department of Child and Family Services reviewed the treatment of the agencies that "discriminate" against same-sex couples by refusing to treat them as married. Intimidated by the potential costs of litigation, and given no specific religious liberty protection in the law, Rockford Catholic Charities decided to close.[148] Later in 2011, Catholic Charities was notified that Illinois would not renew its contract for placement services because it "would not provide those services to unmarried cohabiting couples," a policy that "was in direct violation of the Illinois Religious Freedom Protection and Civil Union Act."

An Illinois Circuit Court said Catholic Charities "do not have a legally recognized protected property interest in the renewal of its contract for foster care and adoption services."[149] As a result of this court decision, placements of some two thousand children in Illinois are endangered. Some parents who were recruited through Catholic Charities say they do not feel comfortable working with the state government that refuses to respect their religious views.

The response of gay marriage advocates to such cases is instructive about what "marriage equality" means.

Kendall Marlowe, a spokesman for the Department of Child and Family Services, told the *Chicago Tribune*: "Social intervention such as adoption laws and practices inevitably reflect their communities. Illinois as a state has grown on this (gay rights) issue as evidenced by (civil union legislation). Adoption law and practice should reflect the values of the people of Illinois." The *Tribune* also reported: "Benjamin Wolf of the American Civil Liberties Union of Illinois, an attorney who represents juvenile state wards as part of a court-monitored consent decree with DCFS, said limiting the pool of prospective foster care parents because certain religious traditions believe same-sex relationships are sinful is irresponsible when children are in need."[150]

After the circuit court confirmed the exclusion of Catholic Charities from the adoption and foster care business, the *Huffington Post* reported: "LGBT advocates, on the other hand, were pleased by the decision. Veteran gay activist Rick Garcia described it as 'a victory not only for fairness and decency but also [one that] sends the message that discrimination is unacceptable even if done in the name of religion' in a statement."[151]

As a gleeful pro–gay marriage blogger put it: "Take that 'Catholic' charities that would rather keep orphans homeless than placing them in loving homes: an Illinois judge has ruled that you cannot discriminate against same-sex couples looking to adopt."[152]

The *State Journal-Register* editorialized in favor of the decision:

> This case had less to do with any religious organization's acceptance or recognition of civil unions than it did with reinforcing the anti-discrimination element of the law that created civil unions in Illinois.... Catholic Charities has done admirable work over its four decades working with the state helping match children with families. Its mission in this area is invaluable. With or without government contracts, we hope this work goes on.
>
> But while the church's definition of family has not changed, society's has. In passing the civil union act, Illinois government recognized this, and Schmidt's ruling was an important step in protecting the rights it guarantees.[153]

Gatekeeper professions, like marriage counseling and social work, are being closed to supporters of traditional understanding of marriage. In Georgia, a contract counselor with the Centers for Disease Control referred an employee in a same-sex relationship to another counselor because of the counselor's religious objection to facilitating a same-sex relationship. Although the second counselor was satisfactory, the employee "felt 'judged and condemned'" and "that plaintiff's nonverbal communication also indicated disapproval of her relationship." After an investigation, the counselor was laid off.[154] In Maine, a licensed school guidance counselor was the subject of a complaint seeking to have his license revoked after he appeared in a television commercial in favor of a ballot referendum that would have restored the definition of marriage in Maine as the union of a man and a woman.[155]

Students who wish to join these professions are confronting new "marriage equality" moral and professional codes designed to screen them out of these jobs. A social work student in Missouri was accused of violating her school's code of conduct when, for reasons of her faith, she refused to sign a letter to the state legislature advocating adoptions by same-sex couples. After she filed suit, the university quickly settled and took corrective action to clear the student's name and make other restitution.[156] A graduate student at Eastern Michigan University was dismissed from the school's counseling program after asking for permission to refer a client to another counselor because she was uncomfortable affirming the same-sex relationship of the client.[157]

What difference will gay marriage make to core supporters of our existing marriage tradition? Five years after the advent of same-sex marriage in Massachusetts, the NOM survey noted above found:

> Thirty-six percent of all Massachusetts voters agreed with the statement, "Some people I know personally would be reluctant to admit they oppose gay marriage because they would worry about the consequences for them or their children." (Twenty-four percent agreed strongly.)
>
> While the majority of Massachusetts voters reject the idea that gay marriage opponents should stay silent, a surprising number expressed open support for (presumably moral) intimidation of those who oppose gay marriage. When asked to what extent they agree with the statement, "People who think marriage is only between a man and a woman SHOULD feel intimidated, because they are engaging in discrimination and no one should feel free to be for discrimination," almost one in five voters strongly agreed, and an additional 8 percent agreed, but not strongly.[158]

When I first began in 2003 to speak against gay marriage, on the grounds that marriage aims to reinforce and support the idea that children need a mother and father, gay marriage advocates responded mostly with puzzlement. Today if you publically advocate for the idea that children need a mom and dad, you will be told that idea itself is homophobic, hateful, and discriminatory.

This is not a complaint; merely an observation that logic plays out in life. The people who say these things about traditional-marriage supporters are not being mean or intemperate. They are living up to the moral principle behind gay marriage: it's wrong to distinguish between same-sex and opposite-sex unions; people who do so are bad, like the people who oppose interracial marriage. That's the logic of "marriage equality" and it is unfolding before our eyes.

The gay marriage license, publicly and institutionally speaking, is a license to stigmatize and exclude from posts of public honor and culturally influential professions people who attempt to hold to the ideas about marriage embedded in Genesis: marriage brings together in love the two great halves of humanity, male and female, in the service of creating new human life.

The burden of proof, at this point, is on gay marriage advocates. If you deny that you support using the law of marriage to marginalize the traditional understanding of marriage, if you deny that it is your intent to intimidate into silence those who support the traditional view, if you truly believe that gay marriage represents but a trivial accommodation with little discernible effect on the public goods provided by marriage, you must prove that when you say "marriage equality," you don't really mean it.

You must prove that when you say there is no difference between gay and straight when it comes to marriage, the essential claim of "marriage equality," you don't really mean it.

You must prove that when you accuse those who support our marriage tradition of bigotry, the logical implication of "marriage equality," you don't really mean it.

You must prove that when you say that people who oppose gay marriage are like those who oppose interracial marriage, you don't really mean it.

And then you have to prove that, just because you personally don't hope that enshrining gay marriage into law will cause these things, you can stop it from happening. But you almost certainly can't, because the reasonable result of gay marriage will be a world in which even the transmission of the core ideas undergirding marriage will become increasingly difficult and expensive; and their public transmission through government action or public policy will be impossible.

WILL GAY MARRIAGE HELP GAY PEOPLE AND THEIR CHILDREN?

Our experience with gay marriage is modest, but one thing is already fairly clear: the so-called "conservative" case for marriage is very weak. The conservative case says gay marriage won't so much transform marriage as obtain for gay people and their children the traditional benefits of marriage. This is untenable on the evidence so far.

It is untenable first because only a minority of gay people will choose to enter a same-sex marriage and only a minority of those unions will last. Gay marriage is not being sought as a moral norm limiting and directing adults' behavior in the gay community; it is being sought and celebrated as an individual right. Obtaining a right and choosing to enter into an institution are not at all the same.

Ten years of experience with gay marriage in the most gay-accepting country in Europe[159] suggests that the majority of gay people will never marry, a much larger majority of those who do (compared to opposite-sex couples) will see their unions dissolve, and children adopted or created in the context of a same-sex union (as opposed to inherited from a previous, sundered opposite-sex relationship) are rare.

Radio Netherlands explained on the tenth anniversary of Dutch gay marriage: "Just 20 percent of Dutch homosexual couples are married, compared with 80 percent of heterosexual couples—this is according to new figures published by Statistics Netherlands as the country marks ten years of officially sanctioned same-sex marriage."

Vera Bergkamp, head of a Dutch gay rights organization, "sees three main reasons for the lack of nuptial enthusiasm among gay couples: less pressure from family and friends, fewer gay couples marrying to have children than their straight counterparts, and a more individualist, less family-orientated mindset among many homosexuals."

One out of five same-sex *couples* chooses to marry. But the proportion of gay individuals who marry is even smaller: after ten years, only about "about eight percent of gay and lesbian people have chosen to marry" according to one estimate.[160]

Same-sex unions have very high dissolution rates, even higher than opposite-sex couples. Formal divorce rates may not capture relationship dissolutions among gay couples, who in the absence of children (or social norms banning adultery) may have fewer reasons to consult the state when they break up. But Sweden keeps records on where and with whom every Swede lives. A study found that gay male couples in legal unions were 35 percent more likely to dissolve their relationship and lesbian couples were twice as likely to divorce as married opposite-sex couples.[161]

What difference did the word marriage make?

Gay marriage advocates may be seriously overestimating the benefit to gay people of civil gay marriages. Studies on the effects of gay marriage or civil unions on same-sex couples are in their infancy. But researchers have been surprised to find in many cases there is little evidence of difference between same-sex couples in civil unions and those who choose not to enter a legal status where available, or between civil union and marriage itself for same-sex couples. What research we have (which is extremely preliminary and limited) suggests the legal structure of gay relationships have relatively little affect on these relationships, at least compared to opposite-sex couples.

In their 2008 study comparing couples in same-sex marriages in Massachusetts, domestic partnerships in California, and civil unions in Vermont, Rothblum and colleagues ask "does the ability to call one's relationship marriage make a difference?" and found no difference in relationship quality, no difference in relationships with family or friends, and no difference in experiences of discrimination among same-sex couples in these different types of unions.

For example, on the experience of discrimination they note, "There were no significant gender or interstate effects for having LGB people at work, having had problems at work as a result of being LGB, having lost or been refused a job as a result of being LGB, or having been refused a place to live as a result of being LGB."[162]

This data is preliminary as these couples had not been in legal unions for long.[163] But this preliminary research does suggest the institutional (or public) meaning of same-sex marriage is not clear even for—or especially for—gay couples who enter civil marriages: "every same-sex couple who chooses to get married or legalize their relationship is making a political and highly personal statement."[164]

In another study, these same researchers summed up their finding this way: "Results indicate few differences between same-sex couples in civil unions and those not in civil unions, particularly for women...In contrast, both types of same-sex couples differed from heterosexual married couples in numerous ways....In sum, whatever civil union legislation means for couples who choose it, same-sex couples are quite different from heterosexual married couples."[165]

A three-year follow-up by these same scholars again concluded that, contrary to their own predictions, there were few differences between same-sex couples in civil unions and those who did not legalize their unions: "Because civil unions provide a measure of legal and social validity to same-sex relationships, we expected that the same-sex couples in civil unions would look more like heterosexual married couples, who also enjoy the benefits of a legalized union, and would diverge from same-sex couples without such a legalized union. This hypothesis was not supported in the current study."[166]

Another study suggests legal ceremonies may be less relevant for same-sex couples than personal ceremonies:

> One study of 65 couples gay men found "Couples who had both commitment ceremonies and legal marriages described the commitment ceremony as having the greater impact on their sense of commitment to the relationship and on the degree of social recognition of the relationship in their immediate social circles."[167]

In striking contrast to this gay experience, there is a fairly strong literature documenting the difference marriage makes for opposite-sex couples.[168] For example, while marriage is strongly associated with reduced mortality and longer lifespans for husbands and wives,[169] the only study I could find of the effects of same-sex marriage on longevity, found that same-sex marriage appears to be associated with increased mortality (for reasons unknown, but perhaps a selection effect into marriage unique to gay relationships).[170]

WILL GAY MARRIAGE BENEFIT GAY PEOPLE'S CHILDREN?

As I noted, there is little evidence the formal benefits attached to marriage matter much for child well-being. (Otherwise children who live with remarried parents would fare better, on average, than children living with solo mothers; they do not.) Marriage protects children by making it more likely they will grow up in a family in which their own mothers and fathers are united to teach other as well as to their children.

By definition, same-sex marriages cannot provide a child with his or her own mother and father.

Gay marriage might benefit children if such marriages reduced children's exposure to family transitions (i.e., stabilized their parents' relationship). There is, however, little evidence that gay marriage is important to relationship stability for gay people compared to informal commitment mechanisms.[171]

In any case, the number of children potentially likely to benefit, even if gay marriage has any benefit, is vanishingly small.

According to Census data about one half of one percent of all children live in a household headed by a same-sex couple. Let's assume that half of these enter marriage, if it is available (a much higher proportion than other gay couples). Such households would then account one-quarter of one percent of children. Let's further assume the dissolution rate in same-sex marriage is no higher than that of opposite-sex couples: around 50 percent. In that case, one eighth of one percent of children might experience a stable marriage as a result of gay marriage. Now let's add in the information provided by Gary Gates, the nation's leading demographer of gay people, that likely 80 percent of these children are products of previous heterosexual relationships,[172] meaning the marriage is a remarriage. Remarriage has no known social science benefit to children.

In sum, one-fifth of one-eighth of one percent of children in America might experience a benefit from gay marriage, assuming it stabilized their parent's union more than private commitment ceremonies or civil unions. One-fortieth of one percent of all U.S. children might experience a benefit from gay marriage, if gay marriage adds value to gay unions with children.

Meanwhile 98 percent of the population is subject to strong drives that produce fatherless children, unless powerfully contained and directed. If children were our first or primary concern in the civil institution of marriage, we would not do this. Gay marriage is a decision that the welfare of children is no longer a core public purpose of marriage.

Marriage is a minority taste in the gay community. Do we prefer catering to that minority taste to bolstering marriage as the most important social institution for the protection of children.

IF I HAD MY WAY

If I had my way the place of gay people would be the same as that of any other of the millions of Americans who choose for their own reasons not to marry, at least as our society understands the word. I have entered the gay marriage debate not because homosexuality looms large in my worldview (I have standard Roman Catholic views on sexual morality, but worry most about my own), but because marriage does.

WHY DO I CARE?

It is in one sense difficult to take seriously the prospect of a world in which the core, cross-cultural understanding of marriage, as well as the whole body of traditional Jewish and Christian sexual ethics, is regarded as irrational, hateful, and bigoted. Yet this the world we will have if gay marriage advocates have their way.

I was raised on the lies of the sexual revolution. I was raised and educated to believe that we had separated sex from reproduction, that there are no differences between men and women. That sex can be whatever we want it to be, emotional and affectional or pleasurable without any consequences that need morally concern us.

I learned from my own, and worse, from my own child's experience, what lies these ideas are, and what harm comes when society tries to reorganize itself around a lie.

Having a baby out of wedlock at 22 showed me the untruths which I had been taught. I reasoned my way to basic sexual ethics beginning with one simple premise: you have to do right by your own child. It cannot be right to engage in sexual acts that so often result in children hungry for their fathers. The fact that sex makes babies, the one truth I was formally educated at Yale and in public schools to believe was no longer true, is the one great fact about sex to which we need to pay more, not less attention.

The most important fact about marriage *as a public institution* is not that it satisfies individual desires but that it reduces the harm men and women routinely do to each other in our sexual lives, and most importantly to our children.

So much damage has been done to the family, to children and to society from these great lies.

I do not blame gay men (or women) for not seeing through them. Why should they?

Why should gay people be the ones to recognize that marriage flows from the reality that the sexual act between men and women creates new human life?

This new human child very soon longs to know and be known by, love and be loved by the man and the woman who made him. The child, without the help of, marriage, is all too likely to be denied this great good, because the sexual relationship between men and women is always asymmetrical; only the woman can become pregnant.

I do not blame gay people for gay marriage, I do hold it as a decision point for the rest of us: do we care enough about the danger and damage done by the lies of the sexual revolution to rise up and defend the core principles of marriage?

176 | DEBATING SAME-SEX MARRIAGE

If we were really concerned about the damage done by the lies about the sexual revolution we would not choose gay marriage, we would not choose to cut so decisively and finally in law and culture the link between marriage and the goal of giving every child his own mother and father. We would not tell this most obvious and damaging of lies—that two male or female sexual partners are just like a mom and dad.

We would be calling more attention, not less and less, to what is unique both for good and for evil about unions of male and female. And we would define, as every culture in history has done, the needs of couples who make children as far more important to the society than trendy and incoherent notions such as "marriage equality."

Marriage is a word for the way in which societies throughout history have sought to celebrate and idealize these truths: sex makes babies, society needs babies, and those babies need and long for a mom and a dad. Gay unions cannot serve these purposes. To the contrary, the pretense in law and culture that gay unions are marriages are right now eroding the ideas on which our marriage tradition is founded and the ideals it seeks to realize.

An institution grounded in the laws of nature and Nature's God, is being demoted into a licensing scheme, created by governments, to express and serve adult desires and above all to serve the principle that adult desire trumps the needs of children every time. One of these desires—the wish of gay adults to require everyone else to pretend there is no important difference between gay and straight—is right now being used to create a new America in which those who refuse to profess this lie can be marginalized and persecuted as bigots.

Gay marriage is a government takeover of an institution the government cannot and did not create. Just as governments once used bans on interracial marriage to further a vicious agenda having nothing to do with the nature of marriage, now government proposes to use gay marriage for political purposes foreign to the nature of marriage.

THE CASE FOR MARRIAGE

Our marriage tradition is just and reasonable because it is based on deep and enduring truths about human beings. Unions of husband and wife really are unique, and they serve the common good in a unique way. All of us, married or not, depend on marriage to carry our civilization into the future.

The gay marriage idea is based on a lie. Same sex couples are not like man and wife. Same sex marriage does not do the "work of marriage." Requiring others to act as if gay unions are marriages is fundamentally unjust in the way that requiring assent to a lie is always unjust.

A gay man does not wish to be a husband in the sense of taking responsibility for a woman and any children their unions create together, a responsibility that necessarily includes eschewing all others sexually.

I do not criticize him for this. This is probably a very reasonable decision on a gay man's part. Many people do not marry, for a variety of reasons. The vast majority of unmarried people in this country are not gay. Unmarried people's lives do not therefore become worthless or meaningless. Their civil rights and well-being remain important.

But people who choose not to marry do not therefore have a right to redefine marriage, so the relationships they do choose "fit." None of us have that right.

The first and most immediate consequence of gay marriage is the distortion in the language itself. Words matter because they are at the core of how human beings understand reality. To say the word "mother" must now mean either mother or father would not allow a new class of people to become mothers. It would be to distort our ability to perceive and understand reality, to know what a "mother" is.

Write gay marriage into the law, inscribe it into the culture, and the marriage idea, so utterly, uniquely essential to society becomes hugely more difficult to transmit or sustain. It is not even in the interests of gay people to do this.

Gay marriage is wrong first and foremost not because of its consequences but because it is a lie. But big lies, especially lies about human nature and especially when enforced by government, have terrible consequences.

For fifty years since the sexual revolution, we have tried to ignore, repress, and marginalize from our awareness certain great truths about human beings in their sexual nature. We have done this for our convenience, in service to our desires, and the result has been indecent. In a decent society adults accept the responsibilities that come with the great gift of sex. In a decent society adults make disciplined sacrifices of their own desire to protect the children desire creates.

We cannot blame gay people for gay marriage, for having a blind spot about sex and children, any more than we can blame the adolescents who, fraught with desire and searching for soul mates cannot see the full meaning of their sexuality. It is not reasonable to expect these young people, against all odds, to create or sustain marriage on their own.

It is the rest of us, the 98 percent of adults whose moral courage is being tested.

Will we, with love, stand on these truths and defend marriage?

4

Reply to Gallagher

JOHN CORVINO

■ □ ■

MY FIRST PUBLIC DEBATE WITH Maggie Gallagher was in Oregon. (You can find video on YouTube.) On the way there, I unexpectedly ran into her while boarding a connecting flight, and we decided to sit together on the plane. At one point, I pulled out my phone and showed her a picture of my partner, Mark, displaying his broad, welcoming smile.

"I can see why you call him home," she said.

At first I misunderstood her. "I don't need to call home," I answered. "I just talked to him."

"No—I can see why you call *him* home. He's 'home' for you," she replied.

I nearly spat my complimentary in-flight beverage across the cabin.

Maggie Gallagher is one of America's foremost same-sex-marriage opponents. As the National Organization for Marriage's cofounder, she has probably done more than any other single individual to ensure that, in the eyes of the law, Mark is *not* home for me. And yet, at some level, she seems to "get it."

I've recounted this story before, which has led some people to react that Maggie Gallagher is a phony, a hypocrite, or worse. I do not share their view. Make no mistake: I think Gallagher is seriously wrong on this issue, and in what follows I'll pull no punches in explaining why. I also think she sincerely believes that, whatever Mark and I mean to each other, we should not be allowed to legally marry. In that respect, she is similar to roughly half of Americans today.[1]

In what follows, I respond to key portions of her essay. For reasons of space I will leave many points untouched.

First, a word about the contrast in our essay styles. Gallagher observes that I present a relatively brief positive case and then spend considerable time rebutting others' arguments. I have two reasons for this approach. The first is that, in our shared goal of "achieving disagreement"—that is, understanding where we differ and why—it is crucial to grapple with what the other side is saying. Both sides would benefit from doing more of this. The second is that, at its core, my positive case is really quite simple: *Generally speaking, it is good for human beings to commit to someone else to have and to hold, for better or for worse, and so on, for life. It is good, regardless of whether they happen to be straight or gay. It is good, not only for them, but also for their neighbors, because happy, stable couples make happy, stable citizens. And marriage helps sustain this commitment like nothing else.*[2] There's plenty more to say, and many objections to consider, but there's the positive case in a nutshell.

THE DEFINITIONAL OBJECTION

But is it really *marriage*? Gallagher claims that "the first reason" and "the deepest reason" to oppose treating same-sex unions as marriages is because "it is not true" (98). That is, she endorses the Definitional Objection, and she claims repeatedly that it is not a circular argument. This section is probably the most confused part of her essay, and I will devote considerable attention to it.

Suppose you were to ask me, "Why should I accept your view of marriage?" and I were to respond, "Because it's true." You would justifiably be unsatisfied. Indeed, you would probably be annoyed. "Okay, John," you might reply, "but that doesn't really answer my question: why should I accept your view of marriage as true?" In other words, *accepting* my view of marriage—which includes same-sex couples—means accepting it as true, as correct, as better than the alternatives. That's what *accepting it* means. Yet Gallagher treats "because it's true" as an independent, noncircular argument—indeed, as the most important argument she offers.

Gallagher attempts to clarify by comparing and contrasting the word *marriage* with the words *red, dog, mother,* and *corporation,* and here the confusion simply escalates. She asks us to imagine a world in which the word "dog" means "either dog or cat," but she doesn't appreciate the force of her own example. She claims that in such a world, those of us who know what a cat is or what a dog is would understand that something untrue was being asserted. Actually, no. Definitions only assert something true (or false) insofar as they attempt to capture established usage. But here Gallagher asks us to imagine abandoning established usage in favor of a different one: one where the string of letters D-O-G refers, not only to certain members of *Canis lupus,* but also to members of *Felis catus.* In that case, assuming that other definitions remain constant, the following statements would all be true:

> *Dogs* are popular pets.
> Some *dogs* are Tabbys.
> Not all *dogs* bark; some purr.
> The famous cartoon characters Felix and Garfield
>   are *dogs.*

(I italicize *dogs* to underscore that the term is being used nonstandardly here.)

Of course, there are many good reasons for distinguishing between dogs and cats, as we currently use those terms. But there are plenty of ways of indicating the distinction that differ from our own. For example, like Spanish speakers, we could use the terms *perros* and *gatos* instead of "dogs" and "cats." In Gallagher's hypothetical society, we could use the terms "canine dogs" and "feline dogs"—or as she suggests, "dogs that bark" and "dogs that meow"—without any loss in precision. These different ways of indicating the distinction might be more or less convenient, more or less euphonious, or more or less familiar, but they are not more or less *true*.

Perhaps Gallagher's point is simply that *established usage* requires that the word "marriage" refer only to different-sex unions; this may explain why she spends considerable time reviewing marriage's history. But Gallagher herself concedes that other societies have recognized same-sex unions as marriages. These marriages may not be common, and they may not be "gay marriages" as we understand them, but they show something important: we are not the first generation to recognize that "male-female" need not be part of *the very definition of "marriage."* Moreover, usage changes over time. So if Gallagher is making an empirical claim about English usage, it appears to be a losing one: many competent speakers today use the word "marriage" to include same-sex couples. Language is malleable, and so is marriage: as Gallagher admits, in an apparently unguarded moment, "Marriage is not static. It changes, adapts, and evolves" (107). Precisely!

What Gallagher really wants to say is this: *heterosexual unions are so important, and so different from same-sex unions, that we ought to reserve a privileged term and privileged status for them.* As she puts it, there is "a basic human reality, captured by this word, that deserves to be named as distinct and unique"

(100). That is a meaningful, noncircular claim. But it's not the Definitional Objection, at least not as Gallagher has articulated it. And whatever it is, it's something that requires argument and evidence, not mere assertion.

Consider an analogy to another social practice: baseball. When the designated-hitter rule was introduced—allowing someone else to bat for the pitcher—some purists objected "That's just not baseball!" Today, virtually all competent English speakers use the term "baseball" to refer to a game that includes the designated-hitter rule. We can still argue about whether that rule is a good idea, whether it should have been adopted in the first place, or whether it should be continued. But arguing that we cannot use the designated-hitter rule "because it's not true" would be silly.

Gallagher will surely object that marriage is not like baseball, and that my analogy proves that I've missed the point. Baseball is a conventional institution: it is created by humans for human purposes and can be changed to suit those purposes. In this respect it resembles Gallagher's example of *corporation*, which she contrasts with *marriage*. As she writes, "If 'marriage' is a word like 'corporation' we are launched into a purely consequentialist argument, in which truth claims do not arise" (104). In that case, "marriage means whatever the individuals decide it means," and ultimately, "the term 'marriage' has no outside referent" (100).

Gallagher's confusion here is legion. First, there is her strange claim that "truth claims do not arise" in consequentialist arguments. (Consequentialist arguments, like all sincere arguments, aim to establish true conclusions.) Second, there's the idea that a conventional institution can mean whatever the *individuals* decide it means. This is false. The pile of paper clips on my desk cannot constitute a corporation, even if I say so, and a game that two people play with a deck of cards can't be baseball, although it may nevertheless be worth playing. The whole point of *conventional* institutions is that they depend on shared understanding across a community. Third, absolutely no one in this debate thinks that "the term 'marriage' has no outside referent," as Gallagher bizarrely asserts. We simply disagree about what that referent can be.

Even worse for Gallagher is that her own preferred comparison—between the word "marriage" and the word "mother"—contradicts the very point she is aiming to make. She wants to argue that "marriage" refers to something whose boundaries exist independently of our legal and social customs—what philosophers might call a *natural kind*. The word "mother" is like that: its primary meaning is a biological reality. As Gallagher puts it, "The mother is the person who bears the child with her body" (103).

Except, sometimes, she's not. Two sentences later, Gallagher rightly notes that we have expanded the use of term "mother" to include those who do not meet the biological or "natural" definition: "When the natural mother cannot or will not perform the maternal function for the child, we give a motherless child a mother through the legal process" (103). Precisely. The word "mother" refers to a certain biological relationship, but it can also refer to a certain *social role* that is often (but not always) performed by biological mothers.

Now, my own view—contra Gallagher and the new-natural-law theorists—is that it's strange to treat marriage as essentially a biological reality. But the point is now unnecessary, because even if one insists that "marriage" refers primarily to a biological relationship, Gallagher's "mother" example shows us how to expand the term's use. By performing social roles that are associated with married couples—lifelong romantic partnering, mutual domestic care, and so on—a same-sex couple can marry, even if they don't meet Gallagher's biological criterion.

Let me illustrate by way of a personal example. My parents regularly refer to my partner, Mark, as their "son-in-law." There is in fact no *law* acknowledging Mark as my spouse: both Michigan (where I live) and Texas (where my parents live) constitutionally prohibit same-sex marriage or similar unions. And we clearly don't meet Gallagher's biological requirement. Yet my parents recognize Mark as their son-in-law. Why?

Because Mark is the person who is committed to me for life, and vice-versa—that's why. Because he's the one I share my home and my bed with, for ten years and counting. Because he's the one who cares for me when I'm sick, who comforts me when I'm grieving, who cheers me on at milestones, and who will bury me when I die (assuming I go first). Because he's the one who pulls me aside to tell me that I'm acting like a jerk, or that it's time to trim my nose hair, or that maybe I've had too much to drink. Because he's the one my parents call when they're concerned that I'm working too hard, or they're trying to figure out what to give me for Christmas, or they want to surprise me with a visit. Because he's the one who, on stressful days, brightens my mood with a simple text-message saying "I love you." Because he is, as they say, "my better half."

My parents, who have been happily married for over forty-four years, always wanted me to find such a person someday. When I was growing up, they did not imagine that this person would be a man. But he is, and he's their son-in-law, and don't try to tell them otherwise.

Indeed, here's one place Gallagher and I agree. She writes that the word "marriage" refers "not primarily to the law, but to a phenomenon outside the law, that the law either recognizes or fails to recognize, supports or fails to support, with real-world consequences" (105). I wholeheartedly concur. As vital as it is, the legal reality is not the only important reality. Just ask my parents.

THE INFERTILE-COUPLES PROBLEM, REVISITED

There's another problem with Gallagher's appeal to the Definitional Objection. She wants the word "marriage," like the word "mother," to refer to a biological reality independent of human custom. But she's quite vague on what that reality is.

As I explained in my main essay, the most robust attempt to identify marriage with an objective biological reality comes from the new-natural-law theorists, who define marriage as a comprehensive union which includes the biological union of coitus. But their account has radically counterintuitive implications, including the result that any couple incapable of coitus—such as a heterosexual couple in which the man is a paraplegic—is thereby incapable of marriage.

Perhaps because she recognizes this problem, Gallagher hesitates to endorse the view: "I am not necessarily embracing all of Girgis and colleagues' natural-law philosophical superstructure," she writes (99). It is unclear what she puts in its place, however. She offers, as a simpler account, that "Marriage is the exclusive, enduring sexual union of husband and wife" (99). Must that sexual union include coitus? If so, then Gallagher faces the same paraplegic counterexample. If not, then what's the bar to counting committed same-sex couples as married? Why aren't they just another variety of permanently infertile couples? If the answer is, "Because they're not husband and wife," then the circularity problem looms again. As Richard Mohr nicely puts it, such circular answers treat marriage "as an empty space, delimited only by what it excludes—gay couples."[3]

Gallagher addresses the infertile-couples problem in only one section. There she seems to want to have it both ways: elderly and other permanently infertile couples may marry, because procreative potential is *not* an essential requirement for every marriage, but same-sex couples may not, because marriage is about "regulating procreation." Which is it?[4]

In order to prove that "regulating procreation" is the public purpose of marriage, Gallagher invokes judicial authority: "Long before the law even imagined the existence of gay marriage, even while old people and infertile people were allowed to marry, judicial authorities reiterated again and again that a key public purpose of marriage was regulating procreation so that children do not get hurt and so that society has the next generation it needs" (117).

Put aside the fact that "regulating procreation" is probably not the best way to describe marriage's child-protective function.[5] The main problem is that—when it comes to homosexual couples, but not heterosexual couples—Gallagher can't seem to distinguish between the following two claims:

Protecting children is a key purpose of marriage.

Protecting children is the only definitive purpose of marriage, and any relationship incapable of producing children cannot be a marriage.

The first claim strikes me as obviously correct. As I state explicitly in my main essay: "the welfare of children is a supremely important rationale for marriage. There is no serious debate about this." But the second claim is obviously false (as the infertile-couples example shows), and that's the one Gallagher needs.

All of the evidence Gallagher cites points to the first claim, not the second. Consider some of the judicial language she cites regarding procreation:

> "the first purpose of matrimony...one of the two principal ends of marriage...[o]ne of the prime purposes of matrimony...could be considered one of the major purposes of marriage...a primary purpose...one of the primary purposes...one of the important ends...one of the great purposes...one of the most important functions"...and so on.

One of the important purposes. Not *the definitive purpose, without which there is no marriage.* The difference is crucial.

STAIRCASES, STILL MISSING

So, to take stock thus far: Gallagher argues that "the deepest reason" for opposing same-sex marriage is "because it's not true." But she fails to acknowledge the malleability of both language and marriage. Moreover, she fails to identify precisely the unchanging biological reality to which the word "marriage" supposedly refers, and that failure exposes her to the infertile-couples objection. Although she argues that "regulating procreation" is a key purpose of marriage, she never explains why a same-sex couple's inability to procreate should render them any less eligible to marry than, say, an elderly different-sex couple.

All of this discussion has focused on whether same-sex marriage is *possible*. But unlike Gallagher, I don't think that's the central and morally urgent dispute between us. The Marriage/Schmarriage Maneuver I described in my main essay proves this: *Fine, you don't think it's marriage. You think it's something else. But why not go for it?* The central and morally urgent dispute between us is about whether to give the same legal recognition and social support to same-sex couples and different-sex couples. So that's the question to which I now turn. From here on, in asking "Why can't same-sex couples *marry*?" I'm not asking whether it's metaphysically possible; I'm asking why we shouldn't do what Canada and Massachusetts and other jurisdictions have done—extend legal marriage to same-sex couples.

That, by the way, is what marriage equality means: not that same-sex couples are similar to different-sex couples in every respect, much less that "men and women are just the same," as Gallagher facetiously suggests (112), but that same-sex couples and different-sex couples *ought to be treated equally under the law.* I think that treating same-sex couples equally means letting them marry; Gallagher disagrees. I think that letting them marry would extend a valuable social institution; Gallagher thinks that letting them "marry" would replace that valuable social institution with a different, inferior one. (Henceforth I'll drop the scare-quotes from the word "marriage" and its cognates when discussing Gallagher's views on same-sex marriage.)

Why inferior? Because, according to Gallagher, this new institution would be less able to perform marriage's core task: "The critical public or "civil" task of marriage is to regulate sexual relationships between men and women in order to reduce the likelihood that children (and their mothers, and society) will face the burdens of fatherlessness, and increase the likelihood that there will be a next generation that will be raised by their mothers and fathers in one family, where both parents are committed to each other and to their children" (96). The resulting argument is consequentialist: letting same-sex couples marry would have bad effects, particularly on mothers and children. Gallagher worries about its being "merely" consequentialist, but there's nothing "mere" about it: the alleged consequences are quite serious.

Again, let me make this personal. (It's all personal at some level.) Given her life experience, Gallagher understands the burdens of fatherlessness in a way that I never will. That said, I live in a city, Detroit, where deadbeat fathers are a widespread problem. And I appreciate how great a gift my own parents have given me by being committed to each other and to me since before I was born. I share Gallagher's desire to see as many children as possible receive that gift. But what does this have to do with whether I can marry Mark?

In answering that question, there are a few things to keep in mind. First, like most gay male couples and many straight ones, Mark and I have absolutely no intention of having children. Gallagher points out that intention is not what makes children. True enough, but trust me: Mark and I are not going to get each other—or anyone else—accidentally pregnant.

Second, if we were to have children, we would do so via adoption. The reasons are various, but they mainly have to do with my genuine sorrow that there are existing children who lack families to care for them. In other words, if we were to have children (which we won't), we wouldn't be taking them away from their mothers and fathers. Most likely, we'd be taking them out of the foster-care system.

Third, while there are certainly couples (and individuals) who choose to have children by artificial insemination or surrogacy, the majority of those are not same-sex couples, and most providers do not require such couples to be married. Thus, it remains unclear how prohibiting same-sex marriage is a reasonable and fair means of curtailing such practices, if that is what one is aiming to do. Moreover, recall that the real-world alternative is not for such children to get their own mother and father; it's for them not to be created in the first place.

Now, with those things in mind, how would extending marriage to same-sex couples (including Mark and me) render it less able to perform its core task of binding parents, and particularly fathers, to their offspring? How do we fill in the "missing staircases" between the premise that children on average do best with their own mothers and fathers, and the conclusion that same-sex couples should not be permitted to marry?

Gallagher offers three interrelated answers, as follows:

1. If two men or two women can count as a marriage, then marriage no longer sends the message that children need their mothers and fathers (The Message Argument).
2. If marriage is expanded to include same-sex couples, norms of fidelity and other important rules will no longer be seen as core features of marriage (The Stretching Argument). The result will be more out-of-wedlock births, more divorce, and more broken homes for children.

3. If the state endorses same-sex marriage, private actors who hold traditional views (e.g., children need a mother and father; marriage is a sexually exclusive commitment, and so on) will be marginalized as bigots.

In my main essay I discussed the first two points as the Message and Stretching Arguments, respectively. The third point builds on the first two: if marriage no longer sends this message (point 1) or embodies these norms (point 2), and if those who try to do so independently are marginalized as bigots (point 3), then the message and the norms become much more difficult to impart.

I have already explained why I think the Message and Stretching arguments don't work. Has Gallagher given us reason to reconsider those rebuttals? I don't think so. Let's take each of the three points in turn.

THE MESSAGE ARGUMENT

According to Gallagher, the central function of marriage is to signal the ideal that children need a mother and father. She thinks it's clear that same-sex marriage would repudiate this function: "If two men are a marriage, marriage is obviously not about getting mothers and fathers for children. Period" (124).

Where Gallagher throws down a "Period," I see room for discussion. Marriage is indeed about getting mothers and fathers for children, but it is not *only* about that, and the other functions can be sufficient in themselves. The elderly-couple example proves this. *Their* marriage is not about getting mothers and fathers for children, and yet we still recognize it as worthwhile, because of another important marital theme: no one should have to face life alone.[6] Gallagher imposes a double standard here: when infertile heterosexuals marry, they're just a harmless exception to the general rule, whereas when gays marry, they somehow repudiate the institution's core purpose. (Nussbaum aptly refers to this sort of procreational double standard as "two-faced.[7])

Gallagher takes me to task for "pok[ing] fun" at the idea that protecting children is a key part of the elderly couple's marriage: "[I]f you have seen the pain of children abandoned by their fathers," she writes, "you would not ridicule this part of the public purpose of every marriage" (115). But my point is not to "ridicule" marriage's child-protective function—which, on the contrary, I heartily endorse—but to challenge Gallagher's idea that protecting children is why we support the elderly couple's marriage. Like other social institutions, marriage embodies multiple messages, and not every marriage points to every one.

Gallagher adds that if the elderly heterosexual husband keeps his marriage vows, he will not be "creating fatherless children in other households." True enough. But that point applies equally well to the gay or bisexual man in a same-sex marriage.

She then tries to assemble evidence that gay-rights advocates are explicitly attacking marriage's procreative purpose. It's true that some of my allies' rhetoric "downgrades" procreation—though no more than some of her allies' rhetoric glorifies it. What's interesting, though, is that some of Gallagher's "evidence" directly contradicts her own point (153–155): She claims that Yale law professor William Eskridge considers procreation "relatively unimportant to marriage, to people, and to society," but then goes on to quote him as saying "Procreation is good and important..."

When Andrew Sullivan writes, "From being a means to bringing up children, [marriage] has become primarily a way in which two adults affirm their emotional commitment to one another," she reads him as rejecting the idea "that marriage could still be 'a means to bringing up children' rather than merely 'a way in which two adults affirm their emotional commitment.'" But Sullivan quite explicitly says "primarily," not "merely."

And after Jonathan Rauch takes pains to note, "I hope I won't be accused of saying that children are a trivial reason for marriage. They just can't be the only reason," Gallagher simply ignores his discussion of multiple purposes and pins the following view on him: "the essential purpose of marriage is to provide adults with caregivers." Not *an* essential purpose—which is Rauch's actual view—but *the* essential purpose, which displaces procreation. Gallagher can't seem to get past this false dilemma: for Gallagher, if you are not single-mindedly focused on procreation—if you believe, instead, that adult sharing of life is a sufficient rationale for marriage—then you cannot allow procreation a significant role at all.

Gallagher makes the same mistake when she argues that various pro-marriage-equality judicial decisions require "downgrading or eliminating the idea that mothers and fathers matter" (158). Take, for example, the passage she cites from the Connecticut Supreme Court: "even though procreative conduct plays an important role in many marriages, we do not believe that such conduct so defines the institution of marriage that the inability to engage in that conduct is determinative of whether same-sex and opposite-sex couples are similarly situated for equal protection purposes, especially in view of the fact that some opposite-sex couples also are unable to procreate, and others choose not to do so."[8]

Notice what the Court actually says: not that procreation is unimportant, much less that mothers and fathers don't matter, but that the inability to procreate doesn't determine "whether same-sex and opposite-sex couples are similarly situated for equal protection purposes."

Like Gallagher, and unlike E. J. Graff, I don't see how we'll ever cut the link between sex and diapers. As Gallagher rightly reminds us, "sex makes babies." But let's not miss Graff's underlying point: there are important rationales for marriage besides protecting children, and important messages it sends besides "Children need their mothers and fathers." Significantly, it sends a message about mutual commitment and responsibility, about putting another person's needs before one's own selfish desires. The courts have recognized this point at least since *Griswold v. Connecticut* (1965), which upheld the right of married couples to purchase contraceptives. As the Griswold court noted, in a passage approvingly cited by Gallagher, "Marriage is a coming together for better or for worse, hopefully enduring, and intimate to the degree of being sacred. It is an association that promotes a way of life, not causes; a harmony in living, not political faiths; a bilateral loyalty, not commercial or social projects. Yet it is an association for as noble a purpose as any involved in our prior decisions." The "noble purpose" referred to here is the way of life, the harmony in living, the bilateral loyalty. Of course such commitment is important for any children that arrive, but it is also vital for childless adults.

Finally, I refer the reader back to my previous discussion of whether children's "need" for their own (biological) mother and father is what Gallagher treats it as being: a mandatory requirement, rather than an ideal rooted in a statistical overgeneralization (Corvino, 45–48).

THE STRETCHING ARGUMENT

Gallagher also argues that same-sex marriage will undermine key marital norms. Because of differences between heterosexual relationships, gay male relationships, and lesbian relationships, she worries that having one institution to cover all would dilute the ways marital norms currently serve heterosexuals—and especially their offspring. She's particularly concerned about sexual exclusivity, although she also raises questions about other norms: Why only two? Why sexual? Why not sisters? Why coparenting?

In my main essay (especially the polygamy section), I addressed several of these questions.[9] Here, I want to say a bit more about sexual exclusivity.

It is important to understand Gallagher's argument. She is not simply arguing "Gay men are promiscuous, therefore, they should not be allowed to marry." Her reasoning is more nuanced. She begins by noting that, for many gay male couples, sexual exclusivity does not correlate with relationship success in the same way that it does for heterosexuals or lesbians. I believe she exaggerates the gap here, by leaning on convenience samples from urban centers like San Francisco, but I'll grant the general point: on average, sexual exclusivity appears less important for gay men's relationship success (longevity, satisfaction, etc.) than it does for that of heterosexuals or lesbians. She then ties this point into an argument about marriage equality. Imagine a gay male couple in an open relationship: let's call them Romeo and Jules. If Romeo and Jules are just as married as anyone else, then marriage no longer *means* forsaking all others sexually. So Gallagher's Stretching Argument ties in to a Message Argument, and even into a kind of Definitional Objection, as follows:

As it is currently understood, marriage means sexual exclusivity—at least, that's the ideal. If Romeo and Jules count as married, marriage will no longer embody that message. The likely result is that fewer heterosexual couples will be sexually exclusive, which would mean more out-of-wedlock births, more divorce, and more broken homes for children.

The first thing to notice is that Gallagher's Stretching Argument rests upon a rather implausible empirical claim about same-sex couples' power to topple majority norms. Gays are, and always will be, a relatively small percentage of the population.[10] So same-sex couples will be a small fraction of marriages, *male* same-sex couples will be about half of those, and male same-sex couples *in open relationships* will be a smaller subset still. Yet somehow, this tiny subset of marriages would change the institution's meaning generally, even to the point of causing heterosexual fathers to cheat on their wives and abandon their children? Even Gallagher acknowledges that the "free love" movement among heterosexuals never quite caught on. Why should we think that gay males will affect heterosexual marriage in a way that straight swingers never did? It seems just as likely, if not more, that mainstream marital norms will affect gay males' behavior—although this sort of effect will take time, as the marriage culture takes root in the gay community.

Most people understand that what works for some married couples doesn't necessarily work for all, or even most. Consider a real-life couple I'll call "Simone" and "Jean-Paul." Simone was a close friend of mine in graduate school; Jean-Paul was her husband. They had an open relationship—uncommon for straight couples, though perhaps less so for academic straight couples who grew up in the sixties. When they married (in the 1980s), they deliberately left fidelity out of their wedding vows. Some might object, "That's not a real marriage." Private observers are free to say so, just as they may voice similar opinions about other marriage subsets: those who don't marry in church, for example, or those whose members have grown emotionally cold. Yet, in the eyes of the law, Simone and Jean-Paul were just as married as any other legally wedded couple.

Given that we allow heterosexual couples like Simone and Jean-Paul to marry (and always have), on what grounds can we deny legal marriage to Romeo and Jules—or for that matter, to the gay male couples who do promise and expect and achieve sexual exclusivity? And what about the lesbians, who here (as elsewhere) seem to be largely ignored? In effect, the Stretching Argument denies marriage to *all* same-sex couples because *some* married straight men who notice the sexual openness of *some* married gay men might start pushing for open marriages and producing out-of-wedlock children. Empirical implausibility aside, the argument is unjust on its face.

I don't doubt that there are general differences between heterosexual couples, gay male couples, and lesbian couples. But let's not forget the important similarities, some of which Gallagher mentions: successful relationships depend on "good communication, trust, loyalty, caretaking and the ability to manage conflict," for example (129). And let's not forget the differences among *heterosexual* marriages, despite the endurance of general norms. In terms of raw numbers, there are probably more straight "swingers" than there are gay men, and yet (as Gallagher documents) people still overwhelmingly expect sexual exclusivity in marriage. There are "commuter marriages," and yet people still associate marriage with cohabitation and mutual domestic care. There are marriages where spouses are scarcely apart, and marriages where they take separate vacations; some with frequent sex, some with infrequent sex; some with a highly gendered division of labor, some that defy gender expectations, and so on.

My point is that marital norms endure even while individuals know how to think for themselves. Do I think that married gay men would be more likely to flout the exclusivity norm than others? Yes. Do I think that this would change the exclusivity norm generally? No. Do I think that this is a good reason to deny marriage to *any* same-sex couple, including those who promise exclusivity? Surely not.

THOSE PROMOTING TRADITIONAL NORMS WILL BE BRANDED AS BIGOTS

Finally, Gallagher worries that letting gays marry "will almost certainly lead to new efforts to stigmatize and repress the traditional view of marriage" and ultimately to treating marriage-equality opponents "like bigots who oppose interracial marriage" (126). When that happens, the view that children need mothers and fathers will become much harder to sustain.

Let me begin by addressing the bigotry charge head-on. I generally avoid labeling my opponents as bigots. Doing so is a conversation-stopper, and I believe we need more dialogue here, not less. To call someone a bigot is to say that his or her views are unworthy of discussion. That's an approach that should be used sparingly.

At the same time, I know firsthand that antigay bigotry is real. I've had food thrown at me by people yelling "Faggot." I've been attacked in a parking lot by teenaged gay-bashers. I've been harassed by a Texas state trooper for kissing another man. (Yes, just kissing: I filed a complaint, and the trooper was disciplined.[11]) And I've experienced the subtle-yet-powerful cumulative effects of being told from a tender age that my deep romantic longings are sick, unnatural, and evil.

Like it or not, that's the social context in which many of us experience the marriage debate. Gallagher understands that marriage is a social institution with messages. Among these is a powerful signal of affirmation: *we the community take your love and commitment seriously.* Whether or not it follows logically, here's the corollary people draw when denied marriage: *your love isn't worthy; your relationship doesn't matter.* For those of us who have been told repeatedly that our deep romantic longings are sick, unnatural, and evil, such denial can feel like an additional slap. Indeed, the section of Gallagher's main essay I found most infuriating was the one where she argued that marriage doesn't make much difference to gay couples. Easy for her to say.

And this is one reason why the marriage debate is so hard. When we ask for marriage, we are not just asking to be left alone. If we were, we could get married on our own and not worry about the state or society. And we're not *only* asking for legal rights and responsibilities, although those are crucial, and their denial can be devastating. When we ask for marriage, we are also asking for inclusion, for affirmation, for equal respect. We should not be ashamed to seek such things: we're social creatures like everyone else. But it's important to remember that, given the affirmative message that marriage carries, asking for marriage means asking other people to grant us something. It's not just a personal relationship between spouses; it's also a relationship between the couple and the community. What we are seeking is the institutional support that our heterosexual fellow citizens take for granted.

Let me be clear: the state cannot force private individuals to affirm or respect anyone. That is, and always will be, a personal choice. But it can, and should, require equal treatment under the law. Citizens in a free society deserve no less from their government.

When people are unwilling to grant same-sex couples inclusion, affirmation, and respect, does that make them bigots? The analogy to interracial marriage can be illuminating here, although perhaps in different ways than you think.[12]

Again, let me illustrate from my own experience. My grandparents—like many other whites of their generation—opposed interracial marriage. I loved, admired, and respected my grandparents. (Still do: one is still living.) Their racism was not the sneering, epithet-wielding, block-the-schoolhouse-door variety. Their stated reasons against interracial marriage seemed noble enough: it was bad for the children, they'd say, or it's not what God wants, or sometimes: "it's just not right." They didn't make a fuss about it, and they didn't organize around it politically, but they deeply believed it.

Were my grandparents bigots? I can understand why many would say so. As someone who loves them, I prefer to think of it this way: my grandparents—like all of us, me included—had their moral blind spots, and racism was among them.

Some people balk at any comparison between same-sex marriage and interracial marriage: "Race and sexual orientation are not the same thing!" Of course they're not. I've never said otherwise. When we make an analogy, we're not saying that two things are the same. We're saying that they're similar in some relevant respects. They may be quite dissimilar in others, and both the similarities and the differences can be instructive.

What can we learn from looking at the history of racial discrimination and interracial marriage? Several relevant things. That couples experience the denial of marriage as a powerful deprivation. That human beings often hide behind religion to absolve their views from rational assessment ("It's not me who says this; it's God!"). That people sometimes invoke what's "natural," or what's bad for the children, to justify their biases. That fear sometimes eclipses reason. That even good people can have serious moral blind spots.

Most relevant to my point here, we can learn how bigotry can have a gracious, even noble-looking face. It's not always about yelling epithets, or throwing food at people, or physically blocking doors. Sometimes it involves kindly grandparents who can't quite wrap their minds around social change. Sometimes it's about metaphorically blocking doors.

Gallagher complains that my allies think of her allies as irrational and bigoted. Indeed, many do. But her allies often think of mine as irrational and perverse, and I don't try to spin an additional argument out of it. Notice Gallagher's peculiar habit of double-counting our arguments: for any one we make, she complains both that we make the argument and that we say that anyone who disagrees is a bigot. Of course, I could employ the same tactic: for any of my opponents' arguments, I could complain both that they make the argument and that they say that anyone who disagrees is perverse—or deviant, or antifamily, or whatever. But the second step is a distraction: it gripes about name-calling rather than engaging the argument's substance. Like the Definitional Objection, it's an avoidance maneuver.

Whichever side prevails in this debate, the other's views will be marginalized. There's no getting around that. (That's what prevailing in a debate *means*.) It needn't be ugly, although it sometimes is. Let's not pretend, however, that either side has a monopoly on nasty rhetoric. When Focus on the Family founder Dr. James Dobson accuses gays of seeking "the utter destruction of the family," or when former U.S. Senator Rick Santorum compares same-sex relationships to "man on dog" sex, or when Congresswoman Michele Bachmann says that homosexuality is "part of Satan," they marginalize and dehumanize their opponents.[13] Traditionalists should think twice before playing the victim card: it is legal in more than half of U.S. states to fire someone from a job simply for being gay. Until recently, gay citizens had to lie about their close relationships in order to serve in our nation's military. And as recently as 2003, until the U.S. Supreme Court struck down anti-sodomy laws in *Lawrence v. Texas,* I could be charged with a felony for having private intimate relations with my partner.[14] Many of Gallagher's allies openly supported such laws. Some still do.

The view that same-sex couples are unworthy of marriage is a wrongheaded one, which should, and will, be marginalized. But what about the view that children need mothers and fathers? If Gallagher is trying to connect the dots between that premise and her opposition to same-sex marriage, we should focus more specifically on this question: will people be stigmatized, and even branded as bigots, simply because they believe that children do best with their own (biological) mother and father?

Honest answer: it depends.

Specifically, it depends on how they frame their point. If they make their focus child welfare, they should be fine. Indeed, on certain points, they may find surprising allies. I too lament the fact that many men don't take their responsibilities as fathers seriously. I'd like to see the divorce rate reduced, especially when children are involved. I recognize teen pregnancy as a real social problem, particularly in poor minority communities. If the focus is on getting everyone to take more responsibility when it comes to sex and procreation and childrearing, then sign me up.

But that, sadly, has seldom been the focus. Instead, "the traditional view of marriage" has become code for "no gays allowed." Consider the National Organization for Marriage, which Gallagher cofounded. What do they do to protect children and strengthen marriage? Not a single thing. Their sole mission is to keep gays out. Worse yet, their scapegoating diverts resources away from measures that might actually help children.

If you don't want your child-welfare convictions to get branded as discrimination, then you shouldn't cloak them in a discriminatory message: *no gays allowed.* Regrettably, that's the path that Gallagher and her allies have consistently chosen.[15]

CONCLUSION

Love is not all: It is not meat nor drink
Nor slumber nor a roof against the rain,
Nor yet a floating spar to men that sink
and rise and sink and rise and sink again.
Love cannot fill the thickened lung with breath
Nor clean the blood, nor set the fractured bone;
Yet many a man is making friends with death
even as I speak, for lack of love alone.

—EDNA ST. VINCENT MILLAY, *from Sonnet XXX of Fatal Interview*

It is odd, perhaps, that a book about marriage has said so little about love. So I'd like to conclude by returning to that theme.

When discussing love and marriage, most people think immediately of romantic love. That's an important aspect, to be sure. But even more important is *love as commitment*—an ongoing activity, not an ephemeral feeling. Marital love is not just something people *feel*, it's something they *do*.

Does getting married make a difference for this kind of life-sustaining love? Gallagher says *yes* for straight people, but *no* for gay people. As evidence she notes that, in one study, "[Gay couples] who had both commitment ceremonies and legal marriages described the commitment ceremony as having the greater impact on their sense of commitment to the relationship and on the degree of social recognition of the relationship in their immediate social circles."[16]

This finding did not surprise me. After all, most gays grow up without legal marriage as an option. We cobble together what supports we can, and we take those very seriously. I am reminded here of Moisés Kaufman's short play *London Mosquitoes*, in which a character, Joe, stands by a casket and eulogizes his late partner, Paul. At one point Joe recalls raising the subject of marriage:

> When this whole "marriage conversation" started and our friends began getting married, I asked him about it: Should we get married? He didn't reply, he just turned and walked out of the room. Every time I tried to bring it up, he'd get upset and storm out. Finally, I told him: I don't care much one way or another, but why don't you want to get married?
>
> Paul yelled at me and said, "If we married now, we'd be having our one-year anniversary next year. What would that say about the last forty-five years? That we were just messing around? Messing around for all that time?"[17]

Those of us in same-sex relationships, and those close to us, know that we're not just messing around. Our love and commitment are real. We don't need the state to authenticate that.

Unfortunately, some of us also know what it's like when the legal and social realities don't quite match the personal reality. There are countless tragic examples. Here's one.

Janice Langbehn and Lisa Marie Pond met and fell in love while in college.[18] On February 18, 2007, they were in Miami with three of their adopted children, about to depart on a cruise celebrating their eighteenth anniversary, when the 39-year-old Lisa collapsed from a brain aneurysm.

Lisa was rushed by ambulance to Jackson Memorial Hospital's Ryder Trauma Center at around 3:30 PM. When the distraught Janice arrived minutes later, she was bluntly told by an emergency-room social worker that they were in an "antigay city and state" and that she should not expect to receive any access to, or information about, her partner. The social worker then turned and walked away.

As I said at the opening of the book, marriage may be "for better or for worse," but it's during the "for worse" when the legal incidents become most urgent. As it happens, Janice Langbehn is herself an emergency-room social worker. Although one can never fully prepare for this sort of nightmare, she and her partner had taken what legal steps they could, executing advance directives, living wills, and powers-of-attorney. Janice immediately called a friend back home, and within a half hour their documents were faxed to the hospital.

It didn't matter.

Despite the documents, and despite repeated pleas, hospital staff refused to acknowledge Janice and the children as family for eight full hours. They refused to accept information from Janice about her partner's medical history or to provide her with regular updates about Lisa's condition. They refused to let Janice and the children see her, even after doctors acknowledged that there was no medical reason preventing visitation. Meanwhile Lisa—who had been semiconscious and responsive upon arrival—slipped into a coma.

Janice was admitted to Lisa's bedside once, for five minutes, when a priest arrived to administer last rites.

Eventually Lisa was transferred to another unit, but no one told Janice. It was not until 11:30 PM, when Lisa's sister (a blood relative) arrived, that hospital staff finally acknowledged the family, informed them of the transfer, and allowed Janice and the children to be with their now-comatose wife and mother. She was pronounced dead the next morning.

The next year, in 2008, Florida voters passed the following amendment to their state constitution: "Inasmuch as marriage is the legal union of only one man and one woman as husband and wife, no other legal union that is treated as marriage or the substantial equivalent thereof shall be valid or recognized." Florida already had statutes defining marriage this way. That's precisely what the emergency-room social worker meant when referring to Miami, Florida as an "antigay city and state." And it's a big part of why Lisa Marie Pond died alone, without her beloved partner by her side. It didn't matter that Langbehn and Pond had been together for two decades, or that they had adopted and reared four children together, or that they had executed powers of attorney for healthcare. In the eyes of Jackson Memorial Hospital and the State of Florida, Janice Langbehn and Lisa Marie Pond were not family.

Is letting gays marry the only way to prevent such nightmare scenarios? No. But it's the only way to get the legal reality and personal reality fully in synch. It is the only way for the state and society to properly acknowledge that Janice and Lisa were *home* for each other—not friends, not "roommates," but family.

In her conclusion, Gallagher writes,

> The gay marriage idea is based on a lie. Same-sex couples are not like man and wife. Same-sex marriage does not do the "work of marriage." Requiring others to act as if gay unions are marriages is fundamentally unjust in the way that requiring assent to a lie is always unjust (177).

"Same-sex marriage does not do the work of marriage."
Tell that to someone who is fighting in vain to be near her
partner of two decades, the co-mother of their children, as she
lay dying in a hospital. Tell that to any committed gay couple
who have made loving sacrifices for each other, and for their
jointly adopted children, for eighteen years. Tell that to Janice
Langbehn.

Of all of the differences between Gallagher and me, this is
perhaps the deepest: when she looks at Janice Langbehn and
Lisa Marie Pond, she sees two unrelated individuals. I see a
family.

5

Reply to Corvino

MAGGIE GALLAGHER

■ □ ■

HOW MUCH PROGRESS HAVE WE MADE in achieving disagreement on same-sex marriage?

I want to thank John Corvino, who is not only an able and civil spokesman for his cause but a kind man who seeks to reach out and recognize moments of common humanity in the midst of a fierce and often painful debate—which is something very few people on either side of this debate attempt to do.

(I suspect his generous impulses may not win him many kudos from some on his own side, at this point in history, which only underscores his own principled grace of character.)

I am not going to use these last few words to defend every argument that has ever been made against gay marriage by other people, and not because I do not think they are defensible (in most cases I think they are).[1]

But whether other people's arguments are true or false, defensible or indefensible, I would still oppose gay marriage, for the reasons I lay out and defend here.

For similar reasons, I am going to respond only briefly in a footnote to Corvino's complaints about me and the National Organization for Marriage, and for the same reason: whether these complaints are just or unjust would not affect whether the argument I am laying out here is true or untrue.

The fundamental problem with arguments that are, formally speaking, ad hominem is not that they are mean-spirited (Corvino's certainly are not), but that they fail as a matter of logic for serious readers. Whether the National Organization for Marriage ought to be taking on more issues than gay marriage tells us little about whether or not marriage should be sustained as a union of husband and wife.[2]

Let me begin by looking at the things on which I think Corvino and I agree.

We agree (it should go without saying, but it does not) that gay people exist, that they should be treated with social respect, that loving, caretaking relationships they create are deserving (like all such caring relationships) of respect.

We agree that marriage matters, that it is more than romantic feeling, that it involves a commitment to caring and caretaking for someone for better or for worse.

Moreover, unlike many defenders of same-sex marriage, Corvino and I agree that the capacity of sex to create new life and create "biological relationships" matters, though exactly how much and why is not necessarily something either of us clearly understands, much less agrees on.

We disagree on whether keeping our current definition of marriage says or implies that Josh and Boyd's relationship is NOT worthy of respect, that doing so is a slap at gay people. There are many relationships worthy of respect; they are not therefore all marriages.

We disagree about whether same-sex marriage is necessary or adequate to protect (legally speaking) children with gay parents, and indeed whether gay marriage will likely help these children at all.

Do we agree that ideally children need a mom and a dad? Corvino is ambivalent, acknowledging the significance of biological connections—at least at some deep personal level—while relying on the opinions of professional organizations that dispute the scientific evidence on whether and how much children need mothers and fathers.[3]

We disagree on how likely it is that the small number of gay people who marry can affect marriage and the norms that sustain it.

We disagree on whether (or how) a definition of marriage can be true or false.

Most of all, we do not see eye to eye on whether changing the understanding of marriage from faithful, loving sexual union of male and female to "union of two people committed to making each other their number one line of defense in the world" can possibly make a difference to anyone else.

Because gay people are such a small fraction of the population, Corvino claims they can no more affect the culture of marriage than nudists can become fashion trendsetters. Individual couples, he says, can still figure out whether or not fidelity is right for them.

In saying this, Corvino doesn't appear to understand how norms work—they are not created by numerically adding up what people do. And he doesn't appear to understand that to say individual couples can still think about whether a former marriage norm such as fidelity fits their marriage—is to say the norm will no longer be a marriage norm.

Where I see a large and obvious staircase, Corvino continues to blink and see only a blank wall.

THE "MISSING STAIRCASE"

Corvino sees a "missing staircase" because "[s]ame-sex marriage never takes children away from competent biological parents who want them." He makes the argument reductio ad absurdum style: "To put it bluntly, what would follow is that gay and lesbian couples should not kidnap children from their own married biological parents. Back on Planet Earth, where gay men and lesbians are not involved in a mass-kidnapping scheme, it's less clear what would follow. Same-sex marriage never—and I mean *never*—takes children away from competent biological parents who want them."

Indeed, there are several obvious pathways by which gay marriage will likely increase the number of children who will be raised without a mom and a dad.

Same-sex couples may well believe, as Judge Walker has ruled, that the constitutional case for marriage rests in part on the idea that children benefit from having a mother and father and that this idea has been scientifically disproved beyond a reasonable doubt. If so, gay marriage will increase same-sex couples' willingness to create motherless or fatherless children and raise them together. Social workers, under the same impression, may prefer giving a child to a gay couple over a married mom and dad. If gay marriage leads, as civil unions already have in Illinois, to putting religious adoption agencies out of business, it will most probably directly reduce the pool of religious, married mothers and fathers who are available to adopt children.[4]

But these minor staircases, although pretty direct, are not my main concern.

Can marriage continue to be viewed as rooted in the necessary task of bringing together men and women to make and raise the next generation if gay unions are approved by law and society as marriages?

The answer is clearly "no." Some or many individual marriages may perform this task, but marriage as a concept will no longer have this task.[5]

Instead, marriage will become, definitively and in a new way, what Corvino describes: the way we designate a "main line of defense in the world."

That which makes opposite-sex couples unique will have to be dubbed of only secondary importance to marriage, or the common good, for fear of running afoul of the new public morality embodied in "marriage equality."

Here, Corvino mistakes an analysis for a personal complaint, that is, "Gallagher complains that my allies think of her allies as irrational and bigoted" and concludes (in classic circular fashion) that the solution is for supporters of our traditional understanding of marriage to simply change their views and drop the "no gays allowed" view.

For the record: I am not complaining that Corvino or anyone else has said something mean or uncivil about me or anyone else with my views.[6] I am asking gay marriage advocates to own up to the truth that this is in fact what "marriage equality" *means.*

If the law endorses the idea that same-sex unions are marriages on the grounds that equality requires it, then people who continue to believe that marriage is a union between a husband and wife that can give children a mother and father will be treated the way we would treat someone who believes that only a marriage between people of the same race is a marriage.[7] That's what "marriage equality" *means.*

As Corvino acknowledges, "marriage equality" is not just a private right of action by gay people to do something they want to do in their own lives, but a new affirming public norm, a bond between the couple and the community, which will replace the older marriage idea, in part by suppressing the benighted people who cling to it (along with their God and their guns, as President Obama might well say).

This is not just a theoretical process; it is the process visibly unfolding in the public square and actively pushed now by major gay marriage advocates.

This month, Hamline University professors objected to a former gubernatorial candidate who was offered a post as

adjunct professor teaching business law, Tom Emmer, because
he opposes gay marriage. He was denied the position, he says,
because of his position on marriage (and he says he has even
been "physically threatened" as a result).[8] Damian Goddard was
fired as a Toronto sportscaster the day after tweeting to his personal twitter account that he believes in the "true and authen-
tic meaning of marriage." Peter Vidmar, the most decorated
male Olympic gymnast in U.S. history, stepped down from a
post of honor rather than face a firestorm after his donation to
Proposition 8 became known. King and Spalding dropped the
House of Representatives as a client, rather than face the wrath
of the Human Rights Campaign.[9]

The use of class networks of power to punish as bigots
people who disagree with gay marriage is not something that
will happen in the future—it is something visibly beginning to
happen now; it is happening not because people are misbehav-
ing or being mean-spirited, but because this is what "marriage
equality" *means.*

*People are beginning to act as if they really believe what they
say: opposition to gay marriage is like opposition to interracial
marriage; only irrationality or hatred explains why the American
people rather stubbornly continue to insist that to make a marriage you need a husband and a wife, who can give to any children their unions creates a mother and a father.*

I am not making a complaint or a plea for better treatment;
I'm insisting, as a matter of justice, on simple honesty about
what the underlying principle of gay marriage is, and what it
will mean to people who hold the contrary, traditional understanding of marriage. Marriage in the public square will not
simply go on unchanged because gay marriages will be such a
tiny fraction of the married population.

The rhetoric, the rules, and the norms of marriage will have
to shift and adapt to accommodate the new overarching organizing principle of "marriage equality under the law."

Yes, as Corvino points out, individual couples will still be free to think about whether fidelity is right for them. Yes. Just so. The difference between that—between individuals carefully considering what features of the newly flexible marriage institution are right for them—and a social norm about marriage, is part of the cost of institutionalizing gay unions as marriages.[10]

Corvino says you may be permitted to make arguments like "children need mothers and fathers," but only if you can somehow figure out a way to do it that does not run afoul of the new marriage-equality public morality.

> The view that same-sex couples are unworthy of marriage is a wrongheaded one, which should, and will, be marginalized.
>
> But what about the view that children need mothers and fathers?... [W]ill people be stigmatized, and even branded as bigots, simply because they believe that children do best with their own (biological) mother and father?
>
> Honest answer: it depends.
>
> Specifically, it depends on how they frame their point. If they make their focus child welfare, they should be fine.... If the focus is on getting everyone to take more responsibility when it comes to sex and procreation and childrearing, then sign me up.
>
> But that, sadly, has seldom been the focus. Instead, "the traditional view of marriage" has become code for "no gays allowed."...
>
> If you don't want your child-welfare convictions to get branded as discrimination, then you shouldn't cloak them in a discriminatory message: *no gays allowed*. Regrettably, that's the path that Gallagher and her allies have consistently chosen.

In other words, Corvino responds that if you try to stand for the idea that marriage matters because children need a mom and dad, and get dubbed a bigot, it's your own fault for not getting on the gay marriage bandwagon.

This may be true, but it is not an answer to the charge that gay marriage will have consequences for marriage as a social ideal and as a norm.

Any robust defense of the traditional understanding of marriage will clearly run afoul of the lines Corvino draws and seeks to enforce. And not just Corvino.

I have actually experimented with this problem in my many public engagements. For example, after a debate at Columbia Law School, a mother with a gay son came up to me afterward, not angry but clearly very disturbed by my arguments that marriage as a cross-cultural human institution is rooted in the idea and the ideal that a child needs a mom and a dad.

"My son is gay and he wants to have kids," she told me, making it clear that the idea that the ideal for a child was a mom and a dad united in marriage was insulting to her son.

"Help me," I said to her. "I do not want to insult your son. Is it what I am saying or the way I'm saying it? Is there any way for me to say 'The ideal for a child is a mom and dad' without insulting your son?" She thought about it and replied, "No, it's not the way you say it, it's the idea itself."

"You can say kids need two parents," she added helpfully.

For her, and for most candid gay marriage advocates, it is the idea itself that contradicts "marriage equality."

After accepting gay marriage, you just can't say that there's anything especially important, normative, crucial to the common good, or ideal for children or society about the man and the woman who make the baby sticking around and loving each other and the baby, too.

This mother of a gay son is not saying something that should surprise any of us. She is speaking out the depths of having internalized what "marriage equality" *means*.

The organizing idea of a public and social institution is a powerful thing, especially when backed by law. Gay marriage advocates who never imagined ten years ago that, say, the government might kick Catholic Charities out of the foster care business if they don't do same-sex couples placements, now think that is perfectly reasonable because the government shouldn't cooperate with institutions that are bigoted and discriminatory.

Mothers who would have been perfectly content with a public space in which their sons can safely live their life as they choose, now seek a public square purged of any suggestions that same-sex couples are in any way different from opposite-sex couples. Their gay son should not have to hear such things said in polite society any more than a black person should have to hear openly racist comments. Gay rights groups, in some cases, now openly call for "bigoted" people to be fired from their jobs.[11]

(In England, it has reached the point where at least one government social worker told a black married couple they were unfit to be foster parents, unless they would tell a 5- to 8-year-old child that homosexuality is right.[12])

The power of the underlying ideas played out in the public square—this is the thing Corvino calls the "missing staircase," the thing he cannot see or acknowledge, but which is already powerfully at work making people feel it is now dangerous to support traditional understandings of marriage or the principles on which this traditional understanding is based.

I vividly remember the first time I pointed out to a Yale law student all the ways in which the law disadvantages people opposed to interracial marriage: her eyes widened. She had never thought of that. Then she turned on a dime and said "You are right, that's how we should treat bigots." "Okay," I told her, "that's what you think. I accept that. But you can't therefore also simultaneously claim that gay marriage is not going to affect anyone but gay people."

Using the power of law and culture to suppress alternative conceptions of marriage and sex (because gay people find these

216 | DEBATING SAME-SEX MARRIAGE

ideas hurtful and insulting to the newly internalized equality norm) is not a bug in the gay marriage system, it's a feature. It's part of, if not the main point.

Again as a point of personal privilege, I am not raising this as a complaint, because I do not consider the future of Maggie to be of interest to anyone but me and my mama.

I am raising it because doing so is a necessary part of a laying out and making visible what Corvino calls the "missing staircase"—the mechanisms through and by which gay marriage is going to affect the culture of marriage, that is our capacity to see and pay attention to the underlying realities, deeply rooted in human nature, that give rise to marriage as a universal human social institution in diverse cultures across time and space.

The "marriage equality" norm, institutionalized in law, will run psychic interference, because that is what norms and institutions do: they affect people's behavior by affecting the way they think and perceive reality.

There will be contests about where exactly to draw the line, but it is already clear that equality trumps not only a robust conception of religious liberty but pluralism itself in American liberal thought.

That the lines of public morality will be redrawn, if we accept the premises of gay marriage, so that traditional understandings of marriage are seen as dangerous to express is very clear; Corvino does not contest that; in fact, he reinforces and affirms it.

The organizing idea of a social institution—especially one backed by law—is the most important thing about a social institution. The ideas that constitute marriage are not extraneous; they are the bulk of how and why marriage makes a difference— far more than the legal incidents of marriage, which are at this point in history quite weak and relatively unimportant.

If this were a debate about helping Janice and Lisa Marie see each other in the hospital, it would be fairly easy to resolve.

President Obama's recent directive to hospitals should help. If more is needed, we can do more.

But Corvino makes it clear that retaining our historic understanding of marriage is itself the problem. The benefits are useful, but the moral message of quasi-sacred social affirmation is the main prize.

Corvino's very slim reed for asserting that our public understanding of marriage as related to "responsible procreation" will not be dramatically altered by gay marriage is the idea that some people who do not or cannot procreate are currently married. Therefore adding a new set of people who do not procreate will not change marriage.

That's it.

To call this response weak is an understatement. It has an air of utter disconnect from reality, as so many abstract legal arguments so often do.

As a matter of hard fact, I can promise you the presence of people who do not currently have (and may never have)[13] children in the marriage pool, never disconnected marriage from procreation. Childless and elderly couples are part of the natural life cycle of marriage. They do not change its public understanding by being acknowledged as marriages.

But a sexual union of two males, endorsed by law and society as a marriage under a new governing norm of "marriage equality," will change the public perception of the relationship between marriage and procreation both in itself and by making this older understanding virtually unsayable.

Meanwhile, as the "marriage equality" norm permeates law and society, those segments of our society most interested in and committed to marriage's traditional public purpose—the great unwashed Orthodox of every denomination—will find it hard to participate in strengthening marriage and its norms in the public square.

Participating in marriage as a legal and public institution will require endorsing gay marriages on an equal basis, something traditional religious people will find virtually impossible to do. Some will retreat within their denominations, to the extent the law permits them, ceding public space to those who are less passionate and committed to marriage as an institution.

A big chunk of traditional religious people, responding to these cross-pressures and tensions, will join the Hard Left in urging government to get out of the marriage business altogether. Abolishing marriage as a legal status will move from a Marxist dream to a conservative Christian demand. Separation of marriage and state is one of the more likely long-term consequences of same-sex marriage.

Contemplate this: the man who leads or comes second in the polls in Iowa, the most conservative state in the nation as I write this, on the eve of Christmas 2011, does not support gay marriage. Instead, Ron Paul argues for getting the government out of the marriage business. And this message clearly resonates with some deeply conservative Christians in Iowa, a state that has court-ordered gay marriages.

Gay marriage is clearly already putting nearly all the once-settled institutional features of marriage—including the involvement of the law itself—into new play. Marriage's foundations in human nature and human necessity are toppled by gay marriage; its once-core features become simply less coherent and less intelligible as a result of internalizing the "marriage equality" norm.

In the end, a social and legal social institution whose core mission is so deeply personal and so little public—"getting a beloved number one for people who want one"—is going to have a far more difficult time sustaining itself under the stress of postmodern tensions and attacks over the long haul.

Yet Corvino somehow maintains that, once law and society adopts the "marriage equality" norm, the rules and norms that sustain enduring opposite-sex unions will not be affected.

He does not dispute that the "default rules" governing successful same-sex and opposite-sex unions are likely to be quite different, especially around norms affecting children (including fidelity).

He reverts to the frame that individuals will still be free to reason their way on their own to the best solution for their particular marriage.

Just so.

That's what happens when a norm dwindles.

Individuals reason their way on their own to better or worse outcomes, because nothing significant to the wider society is at stake in whether they get these rules and norms right.

People who are better at reasoning, and who have more personal examples of marital success, will do a better job on average of personally reasoning to the rule for their personal relationship. (Witness the "blue family" of which Corvino speaks). The weak and the vulnerable and the less powerful, above all children—all those who need a social norm—will be most at risk in the process of reducing marital norms to personal choices.

The evidence is mounting that gay marriage is not just a tiny number of extra people in an existing institution, but a fundamental revision of marriage, a decision we are making about whether to retain and redirect marriage around its historic purposes or launch into the genderless soul mate theory of what marriage really is.

In what sense is it true that gay unions are not marriage? They are not marriages because they do not do the same work or serve the same purposes that marriage has served, in our own culture or across time and space. The distinctions between same-sex and opposite-sex unions are not irrational or arbitrary, they are real and rooted in human nature in ways that government fiat cannot overturn.

As the core organizing principle for what counts as a marriage, what drops out once we adopt the idea that marriage is the word for dubbing another human being our number-one line of defense in the world?

Sex is optional, a taste or a preference, a common but not a necessary part of choosing someone to be your number one.

Fidelity is a working rule that works for some people—maybe even most people—but not integral to the marriage project, especially for same-sex couples whose equal dignity and worth marriage is now committed to protecting as its first rule.

Parenting is great when it happens, but has no necessary integrated relationship with marriage as a public or personal project—not only in the sense that some couples do not have children but that marriage itself is no longer designed around rules to protect and encourage the childbearing family.

Here's what Corvino's definition of marriage has going for it: it is perfectly consistent with some powerful strains in our very contemporary emerging marriage culture especially among the young—what some have dubbed "soul mate" marriage.

Clearly, we live in a time when the felt need for someone who is one's "main line of defense"—for an identity forged on intimate connection—is particularly powerful.

(So strong that Andrew Sullivan in 2011 told me, in a public debate at Georgetown University, that Catholic moral theology, in refusing to endorse sexual love between two men, would be depriving a person of all forms of love, of Love per se.[14])

As an organizing principle for contemporary, postmodern marriage, Corvino's definition has a lot going for it. But it simply cannot explain most features of marriage in our tradition, or why marriage uniquely reappears across multiple cultures—in many of which this definition of the spouse as best friend or "Number One Person" would be unintelligible.

The greatest blindness, and it is hard not to see it as willful in some sense, is the inability to recognize the powerful change to marriage that same-sex marriage requires, presupposes, and reinforces.

What Corvino dubs "the missing staircase" (proffered along with many reductio ad absurdums along with a few ad hominems for good measure) is his and other gay marriage advocates' refusal to acknowledge the obvious: seeing two men as a marriage requires changing the concept of what marriage means, editing out certain features long considered core or integral, and emphasizing or accelerating the features that "fit."

Loving and caretaking can stay.

What drops out? What drops out is the big chunk of marriage that makes it a universal human institution, and not just one bound to a particular time and culture.

Because sexual unions of male and female produce children, the rules and norms that govern them are different from other kinds of unions: sex and sexual fidelity are integral, not optional, not only to the public but the private purposes of marriage. Children are core (even where children are not produced). The institution is designed around them, designed to unite the core goods marriage alone produces, and to unite them without individual couples having to think up the norms and rules on their own.

This is what an institution—and a norm—does; it replaces the process of individuals thinking on their own about what is best for them, in the service of creating a common good.

Institutions arise to answer problems that are social. If a problem is merely individual (what kind of relationship best suits me, fidelity or polyamory?) then individuals find, or fail to find, the answers.

When a problem is social—institutions arise to help, in fact, think for individuals.

Young people may want nothing more than a soul mate, a number one line of defense in the world, deep romantic attachment. But marriage as a social institution guides their path: it tells them to unite money, sex, and parenting with love. It says: live together, have sex only with each other, share your worldly goods, give your children a mother and a father.

222 | DEBATING SAME-SEX MARRIAGE

Twenty-five years ago, only a minority of gay people experienced our understanding of marriage as a deprivation, much less a personal insult. Until Proposition 8, I regularly received letters from gay men telling me they did not see marriage as a big deal, though they did want the benefits.

If that happens very seldom now, it is because the sense that our marriage laws are rooted in irrational hatred of gay people has been carefully cultivated, primarily by gay marriage advocates. This too is part of what "marriage equality" *means.*

Not only homophobia, but heternormativity has got to go.

Not everyone is called to marriage. The majority of people who will never marry in this society are not gay. The majority of Americans who do not see gay unions as marriage are more than willing to approve ways to make sure that Janice and Lisa Marie are able to see each other in the hospital.

Let's return for a moment to the very beginning of this debate, where John Corvino makes a claim that is truly astonishing, the claim that really goes to the heart of our disagreement.

Of Josh and Boyd's wedding, Corvino says, "Were it not for the absence of a bride, you'd have a hard time distinguishing the scene from any other wedding."

My jaw drops when I read and reread this sentence.

You cannot simply take the woman out of the wedding and proceed as if nothing significant has been removed.

What happens to a wedding when you take the bride out of the equation? What you lose above all are the things that give marriage, even to the nonreligious, its quasi-sacramental status, the sense that we are participating in a heightened way in the necessary conditions of our own being.

Take the woman out of the wedding, and you take out the link between the generations, the sense that in that moment we stand at the crossroads of history, that we are in this couples' act of marriage recreating that moment from which we come, while forging a link to the future.

Surely every mother, like Boyd's mother, wants her child to be taken care of, to have a "special someone." Josh and Boyd's wedding can express adults' yearning for a sense of home.

But it does so at the cost of severing the wedding from the associations that make it larger than the two beings who enter it, the sense of participating in the great chain of being itself, rooted in a natural call that is larger than any one person's desire.

Marriage as the key link in the great chain of being. That is what you lose when you take the woman out of the wedding.

Since I was a girl, in the middle of a sexual revolution, I was repeatedly taught that we had separated sex from reproduction; not only practically speaking but conceptually speaking, sex no longer represented procreation. Under the influence of this teaching, whole generations of formerly young women of my age grew up shocked, shocked to discover they are pregnant, and the men who impregnate them feel minimal responsibility. They had consented to sex, not to babies, and what did sex have to do with babies? Women control the abortion decision, so how can one simple act of pleasure be expected to change the whole course of their life?

Same-sex marriage is the end point, the ultimate institutionalization of this view of sex, gender, and marriage, and it is false. Sex between men and women is freighted with the reality that this is the act that creates new human life, even if in any particular instance, new life never takes place. Sexual union of male and female cannot, without distorting or ignoring reality itself, become the same as a union of two men or two women.

Words have to cease to have meaning, cease to attempt to capture truth or reality, before the word "marriage" can mean "genderless union of two people seeking a home in one another" without an enormous change in public understanding.

That "sexual union of male and female" points to a real union of the flesh in the child, is the reality we are suppressing, the only perspective from which it makes sense to regard a union of two men as anything like the unions that reach across the challenging gender divide in the service of new life.

This use of the word marriage is true, deeply true, in the sense that it is based on deep human realities that marriage as a word and as a lived institution attempts to capture, and that redefining marriage as a genderless union of would-be soul mates does not capture, would indeed persistently push our attention away from. It would be like insisting the word "mother" mean "either mother or father" because we want equal respect between parents. What you lose is the capacity to express truth about what a mother is, and who exactly is one.

When a man vows to take his masculinity, his sexuality, and put it at the service of a woman and her children, to channel his sexual nature to make it pleasing in a woman's eyes, to make his manhood good for a woman and her children—he becomes a husband. When a man or a woman attempts to pledge love and fealty across the mysterious divide of gender, fraught with the possibility of creating new life—they are marrying.

Take the woman out of the wedding, and marriage is no longer a universal human institution, necessary to the future of the whole society, indeed all of humanity.

Cut off from its deep roots in human nature, marriage loses its past, and quite possibly, its future.

We shall see.

ACKNOWLEDGMENTS

I'd like to thank Maggie Gallagher for agreeing to this project, and for our many vigorous exchanges by e-mail and in person.

Various people have provided helpful comments on my drafts, in whole or in part, including Matthew Lee Anderson, Dale Carpenter, Sherif Girgis, Hayley Gorenberg, Christie Herring, Timothy Hulsey, Timothy Kirschenheiter, Andrew Koppelman, Hugh LaFollette, David Link, Ken Mehlman, Karen Mottola, Kate Paesani, Brad Roth, Glenn T. Stanton, Steve Swayne, Jonah Wacholder, and Evan Wolfson. Jonathan Rauch deserves particular mention, not only for his helpful comments but also for his generous mentoring over the years.

My colleagues in the Wayne State University philosophy department have all given me regular and invaluable criticism; particular thanks go to Lawrence Lombard, Greg Novack, Bruce Russell, Sean Stidd, and Robert Yanal for their especially detailed written comments on portions of the book. My work on the Definitional Objection benefited from a grant from the Wayne State University Humanities Center and from lively discussions in my Fall 2010 Sexual Ethics seminar, as well as at colloquia at the University of Colorado at Boulder and the University of

Oklahoma. Completion of the book was aided by a sabbatical leave and a Wayne State University Career Development Chair.

James Sterba initiated this project and has encouraged my work for over two decades; I am grateful to him. Tiffany Suydam provided helpful research assistance. Additional thanks go to Paul Clemens, Michael Einheuser, Mitchell and Timothy Gold, Robert Hardgrave, Gina Kirkland, Michael LaRocca, Will Lippincott, Richard Mohr, Brian McNaught and Ray Struble, Alastair Norcross, Dennis and Tom Patrick, Jessica Pettitt, Chase Whiteside, and Jennifer Vanasco for indispensable support of various sorts.

Thanks to Peter Ohlin, Lucy Randall, and Justyna Zajac at Oxford University Press, and to various editors and reviewers.

My parents taught me what family means, and continue to do so. I am forever indebted to them, as well as to my sister, Jennifer, not to mention a close circle of Detroit friends who have become family.

Last, but certainly not least, there's Mark, who has shown me more love and patience than I could possibly deserve. Maggie said it best: he's home for me.

—John Corvino

In addition to thanking John Corvino (and all those he thanks who made this book possible), I would like to express my appreciation for the help of William Duncan at the Marriage Law Foundation.

—Maggie Gallagher

NOTES

Introduction

1. "For First Time, Majority of Americans Favor Legal Gay Marriage," May 20, 2011, at http://www.gallup.com/poll/147662/first-time-majority-americans-favor-legal-gay-marriage.aspx.
2. At the time of this writing (December 2011), Connecticut, Iowa, Massachusetts, New Hampshire, New York, Vermont, and the District of Columbia grant marriage licenses to same-sex couples.
3. Arizona voters rejected a broadly worded marriage amendment in 2006—one that would have prohibited same-sex civil unions and domestic partnerships as well—but then passed a narrower one in 2008.

Chapter 1

1. See especially my forthcoming book *What's Wrong with Homosexuality?* (New York: Oxford University Press, expected Fall 2012). See also Corvino 1997, 2005, and 2007.
2. GAO-04-353R, Defense of Marriage Act (January 23, 2004), letter from GAO Associate General Counsel Dayna K. Shah to Senator Bill Frist, dated Jan. 23, 2004. This was an update of the 1997 report, which had listed 1049 incidents.

3. Rauch 2004, pp. 17–18. Rauch has considerably influenced my thinking on the case for marriage, and I am very much in his debt.
4. Waite and Gallagher 2000, p. 4.
5. For a simple, common-sense reason: when there's someone at home taking care of you, that means the state doesn't have to.
6. Gallagher raises this question in her main essay. So do Girgis, George, and Anderson 2010, pp. 271–272.
7. See Rauch 1996 and 2004 (especially chapter 1).
8. Rauch 2004, p. 33.
9. Gallagher, "What Marriage is For" 2003, p. 25.
10. Meezan and Rauch 2005, p. 98.
11. For a discussion of this point, see Pawleski et al. 2006.
12. Much of the information discussed in the next two paragraphs is documented in Coontz 2005.
13. Coontz 2005, p. 10.
14. Coontz 2005, p. 47.
15. Coontz 2005, p. 29.
16. Coontz 2005 p. 29.
17. Coontz 2005, pp. 32–33.
18. For African cultures, see Murray and Roscoe 1998. For Native American cultures, see Roscoe 1998. The Native American "Two-Spirit" tradition (sometimes referred to as *berdache*) is a difficult case. Two-Spirits, who are often revered as spiritual sages by their communities, adopt gender-variant dress and domestic work. They often marry (and may even engage in sexual relations with) persons of the same biological sex. Some argue that such marriages are better understood as "straight" marriages involving a transgender (or "genderqueer" partner than as "gay" marriages. In fact, neither understanding is adequate, since both distort the culture's experience for the purpose of fitting it into our own neat boxes.
19. This is not true of another example sometimes cited by my fellow marriage-equality advocates: *adelphopoiesis* or *adelphopoiia*, the "brother-making" rites discussed by John Boswell in *Same-Sex Unions in Pre-Modern Europe* (also published as *The Marriage of Likeness*). Boswell himself denied that these unions should be

understood as "homosexual marriages" (pp. 298–299), and much evidence suggests that they were not akin to our present subject.

20. Evans-Pritchard, p. 108; cited in Murray and Roscoe 1998, p. 256.
21. Rauch 2004, p. 162–171.
22. Claiborne 1995, p. 41.
23. Graff 1999, pp. 251–252.
24. Gallagher, "The Stakes" 2003.
25. According to one source, Lincoln actually made the comment about a calf. See *Reminiscences of Abraham Lincoln by distinguished men of his time/collected and edited by Allen Thorndike Rice* (1853–1889)(New York: Harper & Brothers Publishers, 1909), p. 242. I found the source here: http://timpanogos.wordpress.com/2007/05/23/lincoln-quote-sourced-calfs-tail-not-dogs-tail/#more-636.
26. Gallagher 2009, "The Maine Vote for Marriage" http://www.realclearpolitics.com/articles/2009/11/05/the_maine_vote_for_marriage_99020.html (accessed 2/21/12).
27. Ventrella 2005, p. 682.
28. Ventrella, p. 683.
29. Knight 1997, p. 297.
30. As Sherif Girgis, Robert P. George, and Ryan T. Anderson put it, "the current debate is precisely over whether it is *possible* for the kind of union that has marriage's essential features to exist between two people of the same sex" (2010, p. 249, emphasis mine). They contrast their concern with "utility-based" reasons for restricting marriage to one man and one woman (275).
31. I'm indebted to Dan Savage for this line.
32. For some examples, see Lambda "Civil Unions are Not Enough" http://data.lambdalegal.org/publications/downloads/fs_civil-unions-are-not-enough.pdf (accessed 2/21/12).
33. For a thoughtful argument for this approach, see Nussbaum 2010, especially chapter 5.
34. They are actually more commonly known as the "new natural lawyers." But since most of them are not lawyers in the ordinary sense, that appellation may be misleading for many readers. Notable new-natural-law theorists include Germain Grisez, John Finnis, Gerard Bradley, Patrick Lee, Robert P. George, Sherif Girgis, and Ryan Anderson among others.

35. "[I]t it is not clear...that acting against a biological power is necessarily wrong, nor is it clear that sodomitical and other non-marital acts are really *contrary* to that direction." Lee and George 1997; reprinted in George 1999, p. 181.

36. Aquinas himself acknowledges the "walking on hands" example, but he doesn't seem to appreciate the problems it raises for his discussion of homosexuality. See *Summa Contra Gentiles* Book 3 (Providence), Part II, Chapter 122.

37. See Lee and George 1997; reprinted in George 1999, p. 183 n. 23.

38. Girgis, George, and Anderson 2010, p. 246.

39. As Girgis, George, and Anderson explain, "Any marriage law at all communicates some message about what marriage is as a moral reality. The state has an obligation to get that message right" (2010, p. 268).

40. See for example Corvino 2005, p. 518.

41. Grisez 1993, p. 689.

42. I'm indebted to Timothy Kirschenheiter for this point.

43. See for example Blankenhorn, *Future of Marriage* 2007, p. 201.

44. Girgis, George, and Anderson 2010, p. 254.

45. For a nice discussion, see Koppelman 2002, pp. 79–93.

46. See for example George, "What's Sex Got to Do With It?" 2006, p. 160 n59.

47. Girgis, George, and Anderson 2010, p. 254.

48. Girgis, George, and Anderson 2010, p. 251.

49. See for example George, "What's Sex Got to Do With It?" 2006, p. 160 n59: "Where one has deliberately frustrated the possibility of conception, it is not clear to me how one can say that an act of sexual intercourse is reproductive in type."

50. Girgis, George, and Anderson 2010, p. 254.

51. Despite what I've written here, Gallagher tries to pin a simple definition on me: In her final rebuttal in this book, she repeatedly reduces my understanding of marriage to whatever makes someone your "number-one line of defense in the world."

52. Blankenhorn, *Future of Marriage* 2007, p. 11.

53. Blankenhorn, *Future of Marriage* 2007, p. 91.

54. Pope John Paul II 1981, p. 218.

55. By "commitment" here, I mean not the act of committing, but the activity committed—something objective, not subjective. My

ongoing dispute with Blankenhorn on this point rests in part on his failure to distinguish between these two senses of "commitment." One can make a similar point about "promise" or other words describing intentional states: they can refer to the subjective act of intending or the objective thing intended.

56. Parke 2003, p. 8.
57. Parke, p. 9 n1.
58. For a discussion of some of the challenges of such research, as well as a useful overview of some of the better recent studies, see Meezan and Rauch, 2005.
59. Committee on Psychosocial Aspects of Child and Family Health 2002, pp. 339–340.
60. Paige 2004.
61. For a summary of these statements, see Cooper and Cates 2006, chapter 3.
62. The American College of Pediatricians website is http://www.acpeds.org/. See also Cooper and Cates 2006, p. 19.
63. In her Reply, Gallagher responds that "there are several obvious pathways by which gay marriage will likely increase the number of children who will be raised without a mom and a dad." But "raised without a mom and a dad" is not the same thing as taking them away from their own competent biological parents who want them. In other words, she completely ignores my "Compared to what?" argument: What is the real-world alternative for these children who are being raised without a mom and a dad? Foster homes? Not being created (by insemination or surrogacy) at all? Would either of those scenarios be better than being raised by two moms or two dads?
64. See for example Hirschfeld 1995(especially the discussion of mortality rates at p. 180, resulting from lack of emergency transport in rural areas), Larson et al. 2008 (discussion of multiple social risks) and Mayer 2010 (parental income).
65. *Turner v. Safley*, 482 U.S. 78 (1987).
66. *Zablocki v. Redhail*, 434 U.S. 374 (1978).
67. Gallagher,"What Marriage is For" 2003, p. 23.
68. Gallagher,"What Marriage is For" 2003, p. 24.
69. For example, here's Rutgers sociologist David Popenoe: "Few propositions have more empirical support in the social sciences

than this one: Compared to all other family forms, families headed by married, biological parents are best for children," Center for Marriage and Families 2006, p. 1.

70. Of course, Boyd and Josh could have children via surrogacy, as could Walter. In that event, the child would be the direct biological offspring of only one parent in either case. What one would then need to distinguish the cases is evidence that, biological connectedness aside, children do better with a mother and father than with same-sex parents—but there is no such evidence.

71. Biblarz and Stacy 2010, p. 5.

72. Biblarz and Stacy 2010, pp. 12–13.

73. Gartrell and Bos 2003. This study too (like all social-science studies) has its limitations, which are acknowledged by the authors. But the findings are consistent with existing research on lesbian co-parents. See Biblarz and Stacy 2003, pp. 10–12.

74. For data regarding some of these factors, see Larson et al. 2008.

75. See Mayer 2010.

76. There's some evidence that gay men who parent tend to adopt more "feminine" parenting practices than typical heterosexual fathers. See Biblarz and Stacey 2010, p. 12.

77. Usually "slippery slope" is applied to the causal version, not the logical version, although I've seen it applied to the latter as well.

78. See Corvino 2005.

79. "Excerpts of Santorum's AP Interview" 2003.

80. Rauch 2004, p. 132.

81. Rauch makes this point at Rauch 2004, p. 127.

82. See Coontz 2005, p. 10.

83. George, "Same-Sex Marriage and Jon Rauch" 2006.

84. George, "Same-Sex Marriage and Jon Rauch" 2006. See also George "Beyond Gay Marriage" 2006.

85. Gallagher, "Beyond Marriage" 2006. . . ." at http://blog.marriagedebate.com/2006/08/beyond-marriage-maggie-gallagher-joins.htm.

86. It's worth noting that relatively few things are wrong "in principle." Even throwing knives at people isn't wrong "in principle": it's wrong because it's harmful, and if it weren't harmful—say, because humans had metal exoskeletons—it wouldn't be wrong (apart from being mildly annoying). Of course, the world would have

to be quite different for that to be so. Similarly, I suspect, the world would have to be quite different for polygamy not to have serious social costs in practice. But public-policy arguments are quite rightly based on the actual world, not on bizarre hypotheticals.

87. Girgis, George, and Anderson 2010, p. 272.
88. Kurtz 2003.
89. Kurtz 2006; citations and hyperlinks removed.
90. McGarvey 2010, p. 2.
91. "Monogamy" (vs. "polygamy") means one spouse, which does not necessarily entail sexual exclusivity. "Fidelity" means faithfulness, which many (but not all) understand to include sexual exclusivity: partners in consensual open relationships generally do not take nonexclusivity to imply unfaithfulness.
92. See Douthat 2011, where he cites Regnerus and Uecker.
93. Gallagher cites some of these studies in her contribution to this book; see for example Blasband and Peplau 1985.
94. Kurtz 2003.
95. No one knows exactly how many, due to the problems of self-reporting among a stigmatized population. In this book, Gallagher confidently estimates us at 2%. Most reasonable estimates are between 2 and 6%. See Laumann et al. 2000, chapter 8.
96. Rauch 2004, p. 153.
97. Yoshino 2006.
98. Blankenhorn, "Defining Marriage Down" 2007.
99. Blankenhorn, "Defining Marriage Down" 2007.
100. Blankenhorn, "Defining Marriage Down" 2007.
101. For some relevant data, see Cahn and Carbone 2010.
102. Finnis 1997, p. 34.
103. See Cahn and Carbone 2010.
104. The relevant sections are available in Card 1997.
105. Card 1997, p. 320.
106. "Beyond Same-Sex Marriage" 2006.
107. George, "Beyond Gay Marriage" 2006.
108. Blankenhorn, *Future of Marriage* 2007, p. 2.
109. Blankenhorn, *Future of Marriage* 2007, p. 3.
110. Wolfson 2003.
111. *North Coast Women's Care Medical Care Group, Inc., et al., v. San Diego County Superior Court* S 142892. Ct. App. 4/1 D045438.

112. "Our Opinion" 2011.
113. Matthew 19:1–9; Mark 10:1–12; Luke 16:18.
114. See Nussbaum 2010, especially chapter 5.

Chapter 3

1. Freedom to Marry. "Moving Marriage Forward: Building Majority Support for Marriage" New York: Freedom to Marry, at http://www.letcaliforniaring.org/atf/cf/%7B7a706b3a-165f-4950-9144-2fc92fe4d8d1%7D/MOVING%20MARRIAGE%20FORWARD%20REPORT.PDF.
2. Wolfson, Evan. "Defending the Motion," *Economist*, January 5, 2011, at http://www.economist.com/debate/days/view/634.
3. For instance, the National Organization for Marriage (nationformarriage.org).
4. See Messner, Thomas M. "The Price of Prop 8," *Heritage Foundation Backgrounder* no. 2328, October 22, 2009, at http://s3.amazonaws.com/thf_media/2009/pdf/bg2328es.pdf. I am not attempting to draw an equivalency between the sustained stigmatization of homosexuality and homosexuals in law and culture, and the comparatively modest cultural and legal pressures now being directed against those who do not favor same-sex marriage. Moral disapproval of homosexuality is an old phenomenon however. The development of a stigmatization process directed at those who believe either than same-sex sex is wrong, or that gay love is good but that gay marriage is wrong, is however a startlingly novel development whose future progression cannot yet be described. For an example of the latter see Rich, Frank. "Two Weddings, A Divorce and 'Glee,'" *New York Times*, June 12, 2010, at http://www.nytimes.com/2010/06/13/opinion/13rich.html?_r=1; Rich, Frank. "A Heaven-Sent Rent Boy," *New York Times*, May 15, 2010, at http://www.nytimes.com/2010/05/16/opinion/16rich.html?scp=1&sq=david%20blankenhorn&st=cse; Rich, Frank. "Smoke the Bigots Out of the Closet," *New York Times*, February 6, 2010, at http://www.nytimes.com/2010/02/07/opinion/07rich.html; Letter of Elizabeth Marquardt et al. to Arthur Brisbane, *New York Times* Public Editor, June 24, 2010, at http://www.familyscholars.

org/asssets/Arthur-Brisbane-Letter-6.23.10.pdf; Carpenter, Dale. "Blankenhorn and Rich," *Family Scholars.org*, June 16, 2010, at http://familyscholars.org/2010/06/16/blankenhorn-and-rich/; Rauch, Jonathan."Letter to the Editor," *New York Times*, June 15, 2010, at http://www.nytimes.com/2010/06/16/opinion/l16rich. html.

5. Denvir, Daniel. "David Boies on the Fight for Gay Marriage," *Salon.com*, June 27, 2010, at http://www.salon.com/news/feature/2010/06/27/david_boies_proposition_8/index.html.

6. Stewart, Monte N. "Judicial Redefinition of Marriage," 21 *Canadian Journal of Family Law* 11 (2004).

7. "Same-Sex Marriage Debate from the University of St. Thomas," *MPR News*, October 19, 2011, at http://minnesota.publicradio. org/display/web/2011/10/19/midday1.

8. See Department of Health and Human Services, *Report to Congress on Out-of-Wedlock Childbearing* (September 1995) at http://www. cdc.gov/nchs/data/misc/wedlock.pdf.

9. Douglas, Mary. *How Institutions Think*, Syracuse, Syracuse University Press, 1986.

10. Girgis, Sherif, George, Robert P. & Anderson, Ryan T. "What is Marriage?" 34 *Harvard Journal of Law and Public Policy* 245, 2010.

11. *Goodridge v. Department of Public Health*, 798 N.E.2d 941, 948 (Mass. 2003) ("Marriage is a vital social institution. The exclusive commitment of two individuals to each other nurtures love and mutual support; it brings stability to our society.")

12. Girgis, Sherif, George, Robert P. & Anderson, Ryan T. "What is Marriage?" 34 *Harvard Journal of Law and Public Policy* 245, 2010; Blankenhorn, David. *The Future of Marriage*, New York: Encounter Books, 2007; Gallagher, Maggie. "(How) Will Gay Marriage Weaken Marriage as a Social Institution," 2 *University of St. Thomas Law Review* 33, 2004.

13. How would marriage advocates like myself understand empirical evidence to the contrary? What if we found that a society that recognizes gay unions as marriage could nonetheless sustain a flourishing marriage culture, such that most children are born to and raised by their married mothers and fathers? In my view, such a society would demonstrate that the civil definitions of

marriage were not, as I reasonably suspect, culturally powerful. In which case, I would still believe that same-sex unions are not marriages, but I would no longer care whether the civil government recognizes them as such, because the law would have been demonstrated to be an impotent player in the public meaning of the social institution.

14. *Griswold v. Connecticut*, 381 U.S. 479, 486 (1965).

15. *Goodridge v. Department of Public Health*, 798 N.E.2d 941, 950 (Mass. 2003).

16. "[T]he plaintiffs in this case have made it clear the harm they allege, quite apart from any practical consequences, is the harm of having their relationships excluded from the 'social meaning' of marriage. They want this court to short-circuit the hard task of persuading their fellow citizens that their unions ARE marriages, by asking this court to re-educate the voters and re-assign the meaning of a word...." "[S]ame-sex marriage works a profound change in the public meaning of marriage; this change in public definition from 'sexual union of male and female' to 'union of any two persons' clearly severs the connections between marriage and its core historic civil mission: increasing the likelihood that children will be born to and raised by their mother and father. If it is rational for the plaintiffs to be concerned about the meaning of the word, it is rational for 7 million California voters to be concerned as well." Brief of Amicus Curiae, National Organization for Marriage, *Perry v. Schwarzenegger*, No. 10–16696 (9th Cir. Sep. 24, 2010) at http://nomblog.com/wp-content/uploads/2010/09/Brief-of-Amici-Curiae-National-Organization-for-Marriage-et-al.-in-Support-of-Defendant-Intervenors-Appellants.pdf.

17. "Marriage and the Law: A Statement of Principles," Institute for American Values & Institute for Marriage and Public Policy, 2006, p. 5 at http://www.marriagedebate.com/pdf/imapp.mlawstmnt.pdf ("Law sometimes *creates* institutions (the corporation is a prime modern example). But sometimes the law *recognizes* an institution that it does not and cannot meaningfully create. No laws, and no set of lawyers, legislators, or judges, can summon a social institution like marriage into being merely by legal fiat. Marriage and family therefore can never be reduced to a legal construct, a mere creature of the state.")

18. Wolfson, Evan. "Marriage Equality: Losing Forward," *Advocate*, October 28, 2004, at http://www.advocate.com/Politics/ Commentary/Marriage_equality__Losing_forward/.
19. See Brown, Donald E. *Human Universals*, New York: McGraw-Hill, 1991; Davis, Kingsley. *Contemporary Marriage: Comparative Perspectives on a Changing Institution*, New York, Russell Sage Foundation, 1985, page 5 ("Although the details of getting married—who chooses the mates, what are the ceremonies and exchanges, how old are the parties—vary from group to group, the principle of marriage is everywhere embodied in practice.... The unique trait of what is commonly called marriage is social recognition and approval... of a couple's engaging in sexual intercourse and bearing and rearing offspring."); Blankenhorn, David. *The Future of Marriage*, New York: Encounter Books, 2007.
20. See Wegner, Judith Romney. "The Status of Women in Jewish and Islamic Marriage and Divorce Law," 5 *Harvard Women's Law Journal* 1, 13 note 51, 1982; Cott, Nancy F. "Passionlessness," 4 *Signs* 222, 1978.
21. 1 Corinthians 7:4 (Revised Standard Version).
22. Matthew 5:28 (Revised Standard Version).
23. Girgis, Sherif, George, Robert P. & Anderson, Ryan T. "What is Marriage?" 34 *Harvard Journal of Law and Public Policy* 245, page 253, 2010. Once again by highlighting certain of Girgis and colleagues' view I am not therefore adopting their entire natural law suprastructure.
24. Polygamy being a common variant among small tribal societies. Campbell, Angela. *How Have Policy Approaches to Polygamy Responded to Women's Experiences and Rights? An International, Comparative Analysis: Final Report for Status of Women Canada*, May 31, 2005, at http://papers.ssrn.com/sol3/papers. cfm?abstract_id=1360230.
25. See Lefkowitz, Mary R. & Fant, Maureen B. *Women's Life in Greece and Rome: A Source Book in Translation* page 187 (2nd ed., 1992) at http://www.stoa.org/diotima/anthology/wlgr/wlgr-private-life249.shtml ("Hilarion to Alis his sister, heartiest greetings, and to my dear Berous and Apollonarion. Know that we are still even now in Alexandria. Do not worry if when all the others return I remain in Alexandria. I beg and beseech of you to take care of the

little child, and as soon as we receive wages I will send them to you. If—good luck to you!—you bear offspring, if it is a male, let it live; if it is a female, expose it."); Boswell, John E. *The Kindness of Strangers: The Abandonment of Children in Western Europe from Late Antiquity to the Renaissance*, New York: Pantheon Books, 1988.

26. Gallagher, Maggie. "(How) Will Gay Marriage Weaken Marriage as a Social Institution: A Reply to Andrew Koppelman," 2 *University of St. Thomas Law Journal* 33, 49–51, 2004.

27. See Whitehead, Barbara Dafoe. "Dan Quayle Was Right," *The Atlantic*, April 1993, at http://www.theatlantic.com/magazine/archive/1993/04/dan-quayle-was-right/7015/.

28. *Why Marriage Matters: Twenty-Six Conclusions from the Social Sciences*, 2nd ed., New York: Institute for American Values, 2005.

29. Ibid.

30. Which does not include children raised by same-sex couples, who were not included in this research review.

31. Moore, Kristin Anderson et al., "Marriage from a Child's Perspective: How Does Family Structure Affect Children and What Can We Do About It?" *Child Trends Research Brief*, Child Trends, June 2002, at http://www.childtrends.org/files/marriagerb602.pdf .

32. Parke, Mary. "Are Married Parents Really Better for Children?", Center for Law and Social Policy, May 2003 at http://www.clasp.org/admin/site/publications_states/files/0086.pdf.

33. American Psychological Association, *Answers to Your Questions For a Better Understanding of Sexual Orientation & Homosexuality*, 5 at http://www.apa.org/topics/sexuality/sorientation.pdf.

34. Meezan, William & Rauch, Jonathan. "Gay Marriage, Same-Sex Parenting, and America's Children," 15 *Future of Children* 97, 2005.

35. Biblarz, Timothy J. & Stacey, Judith. "How Does the Gender of Parents Matter?" 72 *Journal of Marriage and Family* 3, 2010.

36. Sirota, Theodore. "Adult Attachment Style Dimensions in Women Who Have Gay or Bisexual Fathers," 23 *Archives of Psychiatric Nursing* 289, 2009.

37. *Perry v. Schwarzenegger*, 704 F. Supp. 2d 921 (N.D. Cal. 2010).

38. *Why Marriage Matters: 30 Conclusions from the Social Sciences*, New York: Institute for American Values, 2011.

39. Abma, J. et al., "Fertility, Family Planning, and Women's Health: New Data from the 1995 National Survey of Family Growth," 23 *Vital Health Statistics* 28, table 17, 1997 (70.4 percent of births to married women were intended by both parents, compared to just 28 percent of births to unmarried mothers). See also Henshaw, Stanley K. "Unintended Pregnancies in the United States," 30 *Family Planning Perspectives* 24, 28, table 3, 1998; Fu, Haishan et al., "Contraceptive Failure Rates: New Estimates from the 1995 National Survey of Family Growth," 31 *Family Planning Perspectives* 55, 56, 1999; Trussel, James & Vaughn, Barbara. "Contraceptive Failure, Method-Related Discontinuation and Resumption of Use: Results from the 1995 National Survey of Family Growth," 31 *Family Planning Perspectives* 64, 71, 1999.

40. *Why Marriage Matters: 30 Conclusions from the Social Sciences,* New York: Institute for American Values, 2011.

41. Studies show that two out of three children born out of wedlock have nonresident fathers at birth. This percentage climbs as children grow older (though some couples eventually marry). See, e.g., McLanahan, Sara et al., "Unwed Fathers and Fragile Families, Center for Research on Child Wellbeing," Working Paper #98-12 at 7, March 1998. An Urban Institute policy brief explains the impact: "Parents who do not live with their children are unlikely to be highly involved in their children's lives." Sorensen, Elaine & Zibman, Chava. "To What Extent Do Children Benefit from Child Support?" The Urban Institute, January 2000, p. 8. According to the National Survey of America's Families, one in three (34 percent) children with a nonresident parent saw that parent on a weekly basis in 1997. Another 38 percent saw their nonresident parent at least once during the year, though not on a weekly basis. Fully 28 percent of children with a nonresident parent had no contact with that parent during the course of the year. Ibid. Another review of several national surveys found that, by their mothers' estimates, roughly 40 percent of children with nonresident fathers saw their father once a month, while nearly the same number did not see their father at all in a given year. Manning, Wendy D. & Smock, Pamela J. "New Families and Non-Resident Father-Child Visitation," 78 *Social Forces* 87, 89, September 1999; see also King, Valerie. "Variations in the Consequences of Nonresident Father

Involvement for Children's Well-Being," 56 *Journal of Marriage & Family* 963, 1994 (finding half of children with nonresident fathers see their fathers only once a year, if at all, while just 21 percent see their fathers on a weekly basis).

42. See Bridge, G. Michael. "Uniform Probate Code Section 2-202: A Proposal to Include Life Insurance Assets Within the Augmented Estate," 74 *Cornell Law Review* 511, 513–515, 1989.
43. *Skinner v. Oklahoma* (1942) 316 U.S. 535, 541
44. *Maynard v. Hill* (1888) 125 U.S. 190, 211.
45. *Loving v. Virginia* (1967) 388 U. S. 1, 12 (quoting *Skinner v. Oklahoma*, supra 316 U.S. at p. 541 and citing *Maynard v. Hill*, supra, 125 U.S. 190).
46. *Conaway v. Deane*, 903 A.2d 416, 620 (Md. 2007).
47. *Andersen v. King County* (Wash. 2006) 138 P.3d 963, 978.
48. *Baker v. Baker* (1859) 13 Cal. 87, 103.
49. *Sharon v. Sharon* (1888) 75 Cal. 1, 33 (quoting Stewart on Marriage and Divorce, sec. 103).
50. *De Burgh v. De Burgh* (1952) 39 Cal.2d 858, 863–864.
51. *Maslow v. Maslow* (1953) 117 Cal.App.2d 237, 241.
52. *Poe v. Gerstein* (5th Cir. 1975) 517 F.2d 787, 796.
53. *Singer v. Hara* (Wash. App. 1974) 522 P.2d 1187, 1195.
54. *Baker v. Nelson* (Minn. 1971) 191 N.W.2d 185, 186, appeal dismissed for want of a substantial federal question, 409 U.S. 810 (1972).
55. *Heup v. Heup* (Wis. 1969) 172 N.W.2d 334, 336.
56. *Zoglio v. Zoglio* (D.C. App. 1960) 157 A.2d 627, 628.
57. *Stegienko v. Stegienko* (Mich. 1940) 295 N.W. 252, 254.
58. *Gard v. Gard* (Mich. 1918) 169 N.W. 908, 912.
59. *Grover v. Zook* (Wash. 1906) 87 P. 638, 639.
60. *Adams v. Howerton* (C.D. Cal. 1980) 486 F. Supp. 1119, 1124, affirmed on other grounds (9th Cir. 1982) 673 F.2d 1036.
61. *Dean v. District of Columbia* (D.C. 1995) 653 A.2d 307, 337 (Ferren, J., concurring and dissenting).
62. Laurence Drew Borten, "Sex, Procreation, and the State Interest in Marriage," 102 *Columbia Law Review* 1089, 1114–1115, 2002.
63. Barfield, Thomas, ed. *The Dictionary of Anthropology*, Oxford: Blackwell Publishing, 1997, p. 35, assessable online at http://books.google.com/books?id=V5dkKYyHclwC&printsec=frontco

ver&dq=dictionary+of+anthropology&source=bl&ots=jxaVLO
fm6B&sig=HoUQ6FL3O0A_z7o7QelSa2uFaBk&hl=en&ei=w6-
TTa6yLY68sAP3yuXLBQ&sa=X&oi=book_result&ct=result&re
snum=8&ved=0CFIQ6AEwBw#v=onepage&q&f=false.

64. Gough, E. Kathleen. "The Nayars and the Definition of Marriage,"
89 *Journal of the Royal Anthropological Institute of Great Britain
and Ireland* 370, January–June 1959, quoted in Blankenhorn, *The
Future of Marriage*, p. 109.

65. Of course Catholic priests are a tiny fraction of the population,
while the Nayars may have represented as much as 25 percent of
their tribe.

66. Blankenhorn, *The Future of Marriage*, pp. 106–113.

67. See note 39.

68. Graff, E. J. "Retying the Knot," in *Same-Sex Marriage: Pro and
Con: A Reader*, ed. Andrew Sullivan, 1st ed., New York: Vintage
Books, 1997, pp. 134, 135–137.

69. Blankenhorn, David. *The Future of Marriage*, New York: Encounter
Books, 2007, pp. 207–208; Jones, Michael. "Are Marriage Equality
Opponents Bigots?" *Change.org*, May 5, 2010, at http://news.
change.org/stories/are-marriage-equality-opponents-bigots;
McKay, Hollie. "Mark Ruffalo Slams the 'Old' and 'Bigoted' Views
of Those Who Oppose Same Sex Marriage," *Fox News*, July 2,
2010, at http://www.foxnews.com/entertainment/2010/07/02/
mark-ruffalo-slams-old-bigoted-views-oppose-sex-marriage/;
Beyerstein, Lindsay. "If You Oppose Marriage Equality, You
Are a Bigot," *Big Think*, May 4, 2010, at http://bigthink.com/
ideas/19952; Rich, Frank. "The Bigots' Last Hurrah," *New York
Times*, April 18, 2009, at http://www.nytimes.com/2009/04/19/
opinion/19Rich.html?_r=2&ref=opinion; "Maine's Anti-Gay
Marriage Supporters Kindly Request You Stop Calling Them
Bigots," *Queerty*, September 18, 2009, at http://www.queerty.com/
maines-anti-gay-marriage-supporters-kindly-request-you-stop-
calling-them-bigots-20090918/#ixzz1ICR7wZEA.

70. See Wilson, Robin Fretwell, Laycock, Douglas, & Picarello,
Anthony, eds., *Same-Sex Marriage and Religious Liberty: Emerging
Conflicts*, Lanham: Rowman& Littlefield 2008.

71. Side note: I was in Salt Lake City recently and my guide pointed
out a building as a historic men's club. Men's club? Men's club?

Why do they still have men's clubs in Salt Lake City? You may think it's the gender traditionalism of the LDS community, but it is also because Mormons are not supposed to consume alcohol and their men's clubs do not serve liquor. The club wielded by government to gender-integrate private clubs was the withholding of liquor licenses.

72. See Cere, Daniel N. et al., *The Future of Family Law*, New York: Institute for American Values, 2005, pp. 15–16.

73. See Gottman, John M. et al., "Correlates of Gay and Lesbian Couples' Relationship Satisfaction and Relationship Dissolution," 45 *Journal of Homosexuality* 23, 2003.

74. See Corbett, William R. "A Somewhat Modest Proposal to Prevent Adultery and Save Families: Two Old Torts Looking for a New Career," 33 *Arizona Law Journal* 987, 2001.

75. Saad, Lydia. "Doctor-Assisted Suicide is Moral Issue Dividing Americans Most," *Gallup*, May 31, 2011, at http://www.gallup.com/poll/147842/doctor-assisted-suicide-moral-issue-dividing-americans.aspx.

76. Hall, Julie H. & Fincham, Frank D."Psychological Distress: Precursor or Consequence of Dating Infidelity," 35 *Personality & Social Psychology Bulletin* 143, 2009, at http://www.chs.fsu.edu/~ffincham/papers/2009pspb2009hall.pdf.

77. Popenoe, David. *Life Without Father*, New York: Free Press 1996, p. 176.

78. DeMaris, Alfred. "Distal and Proximal Influences on the Risk of Extramarital Sex: A Prospective Study of Longer Duration Marriages," 46 *Journal of Sex Research* 597, 2009.

79. Ibid.

80. Yucel, Deniz & Gassanov, Margaret A. "Exploring Actor and Partner Correlates of Sexual Satisfaction Among Married Couples," 39 *Social Science Research* 725, September 2010.

81. Hall & Fincham "Psychological Distress: Precursor or Consequence of Dating Infidelity."

82. Confer, Jaime C. & Cloud, Mark D. "Sex Differences in Response to Imagining a Partner's Heterosexual or Homosexual Affair," 50 *Personality and Individual Difference* 129, January 2011.

83. See *Perry v. Schwarzenegger*, Trial Transcript, January 13, 2010, pp. 616–625 at http://www.afer.org/wp-content/uploads/

2010/01/2010-01-13-Perry-Trial-Day-03-Chauncey-cross-redirect-Peplau-mini.pdf (testimony of plaintiff's expert Letitia Peplau).

84. James, Scott. "Many Successful Gay Marriages Share an Open Secret," *New York Times*, January 28, 2010, at http://www.nytimes.com/2010/01/29/us/29sfmetro.html.

85. Hart, Trevor A. & Schwartz, Danielle R. "Cognitive-Behavioral Erectile Dysfunction Treatment for Gay Men," 17 *Cognitive and Behavior Practice* 66, February 2010.

86. Mitchell, Jason W. "Examining the Role of Relationship Characteristics and Dynamics on Sexual Risk Behavior Among Gay Male Couples," PhD diss., Oregon State University, 2010, at http://ir.library.oregonstate.edu/xmlui/bitstream/handle/1957/16379/MitchellJasonW2010.pdf?sequence=1.

87. Hoff, Colleen C. et al., "Relationship Characteristics and Motivations Behind Agreements Among Gay Male Couples: Differences by Agreement Type and Couple Serostatus," 22 *AIDS Care* 827, July 2010, at http://www.ncbi.nlm.nih.gov/pmc/articles/PMC2906147/.

88. *Perry v. Schwarzenegger*, Trial Transcript, January 13, 2010, p. 623 (testimony of plaintiff's expert Letitia Peplau).

89. Hart & Schwartz "Cognitive-Behavioral Erectile Dysfunction Treatment for Gay Men."

90. Ramirez, Oscar Modesto & Brown, Jac. "Attachment Styles, Rules Regarding Sex, and Couple Satisfaction: A Study of Gay Couples," 31 *Australian and New Zealand Journal of Family Therapy* 202, June 2010.

91. Hoff, "Relationship Characteristics and Motivations Behind Agreements Among Gay Male Couples: Differences by Agreement Type and Couple Serostatus."

92. "Long Term Relationships Just as Likely Among Gay Couples, Claims Psychiatrist," 28 *Canadian Family Physician* 1478, September 1982, at http://www.ncbi.nlm.nih.gov/pmc/articles/PMC2306581/pdf/canfamphys00247-0023.pdf.

93. *Perry v. Schwarzenegger*, Trial Transcript, January 13, 2010, pp. 617–618 (testimony of plaintiff's expert Letitia Peplau).

94. Ibid., p. 625. Like most research on gay people, this was not based on a probability sample and must be considered less reliable than randomized surveys.

95. Blasband, David & Peplau, Letitia A. "Sexual Exclusivity Versus Openness in Gay Male Couples," 15 *Archives of Sexual Behavior* 395, October 1985.
96. Ibid.
97. Yip, Andrew K.T. "Gay Male Christian Couples and Sexual Exclusivity," 31 *Sociology* 289, May 1997.
98. Harry, Joseph. "The 'Marital' Liaisons of Gay Men," 28 *The Family Coordinator* 622, October 1979.
99. Regnerus, Mark & Uecker, Jeremy. *Premarital Sex in America*, New York: Oxford University Press, 2011.
100. Ibid.
101. Gallagher, Maggie. *Enemies of Eros*, Chicago: Bonus Books 1989.
102. Kaiser, Charles. "For Gays, Cheers and Doubts About Marriage," *CNN*, June 26, 2011, at http://articles.cnn.com/2011-06-26/opinion/kaiser.gay.marriage_1_gay-marriage-gay-community-modern-gay-movement?_s=PM:OPINION.
103. Volokh, Eugene. "Same-Sex Marriage and Slippery Slopes," 33 *Hofstra Law Review* 101, 2006.
104. Morales, Lymari. "U.S. Adults Estimate That 25 percent of Americans are Gay or Lesbian," *Gallup*, May 27, 2011, at http://www.gallup.com/poll/147824/Adults-Estimate-Americans-Gay-Lesbian.aspx. For actual numbers, see Gates, Gary J. "Gay People Count, So Why Not Count Them Correctly?" *Washington Post*, April 8, 2011, at http://www.washingtonpost.com/opinions/gay-people-count-so-why-not-count-them-correctly/2011/04/07/AFDg9K4C_story.html.
105. Oppenheimer, Mark. "Married with Infidelities," *New York Times*, June 30, 2011, at http://www.nytimes.com/2011/07/03/magazine/infidelity-will-keep-us-together.html?pagewanted=all.
106. Ibid.
107. James, "Many Successful Gay Marriages Share an Open Secret."
108. Ibid.
109. Allen, Douglas W. "Who Should Be Allowed into the Marriage Franchise?" 58 *Drake Law Review* 1043, 2010.
110. Douglas, *How Institutions Think*.
111. Allen, Douglas W. "Let's Slow Down: Comments on Same-Sex Marriage and Negative Externalities: Comment," 2010, at http://papers.ssrn.com/sol3/papers.cfm?abstract_id=1722764.

112. Ibid.
113. *Goodridge v. Department of Public Health*, 798 N.E.2d 941, 950 (Mass. 2003).
114. "Marriage and the Law: A Statement of Principles."
115. Pam Belluck, "Gay Couples Find Marriage Is a Mixed Bag," *New York Times*, June 15, 2008, at http://www.nytimes. com/2008/06/15/us/15marriage.html?pagewanted=print.
116. The argument that divorce permits the behavioral conditions of polygamy, but with even fewer protections for women and children, has also been made and certainly has a rational basis. But at least divorce in our culture represents an allegedly necessary evil, a remedy for a marriage that fails, not a core ideal embodiment of the marital institution.
117. Compare *Elisa B. v. Superior Court*, 117 P.3d 660 (Cal. 2005); *C.E.W. v. D.E.W.*, 845 A.2d 1146 (Maine 2004); *E.N.O. v. L.L.M.*, 711 N.E.2d 886 (Mass. 1999); *LaChapelle v. Mitten*, 607 N.W.2d 151 (Minn. App. 2000); *Matter of T.L.*, 1996 WL 393521 (Mo. Cir. 1996); *V.C. v. M.J.B.*, 748 A.2d 539 (N.J. 2000); *A.C. v. C.B.*, 829 P.2d 660 (N.M. App. 1992); *T.B. v. L.R.M.*, 786 A.2d 913 (Pa. 2001); *Rubano v. DiCenzo*, 759 A.2d 959 (R.I. 2000); *In re L.B.*, 122 P.3d 161 (Wash. 2005); *In re Clifford K.*, 619 S.E.2d 138 (W. Va. 2005); *In re Custody of H.S.H.-K.*, 533 N.W.2d 419 (Wis. 1995) with *In re Adoption of Luke*, 640 N.W.2d 374 (Neb. 2002); *In re Adoption of Doe*, 719 N.E.2d 1071 (Ohio Ct. App. 1998); *In re Angel Lace M.*, 516 N.W.2d 678 (Wis. 1994); *In re Adoption of Baby Z.*, 724 A.2d 1035 (Conn. 1999); *Adoption of T.J.K.*, 931 P.2d 488 (Colo. Ct. App. 1996).
118. Stossel, John. "A Libertarians View of Marriage," *Fox News*, August 31, 2011, at http://www.foxnews.com/opinion/2011/08/31/ libertarians-view-gay-marriage/.
119. Douglas, *How Institutions Think*.
120. Hunter, James Davison. "To Change the World," 3 *Trinity Forum Briefing* 2, 2002, at http://71513.netministry.com/images/TO_ CHANGE_THE_WORLD_HUNTER.pdf.
121. Waite, Linda J. & Gallagher, Maggie. *The Case for Marriage: Why Married People are Happier, Healthier, and Better-Off Financially*, New York: Doubleday, 2000, p. 85.
122. Eskridge, Jr., William N. *The Case for Same Sex Marriage: From Sexual Liberty to Civilized Commitment*, New York: Free Press, 1996, p. 98.

123. Ibid., p. 11.
124. Graff, "Retying the Knot," pp. 134, 135–136.
125. Ibid., p. 137.
126. Sullivan, Andrew. "Introduction," in *Same-Sex Marriage: Pro and Con: A Reader*, 1st ed., Vintage Books, 1997, p. xix.
127. Rauch, Jonathan. *Gay Marriage: Why It Is Good for Gays, Good for Straights, and Good For America*, New York: Times Books, 2004, p. 18.
128. Strasser, Mark. *Legally Wed: Same-Sex Marriage and the Constitution*, Ithaca: Cornell University Press, 1997, p.60 (internal citation omitted).
129. Wolfson, Evan. "Enough Marriage to Share: A Response to Maggie Gallagher," in *Marriage and Same-Sex Unions: A Debate*, ed. Lynn D. Wardle et al., Westport: Praeger 2003, 25, 26.
130. US Sen. Subcomm. on the Const., Civil Rights and Prop. Rights, Hearings on The Defense of Marriage Act, 108th Cong. (Sept. 4, 2003) (written statement of Prof. Judith Stacey, Ph.D., Dept. of Sociology, N.Y.U.).
131. Stacey, Judith. "Gay and Lesbian Families: Queer Like Us," in *All Our Families: New Policies for a New Century*, ed. Mary Ann Mason, Arlene Skolnick & Stephen D. Sugarman, New York: Oxford University Press, 1998, 117, 128–129.
132. *Baker v. State*, 744 A.2d 864, 881–882 (Vt. 1999).
133. *Goodridge v. Department of Public Health*, 798 N.E.2d at 961 (quoting portions of Justice Cordy's dissenting opinion).
134. *Halpern v. Attorney General*, (2003), 225 D.L.R. (4th) 529 (Ont. C.A.).
135. *Perry v. Schwarzenegger*, 704 F. Supp. 2d 921, 992 (2010).
136. *Kerrigan v. Department of Public Health*, 957 A.2d 407, 424 note 19 (2008).
137. *Varnum v. Brien*, 763 NW2d 862, 883–884 (2009).
138. *Goodridge v. Department of Public Health*, 798 N.E.2d at 962 (quoting Romer v. Evans, 517 U.S. 620, 633, 116 S. Ct. 1620, 134 L. Ed. 2d 855 (1996).
139. Blankenhorn, *The Future of Marriage*.
140. Ibid., p. 231.
141. Whitehead, Barbara Dafoe &Popenoe, David. "Who Wants to Marry a Soul Mate?" *State of Our Unions 2001*, National Marriage

Project June 2001, at http://www.virginia.edu/marriageproject/
pdfs/SOOU2001.pdf.

142. Comment, "Breaking News: Paul Clement Refuses to Bow Down
Under HRC Pressure, Leaves Law Firm to Defend DOMA,"
NOM Blog, April 25, 2011, at http://www.nomblog.com/7753/;
Galloway, Jim & Rankin, Bill. "King & Spalding to Withdraw
from Defending DOMA; Clement Resigns," *Atlanta Journal-
Constitution*, April 25, 2011, at http://www.ajc.com/news/geor-
gia-politics-elections/king-clement-resigns-923921.html.

143. Prettyman, Kaitlin. "Peter Vidmar Steps Down as Chief of Mission
for 2012 U.S. Olympic Team," *Deseret News*, May 7, 2011, at http://
www.deseretnews.com/article/700133436/Peter-Vidmar-steps-
down-as-chief-of-mission-for-2012-US-Olympic-Team.html.

144. "TV Host Fired Over Sean Avery Debate," *ESPN.com*, May
13, 2011, at http://sports.espn.go.com/new-york/nhl/news/
story?id=6532954.

145. Avila, Daniel. "Same-Sex Adoption in Massachusetts, the
Catholic Church, and the Good of the Children: The Story Behind
the Controversy and the Case for Conscientious Refusals," 27
Children's Legal Rights Journal 1, 2007.

146. Garvey, John. "State Putting Church Out of Adoption Business,"
Boston Globe, March 14, 2006, A15; Gallagher, Maggie. "Banned
in Boston," *Weekly Standard*, May 15, 2006, p. 20.

147. See Boorstein, Michelle. "Citing Same-Sex Marriage Bill,
Washington Archdiocese Ends Foster-Care Program," *Washington
Post*, Feb. 17, 2010, at http://www.washingtonpost.com/wp-dyn/
content/article/2010/02/16/AR2010021604899.html; Smith, Emily
Esfahani."Washington, Gay Marriage and the Catholic Church,"
Wall Street Journal, Jan. 9, 2010, http://online.wsj.com/article/SB1
0001424052748703478704574612451567822852.html.

148. Brachear, Manya A. "Rockford Catholic Charities Ending Foster
Care," *Chicago Tribune*, May 26, 2011, at http://www.chicagotribune.
com/news/local/breaking/chibrknews-rockford-catholic-
charities-ending-foster-care-adoptions-20110526,0,4532788.
story?track=rss.

149. *Catholic Charities v Illinois*, No. 2011-MR-254 (Illinois Circuit
Court) at http://www.aclu-il.org/wp-content/uploads/2011/08/
110818-Order-granting-Def-motion-for-SJ.pdf.

248 | NOTES TO PAGES 165-167

150. Brachear, Manya A. "State Probes Religious Foster Care Agencies Over Discrimination," *Chicago Tribune*, March 2, 2011, at http://articles.chicagotribune.com/2011-03-02/news/ct-met-gay-foster-care-20110301_1_care-and-adoption-catholic-charities-parents.

151. "Illinois Catholic Charities Adoption Battle: Charities' Attorney to Appeal Judge's Decision," *Huffington Post*, August 20, 2011, at http://www.huffingtonpost.com/2011/08/29/illinois-catholic-chariti_n_941040.html.

152. Higbee, Jonathan. "Judge Rules Catholic Charities Cannot Discriminate Against Gay Adoptive Parents," *Instinct Magazine*, August 19, 2011, at http://instinctmagazine.com/blogs/blog/judge-rules-catholic-charities-cannot-discriminate-against-gay-adoptive-parents?directory=100011 .

153. "Our Opinion: Right Call in Catholic Charities Decision," *State Journal-Register*, August 21, 2011, at http://www.sj-r.com/editorials/x386669877/Our-Opinion-Right-call-in-Catholic-Charities-decision.

154. *Walden v. Centers for Disease Control*, Case No. 1:08-cv-02278-JEC, U.S. District Court, Northern District of Georgia, March 18, 2010 (available at http://www.telladf.org/UserDocs/WaldenSJorder.pdf.

155. Kaminer, Wendy. "Gay Rights and Anti-Gay Liberties," *The Atlantic*, March 2010, at http://www.theatlantic.com/national/print/2010/03/gay-rights-and-anti-gay-liberties/37382/.

156. *Brooker v. Missouri State University*, Complaint, Case No. 06-CV-3432 (U.S. Dist., W. Dist. Mo.) at http://www.telladf.org/UserDocs/BrookerComplaint.pdf; Press Release, "Missouri State Settles Lawsuit with Emily Brooker," Nov. 8, 2006, at http://allnurses-breakroom.com/world-news-current/missouri-state-settles-217367.html.

157. *Ward v. Board of Control of Eastern Michigan University*, Case No. 09-CV-11237 (D.Ct. E.D. Mich. 2010) at http://www.telladf.org/UserDocs/WardImmunityOrder.pdf.

158. National Organization for Marriage, "The 2009 NOM Massachusetts Marriage Survey" at http://www.nationformarriage.org/site/apps/nlnet/content2.aspx?c=omL2KeN0LzH&b=5075187&ct=7000219.

159. Sixty percent of the Netherlands agree gay marriage is a good thing; 62 percent agree "there is nothing immoral about homosexuality," on which see Zick, Andreas, Kupper, Beate, & Hovermann, Andreas. "Intolerance, Prejudice and Discrimination: A European Report," Friedrich Ebert Stiftung Forum Berlin, 2011, at http://www.fes-gegen-rechtsextremismus.de/pdf_11/FES-Study%2BIntolerance,%2BPrejudice%2Band%2BDiscrimination.pdf.
160. Duncan, William C. "The Tenth Anniversary of Dutch Same-Sex Marriage: How is Marriage Doing in the Netherlands?" *iMAPP Research Brief*, May 2011, at http://www.marriagedebate.com/pdf/iMAPP.May2011-rev.pdf.
161. Andersson, Gunnar, et al., "Divorce-Risk Patterns in Same-Sex 'Marriages' in Norway and Sweden," paper presented at the 2004 Annual Meeting of the Population Association of America, April 3, 2004, at http://paa2004.princeton.edu/download.asp?submissionId=40208.
162. Rothblum, Esther D., Balsam, Kimberly F. & Solomon, Sondra E. "Comparison of Same-Sex Couples Who Were Married in Massachusetts, Had Domestic Partnerships in California, or Had Civil Union in Vermont,"29 *Journal of Family Issues* 48, 2008, at http://www.queerty.com/wp/docs/2008/05/rothblum-comparison-of-same-sex-couples.pdf.
163. "Same-sex marriages, civil unions, and domestic partnerships are the product of relatively new legislation. Consequently, this study is more about who chooses to have a legalized relationship and less about how being in a marriage, civil union, or domestic partnership changes a relationship—for that, follow-up research is needed, and we plan to continue contact with these couples." Ibid.
164. Ibid.
165. Ibid., p. 51.
166. Balsam, Kimberly F., Beauchaine, Theodore P., Rothblum, Esther & Solomon, Sondra E. "Three-Year Follow-Up of Same-Sex Couples Who Had Civil Unions in Vermont, Same-Sex Couples Not in Civil Unions, and Heterosexual Married Couples," 44 *Developmental Psychology* 102, 110–111, 2008 at http://ts-si.org/files/Same-SexCouplesFollowupdev441102.pdf (although civil union couples were less likely to end their relationship).

167. LaSala, Michael C. "Monogamy of the Heart: Extradyadic Sex and Gay Male Couples," 17 *Journal of Gay and Lesbian Social Services* 1, 2005.
168. *Why Marriage Matters: Twenty-Six Conclusions from the Social Sciences*, 2nd ed., New York: Institute for American Values, 2005; Lamb, Kathleen A., Lee, Gary R. & DeMaris, Alfred. "Union Formation and Depression: Selection and Relationship Effects," 65 *Journal of Marriage and Family* 953, November 2003; Brown, Susan L. & Kawamura, Sayaka. "Relationship Quality among Cohabitors and Marrieds in Older Adulthood," 39 *Social Science Research* 777, 2010; Klausli, Julia F.& Owen, Margaret Tresch. "Stable Maternal Cohabitation, Couple Relationship Quality, and Characteristics of the Home Environment in the Child's First Two Years," 23 *Journal of Family Psychology* 103, February 2009.
169. Waite, & Gallagher, *The Case for Marriage*, pp. 47–64.
170. Frisch, Morten &Brønnum-Hansen, Henrik. "Mortality Among Men and Women in Same-Sex Marriage: A National Cohort Study of 8333 Danes," 99 *American Journal of Public Health* 133, January 2009.
171. One study of 65 gay male couples found: "Couples who had both commitment ceremonies and legal marriages described the commitment ceremony as having the greater impact on their sense of commitment to the relationship and on the degree of social recognition of the relationship in their immediate social circles," LaSala, "Monogamy of the Heart: Extradyadic Sex and Gay Male Couples."
172. Worth, Katie. "SF Same-Sex Couples Increasingly Going Without Kids," *San Francisco Examiner*, June 26, 2011, at http://www.sfexaminer.com/local/2011/06/sf-same-sex-couples-increasingly-going-without-kids-census-shows.

Chapter 4

1. According to a May 2011 Gallup report. See http://www.gallup.com/poll/147662/first-time-majority-americans-favor-legal-gay-marriage.aspx.
2. In saying that it's *good*, I don't mean that it's mandatory. Marriage certainly isn't right for everyone.

3. Mohr 1994, p. 36.
4. In her reply, which follows this essay, Gallagher calls the infertile-couples objection a "slim reed," but she scarcely offers a refutation of it. Instead, she merely promises that allowing permanently infertile heterosexual couples to marry won't affect marriage's connection to procreation, whereas allowing same-sex couples to marry will, because somehow the latter will render the connection "virtually unsayable." I can only surmise that the connection is already unsayable, or else Gallagher would explain it: how do same-sex couples destroy marriage's connection to procreation whereas permanently infertile heterosexual couples preserve it?
5. It's not clear to me that the law can "regulate" procreation any more than it can "regulate" breathing or digestion, and to the extent that government does "regulate" procreation, it often does so unjustly, as in forced abortions. But this is a terminological point.
6. Of course, there are other ways to find companionship besides marriage, but lifelong romantic commitments are unique, and uniquely valuable—for gays as well as straights.
7. Nussbaum 2010, p. 143.
8. *Kerrigan v. Department of Public Health*, 957 A.2d 407, 424 note 19 (2008).
9. I don't address coparenting, although the answer to this question seems pretty straightforward to me: when two people are married, and thus commit themselves fully to each other, it is inconceivable that one could (or should) take on a major life-project such as parenting without involving the other.
10. Again, no one knows exactly how many, though most reasonable estimates are between 2 and 6 percent. See Laumann et al. 2000, chapter 8.
11. "Texas Officer Suspended" 2004.
12. Note: I usually hesitate to say "*the* analogy" in this context, since there are many ways one might draw lessons from the history of racial discrimination, some of them more helpful than others.
13. For Dobson, see "Dobson's Warning against Gay Marriage" 2004. For Santorum, see "Excerpts of Santorum's AP Interview" 2003. For Bachmann, see "Michele Bachmann Calls Gay People 'Part of Satan'" 2004.

14. *Lawrence v. Texas*, 539 U.S. 558 (2003).
15. It is true that—to her credit—she once devoted the bulk of her work to pro-marriage measures that had nothing to do with same-sex marriage: increasing marital permanence, for example. For whatever reasons, that appears to have changed.
16. LaSala 2004, cited in Gallagher, this book, 172.
17. Kaufman 2011, p. 109.
18. Information about their case is taken from Parker-Pope 2009, and from various documents accessible at http://www.lambdalegal. org/in-court/cases/langbehn-v-jackson-memorial.

Chapter 5

1. In most cases, these people have their own platforms for responding, and will do so more ably than I can, to Corvino's arguments, if they deem it important.
2. Let me respond here briefly to John Corvino's questions about me and the National Organization for Marriage. Why does NOM work only on gay marriage? Why did it run an ad suggesting that gay marriage would take away people's freedom? I founded the National Organization for Marriage in 2007 as a grassroots activist organization because I could see the battle for gay marriage would move out of the courts and into the legislatures in blue states, i.e., in places where evangelicals and their social-conservative political and quasi-political organizations have relatively little influence. When there is only one team on the field, in a political fight, that team is going to win. If one has the goal of affecting a live and immediate political battle, as I did, the organizational structure that is most effective is a single-issue organization. That's why NOM is what it is and does what it does. I will say for the record, I'm very proud of what NOM has accomplished and the way it has made arguments in the public square.

   I stepped down first as president in 2010 and in 2011 as chairman of the board of NOM (while continuing to work with the organization in other ways) because running an activist single-issue organization was not my goal—launching one was. In defense of the idea I am acting in good faith—that my concerns about gay marriage really do stem from a concern for marriage

itself, rather than some dark and inexplicable psychological problem with gay people (as Andrew Koppelman, for example, implies
about opponents of gay marriage, see "The Decline and Fall of
the Case Against Same-Sex Marriage," 2 *University of St. Thomas
Law Journal* 4, 2004)—I would note that as for me personally, long
before gay marriage was on the horizon, I devoted the bulk of my
thought and writing—three books, several public reports, numerous op-eds and articles, to making the case that marriage is an
important public institution, because children need mothers and
fathers.

3. In my original essay, I laid out in some detail my reasons for believ-
ing the body of scientific evidence these professional associations
rely on is weak, especially compared to the broad and deep body of
evidence suggesting the natural family—intact married biological
parents—does protect children. For example, before we endorse
planned motherlessness as equally good in every way, perhaps
there should be at least one study that suggests children raised by
gay fathers do just as well as children in other family forms? And
if it is true that gay parents do just as well, then it is also true that
same-sex marriage is not very important to the well-being of children with same-sex parents, since these studies purporting to show
"no difference" are based on gay parents who are not married for
the most part. I do expect, if the scientific debate is not shut down,
that the evidence will eventually emerge that casts new doubt.

Right now the relevant research has simply not yet been under-
taken or published. As judges like Walker make broad pronouncements about what science has proved about child well-being, the
scholars who recognize the very thin basis of evidence on which
these loud pronouncements are being made will grow concerned
enough—if not about gay marriage about the standards of scientific evidence—to actually investigate these claims, in spite of the
sense many scholars have reported to me that doing so, i.e., doing
the objective research based on ordinary standards of sociological
research (including true probability samples) that might finding a
negative result on gay parenting is fraught with danger to their relationships and careers. A prominent family scholar who is a friend
of mine for more than twenty years recently asked me to com-
municate only through a personal email box, not at this scholars'

university address, for one small example. The truth in academia is that it is much harder to get published if your work supports a traditional understanding of sex, gender, or marriage; the standards of what constitutes "good enough" evidence to publish suddenly go up to the max. But it can, and I predict, will be done. I have faith the processes of science are rigorous enough, and enough scholars (including presumably many scholars who favor gay marriage and parenting) care about them, that eventually the scientific debate, which has not yet really happened, will take place.

4. Indeed, some adoptive parents in Illinois say they would likely not have adopted children if religious agencies were not available. See "Schulz, Craigen, Montague," *Marriage Anti-Defamation Alliance*, December 15, 2011, at http://marriageada.org/schulz-craigen-montague/.

5. To answer Corvino's footnote question, "how do same-sex couples destroy marriage's connections to procreation whereas permanently infertile heterosexual couples preserve it?" "Sexual union of male and female" points to, reinforces, and serves marriage's public purpose of responsible procreation in a way that "sexual union of two men" clearly does not and cannot serve. If opposite-sex couples were typically or usually infertile, much less always and certainly infertile, then Corvino's strange assertion that we can incorporate the union of two men or two women as marriage with no change in marriage's underlying meaning or relationship to responsible procreation would make sense. Instead of honestly comparing the public meaning of "sexual union of male and female" to "sexual union of two men or women," Corvino wishes to narrow the comparison—to compare the effect of two men certified as married to merely "permanently infertile heterosexual couples" as married. What's the difference, Corvino asks. The differences are legion, as I have argued, because even when men and women do not or cannot have children, the default rules for their relationships are built around the reality that they are the kind of people who naturally speaking could. An infertile woman does not become, by virtue of her infertility, the same as a gay man.

But more importantly, the presence of infertile couples in the mix of marriages is no signal or change in its meaning or its relationship to procreation because elderly and childless couples are part of the natural life cycle of marriage. The presence of the infertile couple in the marriage mix is invisible and costless to marriage's public purpose. Gay men's presence as marriages will not be similarly invisible and costless, but a highly visible new public norm that everyone who supports marriage in the public square will be obligated to support. The new public norm of "marriage equality" that Corvino explicitly embraces will ensure that. Corvino never denies or refutes the idea that the underlying norms of marriage—the ideal of a mother and father and fidelity—will change as public norms associated with marriage incorporate "marriage equality" at the core. He simply thinks this change is good and just and it is the obligation of people who support ideas like "children need a mom and dad" to figure out how to say it in such a way that it will not conflict with marriage equality. How can the same person embrace the idea "there is no morally relevant difference with regard to marriage between same-sex and opposite-sex couples" and the idea that "marriage matters because the ideal for children is a mom and a dad"? It is logically impossible. That's the staircase Corvino cannot see beneath his feet; it's missing because he's already leapt his way to the top of it.

6. I do also understand that unfortunately, gay people like Corvino have been frequently treated uncivilly in the public square and the amount of vituperation no doubt far exceeds anything I or other traditional marriage supporters have ever experienced.

7. Let me respond here to Corvino's use of the interracial marriage analogy. Actually of course, unlike opponents of gay marriage, opponents of interracial marriage did believe it was possible to have an interracial marriage; that's why it had to be banned. And it had to be banned primarily because marriage was presumed to be the way we create the next generation and give them a mother and father. By creating a mixed-race child and family, interracial marriage prevented the clear racial lines upon which legal segregation depended. The only purpose to redefining marriage so that interracial marriage didn't count was to perpetuate an unconstitutional racist scheme of government. There is no connection, in reality, between racist views of interracial marriage and support for the traditional understanding of marriage, which is rooted in real and significant differences between same-sex and

opposite-sex couples that are directly related to marriage's core public purpose. The main reason (historically and cross-culturally speaking) we have laws about it, unlike other kinds of personal relationships that flourish without legal definition, is that sexual unions of male and female create children.

8. See "Audio: Emmer Discusses Hamline Controversy on Local FOX Radio," *NOM Blog*, December 21, 2011, at http://www.nomblog.com/17018/.

9. See Prettyman, Kaitlin. "Peter Vidmar Steps Down as Chief of Mission for 2012 U.S. Olympic Team," *Deseret News*, May 7, 2011, at http://www.deseretnews.com/article/700133436/Peter-Vidmar-steps-down-as-chief-of-mission-for-2012-US-Olympic-Team.html; "TV Host Fired Over Sean Avery Debate," *ESPN. com*, May 13, 2011, at http://sports.espn.go.com/new-york/nhl/news/story?id=6532954; Galloway, Jim & Rankin, Bill. "King & Spalding to Withdraw from Defending DOMA; Clement Resigns," *Atlanta Journal-Constitution*, April 25, 2011, at http://www.ajc.com/news/georgia-politics-elections/king-clement-resigns-923921.html.

10. If the recent experiences of men like Anthony Weiner and his many Republican counterparts tells us anything, it tells us that people contemplating adultery are not in a state of mind that allows them to rationally contemplate the correct rule for their own relationships, much less all of the society. Moral and social norms are meant to step in where thought so often fails, as part of a social defense against human frailty and irrationality—to think for people precisely in situations where when they can't or won't think clearly for themselves. That norms fail in individual cases is not an indictment against their necessity or usefulness. It is, rationally speaking, a call to strengthen and reinforce the norm, rather than abandon it to individual choice.

11. See Comer, Matt. "Group Criticizes Bank of America, Cisco for Rehiring Anti-Gay Activist," *QNotes*, December 15, 2011, at http://goqnotes.com/13959/group-criticizes-bank-of-america-cisco-for-rehiring-anti-gay-activist/.

12. See "Video: British High Court Rules Christian Couple May Not Foster Kids," *NOM Blog*, February 28, 2011, at http://www.nomblog.com/5395/.

13. How did the common law treat impotent men or paraplegics who wished to marry? In truth, they would be able to marry because a union of male and female is presumptively assumed to be capable of sexual intercourse. If a man or a woman were unable to do so, the marriage could be annulled, even during all the years when divorce was rare. Impotence—and inability to perform "the marital act"—was considered a bar to marriage but infertility was not.

14. See "Georgetown University Event: A Catholic Family Conversation," *Catholics for Equality*, December 8, 2011, at http://catholicsforequality.org/Georgetown.

BIBLIOGRAPHY

Abma, J. et al. "Fertility, Family Planning, and Women's Health: New Data from the 1995 National Survey of Family Growth." *Vital Health Statistics* 23, no. 19 (1997): 1–111.

Allen, Douglas W. "Let's Slow Down: Comments on Same-Sex Marriage and Negative Externalities: Comment," posted December 10, 2010. *Social Science Research Network*, at http://papers.ssrn.com/sol3/papers.cfm?abstract_id=1722764.

———. "Who Should Be Allowed into the Marriage Franchise?" 58 *Drake Law Review* 1043 (2010).

American Psychological Association. "Answers to Your Questions: For a Better Understanding of Sexual Orientation & Homosexuality" (Washington, D.C. American Psychological Association 2008) at http://www.apa.org/topics/sexuality/sorientation.pdf.

Andersson, Gunnar et al. "Divorce-Risk Patterns in Same-Sex 'Marriages' in Norway and Sweden." Paper presented at the 2004 Annual Meeting of the Population Association of America, April 3, 2004, at http://paa2004.princeton.edu/download.asp?submissionId=40208.

Aquinas, St. Thomas. *Summa Contra Gentiles Book 3 (Providence), Part II* translated by Vernon J. Bourke. Notre Dame, IN: University of Notre Dame Press 1975.

"Audio: Emmer Discusses Hamline Controversy on Local FOX Radio." *NOM Blog*, December 21, 2011, at http://www.nomblog.com/17018.

Avila, Daniel. "Same-Sex Adoption in Massachusetts, the Catholic Church, and the Good of the Children: The Story Behind the Controversy and the Case for Conscientious Refusals." 27 *Children's Legal Rights Journal* 1 (2007).

Balsam, Kimberly F., Beauchaine, Theodore P., Rothblum, Esther, and Solomon, Sondra E. "Three-Year Follow-Up of Same-Sex Couples Who Had Civil Unions in Vermont, Same-Sex Couples Not in Civil Unions, and Heterosexual Married Couples." 44 *Developmental Psychology* 102 (2008).

Barfield, Thomas, ed. *The Dictionary of Anthropology*. Oxford: Blackwell Publishing, 1997.

Belluck, Pam. "Gay Couples Find Marriage Is a Mixed Bag." *New York Times*, June 15, 2008, at http://www.nytimes.com/2008/06/15/us/15marriage.html?pagewanted=print.

Beyerstein, Lindsay. "If You Oppose Marriage Equality, You Are a Bigot." *Big Think*, May 4, 2010, at http://bigthink.com/ideas/19952.

"Beyond Same-Sex Marriage: A New Strategic Vision for All Our Families and Relationships," Beyond Marriage.org, July 26, 2006, at http://beyondmarriage.org/full_statement.html.

Biblarz, Timothy J., and Stacey, Judith. "How Does the Gender of Parents Matter?" 72 *Journal of Marriage and Family* 3 (2010).

Blankenhorn, David. "Defining Marriage Down is No Way to Save It." *Weekly Standard*, April 2, 2007, at http://www.weeklystandard.com/Content/Public/Articles/000/000/013/451noxve.asp.

———. *The Future of Marriage*. New York: Encounter Books, 2007.

Blasband, David, and Letitia A. Peplau. "Sexual Exclusivity Versus Openness in Gay Male Couples." 15 *Archives of Sexual Behavior* 395 (October 1985).

Boorstein, Michelle. "Citing Same-Sex Marriage Bill, Washington Archdiocese Ends Foster-Care Program." *Washington Post*, February 17, 2010, at http://www.washingtonpost.com/wp-dyn/content/article/2010/02/16/AR2010021604899.html.

Borten, Laurence Drew. "Sex, Procreation, and the State Interest in Marriage." 102 *Columbia Law Review* 1089 (2002).

Boswell, John. *The Kindness of Strangers: The Abandonment of Children in Western Europe from Late Antiquity to the Renaissance*, New York: Pantheon Books, 1988.

———. *Same-Sex Unions in Pre-Modern Europe* [also published as *The Marriage of Likeness*]. New York: Vintage, 1995.

Brachear, Manya A. "Rockford Catholic Charities Ending Foster Care." *Chicago Tribune*, May 26, 2011, at http://www.chicagotribune.com/news/local/breaking/chibrknews-rockford-catholic-charities-ending-foster-care-adoptions-20110526,0,4532788.story?track=rss.

———. "State Probes Religious Foster Care Agencies Over Discrimination." *Chicago Tribune*, March 2, 2011, at http://articles.chicagotribune.com/2011-03-02/news/ct-met-gay-foster-care-20110301_1_care-and-adoption-catholic-charities-parents.

Bridge, G. Michael. "Uniform Probate Code Section 2-202: A Proposal to Include Life Insurance Assets Within the Augmented Estate." 74 *Cornell Law Review* 511 (1989).

Brief of Amicus Curiae, National Organization for Marriage, *Perry v. Schwarzenegger*, No. 10-16696 (9th Cir. September 24, 2010) at http://nomblog.com/wp-content/uploads/2010/09/Brief-of-Amici-Curiae-National-Organization-for-Marriage-et-al.-in-Support-of-Defendant-Intervenors-Appellants.pdf.

Brown, Donald E. *Human Universals*. New York: McGraw-Hill 1991.

Brown, Susan L., and Kawamura, Sayaka. "Relationship Quality among Cohabitors and Marrieds in Older Adulthood." 39 *Social Science Research* 777 (2010).

Cahn, Naomi, and Carbone, June. *Red Families v. Blue Families: Legal Polarization and the Creation of Culture*. New York: Oxford University Press, 2010.

Campbell, Angela. *How Have Policy Approaches to Polygamy Responded to Women's Experiences and Rights? An International, Comparative Analysis: Final Report for Status of Women Canada*, May 31, 2005, at http://papers.ssrn.com/sol3/papers.cfm?abstract_id=1360230.

Card, Claudia. "Against Marriage." In John Corvino, ed., *Same Sex: Debating the Ethics, Science, and Culture of Homosexuality*. Lanham: Rowman & Littlefield, 1997, pp. 317–330.

Carpenter, Dale. "Blankenhorn and Rich." *Family Scholars.org*, June 16, 2010, at http://familyscholars.org/2010/06/16/blankenhorn-and-rich/.

Center for Marriage and Families. *The Scholarly Consensus on Marriage.* Fact Sheet No. 2. New York: Institute for American Values, 2006, at http://www.americanvalues.org/pdfs/factsheet2.pdf.

Cere, Daniel N. et al. *The Future of Family Law.* New York: Institute for American Values, 2005.

Claiborne, Craig. *The New New York Times Cookbook.* New York: Random House, 1995.

Comment, "Breaking News: Paul Clement Refuses to Bow Down Under HRC Pressure, Leaves Law Firm to Defend DOMA." *NOM Blog*, April 25, 2011, at http://www.nomblog.com/7753/.

Committee on Psychosocial Aspects of Child and Family Health. "Technical Report: Coparent or Second-Parent Adoption by Same-Sex Parents." *Pediatrics*, vol. 109 (February 2, 2002).

Confer, Jaime C., and Cloud, Mark D. "Sex Differences in Response to Imagining a Partner's Heterosexual or Homosexual Affair." 50 *Personality and Individual Difference* 129 (January 2011).

Coontz, Stephanie. *Marriage: A History.* New York: Viking, 2005.

Cooper, Leslie, and Cates, Paul. *Too High A Price: The Case Against Restricting Gay Parenting.* New York: American Civil Liberties Union Foundation, 2006, at http://www.aclu.org/lgbt-rights_hiv-aids/too-high-price-case-against-restricting-gay-parenting.

Corbett, William R. "A Somewhat Modest Proposal to Prevent Adultery and Save Families: Two Old Torts Looking for a New Career." 33 *Arizona Law Journal* 987 (2001).

Corvino, John. "Why Shouldn't Tommy and Jim Have Sex: A Defense of Homosexuality." In John Corvino, ed., *Same Sex: Debating the Ethics, Science, and Culture of Homosexuality.* Lanham, Md: Rowman & Littlefield, 1997.

———. "Homosexuality and the PIB Argument." *Ethics*, vol. 115 (April 2005): 501–534.

———. "Homosexuality, Harm, and Moral Principles." In Laurence Thomas, ed., *Contemporary Debates in Social Philosophy.* Malden: Blackwell, 2007, pp. 79–93.

———. *What's Wrong with Homosexuality?* New York: Oxford University Press, forthcoming, Fall 2012.

Cott, Nancy F. "Passionlessness." 4 *Signs* 222 (1978).

Davis, Kingsley. *Contemporary Marriage: Comparative Perspectives on a Changing Institution.* New York: Russell Sage Foundation, 1985.

DeMaris, Alfred. "Distal and Proximal Influences on the Risk of Extramarital Sex: A Prospective Study of Longer Duration Marriages." 46 *Journal of Sex Research* 597 (2009).

Denvir, Daniel. "David Boies on the Fight for Gay Marriage." *Salon.com*, June 27, 2010, at http://www.salon.com/news/feature/2010/06/27/david_boies_proposition_8/index.html.

Department of Health and Human Services. *Report to Congress on Out-of-Wedlock Childbearing*, Hyattsville: Centers for Disease Control, September 1995, at http://www.cdc.gov/nchs/data/misc/wedlock.pdf.

"Dobson's Warning against Gay Marriage." April 2004, *Christians for Truth* website, at http://www.cft.org.za/articles/dobson.htm; originally found at http://www.focusonthefamily.com/docstudy/newsletters/A000000334.cfm (nonworking link).

Douglas, Mary. *How Institutions Think.* New York: Syracuse University Press, 1986.

Douthat, Ross. "Why Monogamy Matters." *New York Times*, March 7, 2011, p. A21.

Duncan, William C. "The Tenth Anniversary of Dutch Same-Sex Marriage: How is Marriage Doing in the Netherlands?" *iMAPP Research Brief*, May 2011, at http://www.marriagedebate.com/pdf/iMAPP.May2011-rev.pdf.

Eskridge, Jr., William N. *The Case for Same Sex Marriage: From Sexual Liberty to Civilized Commitment.* New York: Free Press, 1996.

Evans-Pritchard, Edward E. *Kinship and Marriage among the Nuer.* Oxford: Oxford University Press, 1951.

"Excerpts of Santorum's AP Interview," taped April 7, 2003, published April 22, 2003, by the Associated Press, at http://www.foxnews.com/story/0,2933,84862,00.html.

Finnis, John. "Law, Morality, and 'Sexual Orientation.'" In John Corvino, ed., *Same Sex: Debating the Ethics, Science, and Culture of Homosexuality.* Rowman & Littlefield: Lanham, Md.: 1997, pp. 31–43.

"For First Time, Majority of Americans Favor Legal Gay Marriage." *Gallup.com* May 20, 2011, at http://www.gallup.com/poll/147662/first-time-majority-americans-favor-legal-gay-marriage.aspx.

Freedom to Marry. "Moving Marriage Forward: Building Majority Support for Marriage" New York: Freedom to Marry at http://www.letcaliforniaring.org/atf/cf/%7B7a706b3a-165f-4950-9144-2fc92fe4d8d1%7D/MOVING%20MARRIAGE%20FORWARD%20REPORT.PDF.

Frisch, Morten, and Brønnum-Hansen, Henrik. "Mortality Among Men and Women in Same-Sex Marriage: A National Cohort Study of 8333 Danes." 99 *American Journal of Public Health* 133 (January 2009).

Fu, Haishan et al. "Contraceptive Failure Rates: New Estimates from the 1995 National Survey of Family Growth." 31 *Family Planning Perspectives* 55 (1999).

Gallagher, Maggie. *Enemies of Eros.* Chicago: Bonus Books 1989.

———. "The Stakes." *National Review Online,* July 4, 2003, at http://article.nationalreview.com/269352/the-stakes/maggie-gallagher.

——— "What Marriage Is For: Children Need Mothers and Fathers." *Weekly Standard,* (August 4–11, 2003): 22–25.

———. "Beyond Marriage: Maggie Gallagher Joins the Fray." *Institute for Marriage and Public Policy* website, August 2006 at http://blog.marriagedebate.com/2006/08/beyond-marriage-maggie-gallagher-joins.htm.

———. "The Maine Vote for Marriage"http://www.realclearpolitics.com/articles/2009/11/05/the_maine_vote_for_marriage_99020.html.

———. "(How) Will Gay Marriage Weaken Marriage as a Social Institution: A Reply to Andrew Koppelman." 2 *University of St. Thomas Law Journal* 33 (2004).

———. "Banned in Boston." *Weekly Standard,* May 15, 2006.

Galloway, Jim, and Rankin, Bill. "King & Spalding to Withdraw from Defending DOMA; Clement Resigns." *Atlanta Journal-Constitution,* April 25, 2011, at http://www.ajc.com/news/georgia-politics-elections/king-clement-resigns-923921.html.

Gartrell, Nanette, and Bos, Henry. "US National Longitudinal Lesbian Family Study: Psychological Adjustment of 17-Year-Old Adolescents." *Pediatrics,* June 17, 2003, at http://pediatrics.aappublications.org/content/early/2010/06/07/peds.2009-3153.abstract.

Garvey, John. "State Putting Church Out of Adoption Business." *Boston Globe*, March 14, 2006, p. A15.

Gates, Gary J. "Gay People Count, So Why Not Count Them Correctly?" *Washington Post*, April 8, 2011, at http://www.washingtonpost.com/opinions/gay-people-count-so-why-not-count-them-correctly/2011/04/07/AFDg9K4C_story.html.

George, Robert P. *In Defense of Natural Law*. Oxford: Oxford University Press 1999.

———. "What's Sex Got to Do with It? Marriage, Morality, and Rationality." In Robert P. George and Jean Bethke Elshtain, eds., *The Meaning of Marriage: Family, State, Market and Morals*. Dallas: Spence Publishing Company, 2006, p. 142.

———. "Beyond Gay Marriage." *First Things*, August 2, 2006, at http://www.firstthings.com/onthesquare/2006/08/robert-george-beyond-gay-marri.

———. "Same-Sex Marriage and Jon Rauch." *First Things*, August 10, 2006, at http://www.firstthings.com/onthesquare/2006/08/same-sex-marriage-and-jon-rauc.

"Georgetown University Event: A Catholic Family Conversation." *Catholics for Equality*, December 8, 2011, at http://catholicsforequality.org/Georgetown.

Grisez, Germain. *The Way of the Lord Jesus*. Vol. 2: *Living a Christian Life*. Quincy, Ill.: Franciscan Press, 1993.

Girgis, Sherif, George, Robert P., and Anderson, Ryan T. "What is Marriage?" 34 *Harvard Journal of Law and Public Policy* 245 (2010).

Gottman, John M. et al. "Correlates of Gay and Lesbian Couples' Relationship Satisfaction and Relationship Dissolution." 45 *Journal of Homosexuality* 23 (2003).

Gough, E. Kathleen. "The Nayars and the Definition of Marriage." 89 *Journal of the Royal Anthropological Institute of Great Britain and Ireland* 370 (January–June 1959).

Graff, E. J. "Retying the Knot." In Andrew Sullivan, ed., *Same-Sex Marriage: Pro and Con: A Reader*. 1st ed. New York: Vintage Books 1997, pp. 134–138

———. *What Is Marriage For? The Strange Social History of Our Most Intimate Institution*. Boston: Beacon 1999.

Hall, Julie H., and Fincham, Frank D. "Psychological Distress: Precursor or Consequence of Dating Infidelity." 35 *Personality & Social Psychology Bulletin* 143 (2009).

Halpern v. Attorney General, (2003), 225 D.L.R. (4th) 529 (Ont. C.A.).

Harry, Joseph. "The 'Marital' Liaisons of Gay Men." 28 *The Family Coordinator* 622 (October 1979).

Hart, Trevor A., and Schwartz, Danielle R. "Cognitive-Behavioral Erectile Dysfunction Treatment for Gay Men." 17 *Cognitive and Behavior Practice* 66 (February 2010).

Henshaw, Stanley K. "Unintended Pregnancies in the United States." 30 *Family Planning Perspectives* 24 (1998).

Higbee, Jonathan. "Judge Rules Catholic Charities Cannot Discriminate Against Gay Adoptive Parents." *Instinct Magazine*, August 19, 2011, at http://instinctmagazine.com/blogs/blog/judge-rules-catholic-charities-cannot-discriminate-against-gay-adoptive-parents.

Hirschfeld, Jerome A. "Emergency Medical Services for Children in Rural and Frontier America: Diverse and Changing Environments." *Pediatrics*, vol. 96, no. 1 (July 1995): 179–184.

Hoff, Colleen C. et al. "Relationship Characteristics and Motivations Behind Agreements Among Gay Male Couples: Differences by Agreement Type and Couple Serostatus." 22 *AIDS Care* 827 (July 2010), at http://www.ncbi.nlm.nih.gov/pmc/articles/PMC2906147/.

Hunter, James Davison. "To Change the World." 3 *Trinity Forum Briefing*, no. 2, 2002, at http://71513.netministry.com/images/TO_CHANGE_THE_WORLD_HUNTER.pdf.

"Illinois Catholic Charities Adoption Battle: Charities' Attorney to Appeal Judge's Decision." *Huffington Post*, August 20, 2011, at http://www.huffingtonpost.com/2011/08/29/illinois-catholic-chariti_n_941040.html.

James, Scott. "Many Successful Gay Marriages Share an Open Secret." *New York Times*, January 28, 2010, at http://www.nytimes.com/2010/01/29/us/29sfmetro.html.

John Paul II, Pope [Karol Wojtyla]. *Love and Responsibility*. San Francisco: Ignatius Press, 1981.

Jones, Michael. "Are Marriage Equality Opponents Bigots?" *Change.org*, May 5, 2010, at http://news.change.org/stories/are-marriage-equality-opponents-bigots.

Kaiser, Charles. "For Gays, Cheers and Doubts About Marriage." *CNN*, June 26, 2011, at http://articles.cnn.com/2011-06-26/opinion/kaiser.gay.marriage_1_gay-marriage-gay-community-modern-gay-movement?_s=PM:OPINION.

Kaminer, Wendy. "Gay Rights and Anti-Gay Liberties." *The Atlantic*, March 2010, at http://www.theatlantic.com/national/print/2010/03/gay-rights-and-anti-gay-liberties/37382/.

Kaufman, Moisés. "London Mosquitoes." In *Standing on Ceremony: The Gay Marriage Plays* pp. 99–111. (c) 2011 by Moisés Kaufman; cited with permission of the playwright.

King, Valerie. "Variations in the Consequences of Nonresident Father Involvement for Children's Well-Being." 56 *Journal of Marriage & Family* 963 (1994).

Klausli, Julia F., and Owen, Margaret Tresch. "Stable Maternal Cohabitation, Couple Relationship Quality, and Characteristics of the Home Environment in the Child's First Two Years." 23 *Journal of Family Psychology* 103 (February 2009).

Knight, Robert H. "How Domestic Partnerships and 'Gay Marriage' Threaten the Family." In John Corvino ed., *Same Sex: Debating the Ethics, Science, and Culture of Homosexuality*. Lanham, Md.: Rowman & Littlefield 1997, pp. 288–302.

Koppelman, Andrew. *The Gay-Rights Question in Contemporary American Law*. Chicago: University of Chicago Press, 2002.

Kurtz, Stanley. "Beyond Gay Marriage: The Road to Polyamory." *Weekly Standard*, August 4, 2003, at http://www.weeklystandard.com/Content/Public/Articles/000/000/002/938xpsxy.asp.

———. "*Big Love*: From the Set." *National Review*, March 13, 2006, at http://old.nationalreview.com/kurtz/kurtz.asp.

LaChapelle v. Mitten, 607 N.W.2d 151 (Minn. App. 2000).

Lamb, Kathleen A., Lee, Gary R., and DeMaris, Alfred. "Union Formation and Depression: Selection and Relationship Effects." 65 *Journal of Marriage and Family* 953 (November 2003).

Larson, Kandyce, Shirley A. Russ, James J. Crall, and Neal Halfon. "Influence of Multiple Social Risks on Children's Health." *Pediatrics*, vol. 121, no. 2 (February 2008): 337–344.

LaSala, Michael C. "Monogamy of the Heart: Extradyadic Sex and Gay Male Couples." 17 *Journal of Gay and Lesbian Social Services* 1 (2005).

Laumann, Edward O., Gagnon, John H., Michael, Robert T., and Michaels, Stuart. *The Social Organization of Sexuality: Sexual Practices in the United States.* Chicago: University of Chicago Press, 2000.

Lawrence v. Texas, 539 U.S. 558 (2003).

Lee, Patrick, and George, Robert P. "What Sex Can Be: Self-Alienation, Illusion, or One-Flesh Union." *American Journal of Jurisprudence* 42 (1997).

Lefkowitz, Mary R., and Fant, Maureen B. *Women's Life in Greece and Rome: A Source Book in Translation.* 2nd ed., 1992, at http://www. stoa.org/diotima/anthology/wlgr/wlgr-privatelife249.shtml.

Letter of Elizabeth Marquardt et al. to Arthur Brisbane, *New York Times* Public Editor, June 24, 2010, at http://www.familyscholars. org/assets/Arthur-Brisbane-Letter-6.23.10.pdf.

"Long Term Relationships Just as Likely Among Gay Couples, Claims Psychiatrist." 28 *Canadian Family Physician* 1478 (September 1982), at http://www.ncbi.nlm.nih.gov/pmc/articles/ PMC2306581/pdf/canfamphys00247-0023.pdf.

Loving v. Virginia (1967) 388 U. S. 1.

"Maine's Anti-Gay Marriage Supporters Kindly Request You Stop Calling Them Bigots." *Queerty,* September 18, 2009, at http://www.queerty. com/maines-anti-gay-marriage-supporters-kindly-request -you-stop-calling-them-bigots-20090918/#ixzz1ICR7wZEA.

Manning, Wendy D., and Smock, Pamela J. "New Families and Non-Resident Father-Child Visitation." 78 *Social Forces* 87, 89 (September 1999).

"Marriage and the Law: A Statement of Principles." Institute for American Values & Institute for Marriage and Public Policy, 2006, at http://www.marriagedebate.com/pdf/imapp.mlawstmnt.pdf.

Mayer, Susan E. "Revisiting an Old Question: How Much Does Parental Income Affect Child Outcomes?" *Focus,* vol. 27, no. 2 (Winter 2010): 21–26.

McGarvey, Bill. "Lesbian, Catholic and Celibate: Eve Tushnet Discusses Conversion, the Theology of Friendship and Her Argument against Gay Marriage." *Busted Halo* August 4, 2010 at http://bust-edhalo.com/features/lesbian-catholic-and-celibate.

McKay, Hollie. "Mark Ruffalo Slams the 'Old' and 'Bigoted' Views of Those Who Oppose Same Sex Marriage." *Fox News,* July 2, 2010, at http://www.foxnews.com/entertainment/2010/07/02/mark-ruffalo-slams-old-bigoted-views-oppose-sex-marriage/.

McLanahan, Sara, and Gary Sandefur. *Growing Up With a Single Parent: What Hurts, What Helps*. Cambridge, Mass.: Harvard University Press, 1994.

McLanahan, Sara et al. "Unwed Fathers and Fragile Families, Center for Research on Child Wellbeing." Working Paper #98–12, March 1998.

Meezan, William, and Rauch, Jonathan. "Gay Marriage, Same-Sex Parenting, and America's Children." 15 *Future of Children* 97 (2005).

Messner, Thomas M. "The Price of Prop 8." *Heritage Foundation Backgrounder*, no. 2328 (October 22, 2009), at http://s3.amazonaws.com/thf_media/2009/pdf/bg2328es.pdf.

"Michele Bachmann Calls Gay People 'Part of Satan.'" Lecture to the National Education Leadership Conference on November 6, 2004, at http://www.towleroad.com/2011/07/bachmannsatan.html.

Mitchell, Jason W. "Examining the Role of Relationship Characteristics and Dynamics on Sexual Risk Behavior Among Gay Male Couples." PhD dissertation, Oregon State University, 2010, at http://ir.library.oregonstate.edu/xmlui/bitstream/handle/1957/16379/MitchellJasonW2010.pdf?sequence=1.

Mohr, Richard. *A More Perfect Union: Why Straight America Must Stand Up for Gay Rights*. Boston: Beacon Press, 1994.

Moore, Kristin Anderson et al. "Marriage from a Child's Perspective: How Does Family Structure Affect Children and What Can We Do About It?" *Child Trends Research Brief*, Child Trends, June 2002, at http://www.childtrends.org/files/marriagerb602.pdf .

Morales, Lymari. "U.S. Adults Estimate That 25% of Americans are Gay or Lesbian." *Gallup*, May 27, 2011, at http://www.gallup.com/poll/147824/Adults-Estimate-Americans-Gay-Lesbian.aspx.

Murray, Stephen O., and Will Roscoe, eds. *Boy Wives and Female Husbands: Studies in African Homosexualities*. New York: Palgrave 1998.

National Organization for Marriage, "The 2009 NOM Massachusetts Marriage Survey" at http://www.nationformarriage.org/site/apps/nlnet/content2.aspx?c=omL2KeN0LzH&b=5075187&ct=7000219.

Nussbaum, Martha C. *From Disgust to Humanity: Sexual Orientation and Constitutional Law*. New York: Oxford University Press 2010.

Oppenheimer, Mark. "Married with Infidelities." *New York Times*, June 30, 2011, at http://www.nytimes.com/2011/07/03/magazine/infidelity-will-keep-us-together.html?pagewanted=all.

"Our Opinion: Right Call in Catholic Charities Decision." *State Journal-Register*, August 21, 2011, at http://www.sj-r.com/editorials/x386669877/Our-Opinion-Right-call-in-Catholic-Charities-decision.

Paige, R. U. *Proceedings of the American Psychological Association, Incorporated, for the legislative year 2004*. Minutes of the meeting of the Council of Representatives, July 28 and 30, 2004. Retrieved at http://www.apa.org/about/governance/council/policy/parenting.aspx.

Parke, Mary. "Are Married Parents Really Better for Children? What Research Says About the Effects of Family Structure on Child Well-Being." Center for Law and Social Policy (CLASP) brief, May 2003.

Parker-Pope, Tara. "Kept from a Dying Partner's Bedside." *New York Times*, May 19, 2009, p. D5, at http://www.nytimes.com/2009/05/19/health/19well.html.

Pawleski, James, et al. "The Effects of Marriage, Civil Union, and Domestic Partnership Laws on the Health and Well-being of Children." *Pediatrics*, vol. 118, no. 1 (July 2006): 349–364.

Perry v. Schwarzenegger, 704 F. Supp. 2d 921 (N.D. Cal. 2010).

Poe v. Gerstein (5th Cir. 1975) 517 F.2d 787.

Popenoe, David. *Life Without Father*. New York: Free Press, 1996.

Press Release. "Missouri State Settles Lawsuit with Emily Brooker." November 8, 2006, at http://allnurses-breakroom.com/world-news-current/missouri-state-settles-217367.html .

Prettyman, Kaitlin. "Peter Vidmar Steps Down as Chief of Mission for 2012 U.S. Olympic Team." *Deseret News*, May 7, 2011, at http://www.deseretnews.com/article/700133436/Peter-Vidmar-steps-down-as-chief-of-mission-for-2012-US-Olympic-Team.html.

Ramirez, Oscar Modesto, and Brown, Jac. "Attachment Styles, Rules Regarding Sex, and Couple Satisfaction: A Study of Gay Couples." 31 *Australian and New Zealand Journal of Family Therapy* 202 (June 2010).

Rauch, Jonathan. "Who Needs Marriage?" In Bruce Bawer, ed., *Beyond Queer: Challenging Gay Left Orthodoxy*. New York: Free Press, 1996, pp. 296–313.

———. *Gay Marriage: Why It Is Good for Gays, Good for Straights, and Good For America*. New York: Times Books, 2004.

———. "Letter to the Editor." *New York Times*, June 15, 2010, at http://www.nytimes.com/2010/06/16/opinion/l16rich.html.

Regnerus, Mark, and Uecker, Jeremy. *Premarital Sex in America*. New York: Oxford University Press, 2011.

Reminiscences of Abraham Lincoln by distinguished men of his time / collected and edited by Allen Thorndike Rice (1853–1889). New York: Harper & Brothers Publishers, 1909, at http://timpanogos.wordpress.com/2007/05/23/lincoln-quote-sourced-calfs-tail-not-dogs-tail/#more-636.

Rich, Frank. "The Bigots' Last Hurrah." *New York Times*, April 18, 2009, at http://www.nytimes.com/2009/04/19/opinion/19Rich.html?_r=2&ref=opinion.

———. "Smoke the Bigots Out of the Closet." *New York Times*, February 6, 2010, at http://www.nytimes.com/2010/02/07/opinion/07rich.html.

———. "A Heaven-Sent Rent Boy." *New York Times*, May 15, 2010, at http://www.nytimes.com/2010/05/16/opinion/16rich.html?scp=1&sq=david%20blankenhorn&st=cse.

———. "Two Weddings, A Divorce and 'Glee.'" *New York Times*, June 12, 2010, at http://www.nytimes.com/2010/06/13/opinion/13rich.html?_r=1.

Roscoe, Will. *Changing Ones: Third and Fourth Genders in Native North America*. New York: Palgrave, 1998.

Rothblum, Esther D., Balsam, Kimberly F. and Solomon, Sondra E. "Comparison of Same-Sex Couples Who Were Married in Massachusetts, Had Domestic Partnerships in California, or Had Civil Union in Vermont." 29 *Journal of Family Issues* 48 (2008).

Saad, Lydia. "Doctor-Assisted Suicide is Moral Issue Dividing Americans Most." *Gallup*, May 31, 2011, at http://www.gallup.com/poll/147842/doctor-assisted-suicide-moral-issue-dividing-americans.aspx.

"Same-Sex Marriage Debate from the University of St. Thomas." *MPR News*, October 19, 2011, at http://minnesota.publicradio.org/display/web/2011/10/19/midday1.

"Schulz, Craigen, Montague." *Marriage Anti-Defamation Alliance*, December 15, 2011, at http://marriageada.org/schulz-craigen-montague/.

Sirota, Theodore. "Adult Attachment Style Dimensions in Women Who Have Gay or Bisexual Fathers." 23 *Archives of Psychiatric Nursing* 289 (2009).

Skinner v. Oklahoma (1942) 316 U.S. 535.

Smith, Emily Esfahani. "Washington, Gay Marriage and the Catholic Church." *Wall Street Journal*, January. 9, 2010, at http://online.wsj.com/article/SB10001424052748703478704574612451567822852.html.

Sorensen, Elaine, and Zibman, Chava. "To What Extent Do Children Benefit from Child Support?" Washington, D.C.: The Urban Institute, January 2000.

Stacey, Judith. "Gay and Lesbian Families: Queer Like Us." In Mary Ann Mason, Arlene Skolnick and Stephen D. Sugarman, eds., *All Our Families: New Policies for a New Century*. New York: Oxford University Press, 1998, pp. 144–169.

Stewart, Monte N. "Judicial Redefinition of Marriage." 21 *Canadian Journal of Family Law* 11 (2004).

Stossel, John. "A Libertarian's View of Marriage." *Fox News*, August 31, 2011, at http://www.foxnews.com/opinion/2011/08/31/libertarians-view-gay-marriage/.

Strasser, Mark. *Legally Wed: Same-Sex Marriage and the Constitution*. Ithaca: Cornell University Press, 1997.

Sullivan, Andrew. "Introduction." In Andrew Sullivan, ed., *Same-Sex Marriage: Pro and Con: A Reader*. 1st ed. New York: Vintage Books, 1997.

"Texas Officer Suspended for Comment to Gay Couple." *Associated Press*, December 10, 2004, at http://austin.ynn.com/content/top_stories/126767/capitol-trooper-disciplined-for-comment-to-gay-couple.

Trussel, James, and Vaughn, Barbara. "Contraceptive Failure, Method-Related Discontinuation and Resumption of Use: Results from the 1995 National Survey of Family Growth." 31 *Family Planning Perspectives* 64, 71 (1999).

"TV Host Fired Over Sean Avery Debate." *ESPN.com*, May 13, 2011, at http://sports.espn.go.com/new-york/nhl/news/story?id=6532954.

US Senate Subcommittee on the Constitution, Civil Rights and Property Rights. Hearings on The Defense of Marriage Act, 108th

Cong. (Sept. 4, 2003). Written statement of Prof. Judith Stacey, PhD, Dept. of Sociology, N.Y.U.

Ventrella, Jeffery. "Square Circles?!! Restoring Rationality to the Same-Sex 'Marriage' Debate." *Hastings Constitutional Law Quarterly* vol. 32, (2005) p. 681.

"Video: British High Court Rules Christian Couple May Not Foster Kids." *NOM Blog*, February 28, 2011, at http://www.nomblog.com/5395/.

Volokh, Eugene. "Same-Sex Marriage and Slippery Slopes." 33 *Hofstra Law Review* 101 (2006).

Waite, Linda J., and Gallagher, Maggie. *The Case for Marriage: Why Married People are Happier, Healthier, and Better-Off Financially.* New York: Doubleday, 2000.

Wegner, Judith Romney. "The Status of Women in Jewish and Islamic Marriage and Divorce Law." 5 *Harvard Women's Law Journal* 1, (1982).

Whitehead, Barbara Dafoe. "Dan Quayle Was Right." *The Atlantic*, April 1993, at http://www.theatlantic.com/magazine/archive/1993/04/dan-quayle-was-right/7015/.

——, and Popenoe, David. "Who Wants to Marry a Soul Mate?" *State of Our Unions 2001*, National Marriage Project, June 2001, at http://www.virginia.edu/marriageproject/pdfs/SOOU2001.pdf.

Why Marriage Matters: 30 Conclusions from the Social Sciences. New York: Institute for American Values, 2011.

Why Marriage Matters: Twenty-Six Conclusions from the Social Sciences. 2nd ed. New York: Institute for American Values, 2005.

Wilson, Robin Fretwell, Laycock, Douglas, and Picarello, Anthony, eds. *Same-Sex Marriage and Religious Liberty: Emerging Conflicts.* Lanham: Rowman & Littlefield 2008.

Wolfson, Evan. "Enough Marriage to Share: A Response to Maggie Gallagher." In Lynn D. Wardle et al., eds., *Marriage and Same-Sex Unions: A Debate.* Westport: Praeger 2003, pp. 25–32.

——. "Defending the Motion." *Economist*, January 5, 2011, at http://www.economist.com/debate/days/view/634.

——. "Marriage Equality: Losing Forward." *Advocate*, October 28, 2004, at http://www.advocate.com/Politics/Commentary/Marriage_equality__Losing_forward/.

Worth, Katie. "SF Same-Sex Couples Increasingly Going Without Kids." *San Francisco Examiner*, June 26, 2011, at http://www.sfexaminer.

com/local/2011/06/sf-same-sex-couples-increasingly-going-without-kids-census-shows.

Yip, Andrew K. T. "Gay Male Christian Couples and Sexual Exclusivity." 31 *Sociology* 289, (May 1997).

Yoshino, Kenji. "Too Good for Marriage." *New York Times*, July 14, 2006, at http://www.nytimes.com/2006/07/14/opinion/14yoshino. html.

Yucel, Deniz, and Gassanov, Margaret A. "Exploring Actor and Partner Correlates of Sexual Satisfaction Among Married Couples." 39 *Social Science Research* 725 (September 2010).

Zick, Andreas, Kupper, Beate, and Hovermann, Andreas. "Intolerance, Prejudice and Discrimination: A European Report." Friedrich Ebert Stiftung Forum, Berlin, 2011, at http://www.fes-gegen-rechtsextremismus.de/pdf_11/FES-Study%2BIntolerance,%2BPr ejudice%2Band%2BDiscrimination.pdf.

INDEX

Information in footnotes is indicated by n after the page number and before the note number.